ONE
HEARTBEAT

The Story of the *1983 University Of Texas Baseball Team,*
and Their Road to the National Championship

JERRY JOHNSON

Other books by Jerry Johnson:

Bombing Chicago (Book 1 of the Peterson Files)
SEVEN: A Novel of Domestic Terrorism
(Book 2 of the Peterson Files)
SIX (Book 3 of the Peterson Files)
CRUISE

"The winning tradition of the University of Texas will not be entrusted to the timid or the weak."

- Billy Disch

Cover picture – Mike Capel, Roger Clemens, Kirk Killingsworth, and Calvin Schiraldi (front)

DEDICATION

This book is dedicated to the entire University of Texas' baseball program – not just the 1983 team, even though that team was something special. This dedication includes all the players that have entertained us over the years, from the kids that used to scramble up Billy Goat Hill in Clark Field to the latest teams that keep getting the Texas team back to Omaha and the College World Series. This is also dedicated to all the coaches that have helped teach the game over the years, the support staff, the umpires, players' families and girlfriends, the media that reported on the games, and even the fans.

A big thank you needs to go out to the people of Omaha, Nebraska, for their hard work each year in putting on the logistical challenge of the College World Series. ESPN deserves a "shout-out" for their support of college baseball over the last 40+ years, helping the sport grow to where it is today.

And a special dedication to Cliff Gustafson. "Coach Gus" came to Texas in 1968, my freshman year at UT. He was hired after a great high school coaching career, but actually took a pay cut to come to Texas. He was asked if he was interested in coming to Texas by then UT Athletics Director Darrell Royal, and Cliff was too excited by the offer to tell Coach Royal that the salary being offered was less than what Gus was already making at South San Antonio High School.

Coach Gustafson coached at UT from 1968 – 1996, compiling a record of 1,466-377 over those 29 years. He won 22 Southwest Conference championships, went to the College World Series 17 times as a coach (after having played there for UT in 1952), and won national championships in 1975 and 1983. His career winning percentage of .792 still ranks second amongst all college coaches.

Tommy Harmon, who played for Cliff and then worked for him for years as an assistant coach, said at Cliff's passing in 2023:

"When you talk about all-time coaching greats at The University of Texas — in all sports — Coach Gus is right up there with the best. The historic run he had in building on the great legacy of our baseball program will never be forgotten, and the stature he took it to continues to this day. He was a man who just loved baseball, loved his players, and every year gave his teams everything he had. There was no doubting it, for Coach Gus, it was Family, Faith, and Baseball … and I'm not sure in which order.

He was driven to succeed, and that fueled us as players. Coach Gus was always prepared, and he scripted practice to cover every possible detail in a game. We worked long and hard, but always knew that we'd go into a game ready for any possible scenario. He was going to outwork and out-prepare his opponents and develop his players, and that led to a lot of great years, championships and a hall of fame career."

Rest in peace, Coach Gus. And may the legacy you helped build at UT continue forever.

CONTENTS

PROLOGUE

There is an entire industry built around the idea that an organization is better if the members of that group "bond" – that is, buy into the concept that their individual efforts are contributing toward the organizational goal and the greater good. An organization can hire consultants, put on seminars, and there are even camps where the "team" can practice doing trust falls, challenge themselves on climbing walls and rope courses, and play various games designed to bring a group together and into focus.

Sports teams are no different. A team that bonds into a single entity is much more powerful than a group of individuals just seeking their own statistics. This is the story of one team that finally found that bond, and what they accomplished.

As Texas Baseball Coach Cliff Gustafson told Sports Information Director Bill Little when the team first arrived in Omaha, "It took a while, but the team is now playing with one heartbeat."

June 11, 1983

Tonight, the Texas Longhorns take on the Alabama Crimson Tide for the 1983 NCAA Baseball Championship in Rosenblatt Stadium – the home every year of the College World Series in Omaha, Nebraska. 1983 has been a special year for the University of Texas, the Centennial Year for the University, and a special year for this baseball team.

After a couple of crushing upsets knocked Texas out of the College World Series in 1982, the 1983 team had a lot of growing to do. UT Coach Cliff Gustafson had some good pitchers returning, but he had to rebuild his entire infield and outfield.

There were a lot of frustrations during the '83 year from the players, coaches, fans, and even the umpires. During the year at least four of the team's stars either thought about quitting or actually quit the team and had to be talked into returning. The team did not look good early in the year, losing to teams that had no business even being on the field with Texas. UT was obviously feeling the pressure that comes with the expectation that the Longhorns were supposed to be one of the best teams in the country. The coaches chewed on the players after losses, and the team had multiple "players only" meetings where they tried to work out their differences.

It was hard. Winning had come so easily in 1982 that the fans (and even some of the players) thought all Texas had to do was roll the ball out on the field and the game was theirs – but 1983 was different. This new team had a disparate mix of returners from '82, an influx of talented freshmen, and a scattering of transfers from various junior colleges, all trying to get on the same page.

And slowly the coaches put together a team that finally bonded and focused on what it took to win it all.

And now here they are, in the finals for the 1983 championship. It has been quite a ride, and this is the story of that team.

CHAPTER 1

THE PAST

This story actually began last year, in June 1982, again in Omaha. The '82 University of Texas baseball team was probably the best team in the country that year. Even the Longhorn baseball coach, Cliff Gustafson, said it was the best team he had ever coached.

Texas won over 30 straight games to start the year in '82, blew through the Southwest Conference regular season, won the conference tournament, and then easily won the Regional (with Milo Choate, with his .176 batting average for the year, getting the key hits in the Regional). The team had outstanding (but mostly young) pitching, good hitting, and the best player in college baseball that year, Spike Owen. He was so good defensively at shortstop that one major league scout opined that Spike, "Could probably start for our major league team right now."

UT won the first two games at the College World Series in Omaha in '82, blasting Oklahoma State 9-1 (a team Texas loved to beat, because their coach, Gary Ward, wouldn't let their team shake hands with the other team, win or lose, after a game – which to most teams was only showing bad sportsmanship). The Longhorns then won a close game against Stanford 8-6 (with Stanford taking UT to extra innings). So, by mid-week, thanks to the tournament's double elimination format (lose two games and you are out), the series was down from the original eight teams to the top four – UT, Miami, Wichita State, and the big underdog Maine. Texas could almost smell that trophy.

But then on Thursday evening Texas lost a one run game to Miami, probably the hottest team in the tournament. Spike scored after a triple in the first, but that was it for UT scoring. Miami held UT to five hits, with their pitchers striking out eight Longhorns, with seven of those batters looking at called third strikes. It was the first time Texas had lost a game in 45 days. Roger Clemens was the losing pitcher, only giving up two runs, but that was one too many on that particular night. The ump that night had a pretty wide strike zone, but that was no excuse – in every game the team needs adjust to what the umpire is calling.

If the ump is going to give the pitcher a half inch off the outside rubber, calling that a strike, then the catcher has to try for a full inch off the rubber, to see how far the umpire is willing to go. Some umps set up a little outside, to try and improve their view over the catcher, making that area off the plate seem like it might be part of the strike zone. And if a catcher gets the ball right where he places his mitt, even if the mitt is located just off the rubber that outlines the plate, or if he is good at "framing" – pulling the catcher's mitt from slightly off the plate back into the strike zone after the ball is caught – then sometimes an ump can be fooled into thinking what should be called a ball is actually a strike. But as long as an umpire is consistent, and calls it the same way for both teams, there should be no complaints from either team about the calls.

The Texas team may have been a little overconfident and looking ahead, might have lost a little focus, or just had a bad night at the plate – but a loss was still a loss.

No problem, though – Texas knew they could beat Wichita State, their next opponent on Friday. UT had swept a double header from the Shockers back in March of '82, shutting them out in both games at Austin's Disch-Falk Field, the Longhorns' home stadium. Texas had Calvin Schiraldi on the mound for this semifinal game in Omaha, and he had one-hit Wichita when UT played them earlier. Beat the Shockers, and the Longhorns would be in the final, probably against Miami again. Texas couldn't see Miami losing to an overachieving Maine Black Bear team that had somehow made the semifinals.

But then in the second inning against Wichita State, a fastball got away from Calvin Schiraldi and he hit Kevin Penner, the WSU batter. Some Texas players, sitting in the dugout, thought Calvin might have killed Penner after hearing the sound of the ball hitting Kevin in the head. Penner eventually had to be carried off the field on a stretcher, and you could tell that it upset Calvin.

Schiraldi was never the same in that game, understandably losing his concentration, and he ended up facing twelve batters and giving up six runs in the third. Texas hit the ball hard the entire game but left too many runners on base. The Longhorns couldn't get the key hit when they needed it. And, just like that, with an 8-4 loss, the UT season was over. Texas finished third in Omaha for the second year in a row.

It was a deathly quiet locker room after the loss. A couple of the guys hung towels over their heads, so that their teammates couldn't see the tears in their eyes. You could tell people like Spike were pretty upset about not going home with the trophy, especially knowing that this was his last collegiate ball game. And, even though Texas had been to Omaha more than any other team, the players knew it was not easy to get here – anything can happen along the way to derail a team's dream of playing in Rosenblatt - so there was no way of knowing when the Longhorns might make it back for another College World Series. At Texas, making it to the College World Series is the goal starting out every year. But not winning the whole thing in '82, considering the talent on this team, was still a huge disappointment. One fan tried to console the Texas coach, Cliff Gustafson, telling the coach, "Well, you can't win them all." Gustafson responded, "You can if you're good enough."

And Texas didn't get to dogpile. Other teams dogpile – jump on top of each other on the mound after almost any big win – be it a conference championship, a no-hitter, or winning a Regional. But Texas has higher goals. They don't dogpile unless they win the last game at Omaha. And they didn't reach that goal in 1982.

The Texas team flew back to Austin on Saturday, June 12, and had a nice crowd of family and fans meet the team and coaches at Disch-Falk Field to celebrate their "successful" season. But it didn't feel that successful to the team. They weren't satisfied and knew they should have won it all with the team they had. This was the end of the college career for the graduating seniors and the juniors drafted by the major leagues that would be moving on to professional baseball careers, and those players were leaving unfulfilled. The people coming back vowed then and there to do better in 1983.

CHAPTER 2

FALL, 1982

Fall baseball means drills. And then more drills. And then more drills. Getting the picture? Texas did scrimmage nearly every day, but most of the time the team was doing drills to get the fundamentals down to as close to perfect as possible. Coach Gustafson commented, "Do it right once, it was probably luck. Do it right 10 times in a row, and you are showing some skill. Do it 100 times, and you are developing a habit."

That 100-time comment might actually be on the low end of how many times the Longhorns repeated plays. Ball is hit back to the pitcher, runner on first, the correct play is to throw to second to try and start the double play. But you didn't put the throw directly over the bag, or a little on the first base side of second to make it easier for the shortstop to continue the play on to first base? Do it again. And again. And again. Outfielders throwing to third or home, and missing the cutoff man? Cutoff man not in the right position? Pitcher not backing up the play? Repeat, ad infinitum. Runners on first and second, no outs, sacrifice bunt coming, need to run the wheel play? If the shortstop isn't on third in time, run the play again. And again.

Plus, as mentioned, UT was scrimmaging (intrasquad) every day – and with Gus, a "game" usually lasted 17 or 18 innings. There was no NCAA rule on how long the team could practice each day, so Coach Gus wanted to get his money's worth out of every day of practice. Often, the guys were on the field playing until dark thirty, and Gus had to call the dining room, asking them to stay open late, so that the team could still get dinner after a quick shower. Players had to have classes over with by noon and be on the field by 1:30. You can get in a lot of practice when the team is doing it 7 hours a day! Most nights everyone was there until at least 8:00 or 8:30, and sometimes even later!

One of Gus' basic tenets is that you are much more comfortable in any given situation if you have faced that situation in the past. Man on second, less than two outs, need to hit the ball to the right side of the field? It helps if you have been at bat in that situation. Man on third, infield drawn in, and you are trying to slap the ball past one of the infielders? Been there, done that! Long scrimmages meant that everyone got a chance to play, and everyone gained experience in situations that are likely to come up in a "real" game in the spring.

With a veteran team, Coach Gus might have cut the team a little slack. But UT had new people at just about every position, so drill they did. Last year Gus took it easy on the team because he had a pretty experienced team coming back from '81. This year, he is being tougher. His style almost instills fear in people – play well, or someone else will be playing your position.

Bill Bethea and Clint Thomas, the assistant coaches, are a little easier going, and with them on the staff players at least have someone approachable if they have a problem. Gus would just sit in his folding chair behind third base with his scorebook, keeping score by hand – and you never knew what he was putting down in his book about how you were playing. Even in the intrasquad games, if you weren't playing well, you might get pulled in the middle of an inning! For the new guys, Gus just sitting there was more intimidating than anything they had experienced in their entire career.

Catcher Jeff Hearron and shortstop Mike Brumley were the only two starting position players returning from last year's team – and Brumley had moved from the outfield to shortstop this year. He probably had the biggest shoes to fill, since he will be replacing Spike Owen, the All-American do everything shortstop that has been the mainstay of this team the last three years. The new UT first baseman, José Tolentino, said that Brumley still had that outfielder mentality, trying to throw as hard as possible on every throw – which made for some errant throws. José said he finally had to talk to Mike about "just flipping the ball" when he had plenty of time to make the throw. Since then, Brumley has been much more accurate with his throws to first. Mike does have a great arm and likes to show it off – but a lot of times the hardest throw is not the best throw.

Hearron and the pitching staff seem to be the team leaders this year. Jeff, with his constant "5 o'clock shadow," looks like he is about to turn 30. Some of the younger players seem to be a little scared of him. The pitching staff has a swagger about them, having had success the previous year, plus they lead by example.

There were a lot of transfers and freshmen that needed to be integrated into the team, and the coaches needed to see if they were talented enough to excel at this top level of competition. A bigger question was could the "old timers" and the new guys bond as a team? To succeed at this level of competition requires a very focused attitude from everyone, with everyone being on the same page. Talent can only carry you so far – effort, concentration, comradery, and the will to win are necessary components of any winning team, and everyone could tell the team was just not there yet. You have to show individual responsibility on and off the field. Are you making all the meals? Attending all the lifting sessions? Going to class? Getting homework assignments done on time? Working on your batting stroke in the cage? Team culture is an important part of winning – and taking responsibility for your actions shows that you are committed to the standard required for University of Texas baseball players.

But even early in the fall, some people were starting to stand out. Freshman Doug Hodo was making consistent contact at the plate but having problems hitting sliders – a pitch he said he had never seen before. Steve Labay, a transfer from Angelina Junior College, showed he can both pitch and hit, and looked like the best left-handed pitcher on the team. Bill Bates, another freshman, was beginning to look so smooth at second base that he will probably win that job. Gus was probably a little disappointed, in that he was secretly hoping his son Deron would win the starting spot at second this year, but it was pretty obvious as the fall practices progressed that Bates was the better player.

A couple of notes on Bates – he had a little trouble adjusting at first to the speed of the artificial turf infield, and how quickly the ball would get to him, but the coaches said he didn't make a bad throw to first during the entire fall series of practices. Bates did have a tendency to throw a little sidearm, so the guy playing first – usually José Tolentino, has to be prepared for the ball to curve. The coaches can see Bates' curve ball from the coaching box at first when he throws – Bill might make a decent pitcher! Once, while playing in one of the fall junior college scrimmages,

Bates started to steal second, only to realize that the catcher had called a pitchout and already had the ball headed to second base. Bates stopped halfway to second, reversed himself, and easily beat the return throw to first base. That is probably the first time the rest of the team realized just how fast the kid was – he could move!

When at the first fall practice Bill Bethea had everybody in the stands and was introducing the team to each other, he named Bill Bates, and added, "Probably the worst fielder on the team." So, Bates went to Bethea after the introductions ended, and said, "What can we do about that?" Bethea told Bates to stay after practice every night, and Bethea would hit fungos to Bates. It worked. By the end of the fall, Bates had gotten used to the speed of the turf and become a pretty slick infielder.

Speaking of Tolentino, he and Jamie Doughty transferred in from Seminole Junior College (where they finished in second place in the junior college national championship tournament last year). They were playing in the Alaska Summer League in July 1982, when they got a call from Doug Gassoway. Doug was a major league scout, and good friend of Cliff Gustafson. Doug had helped UT recruit so many kids that he had a reserved parking spot with his name on the sign right next to Cliff's at Disch-Falk Field. Gassoway told José that if he and Jamie signed with Texas, they would win the National Championship in '83 – and that was good enough for José. He and Doughty agreed to sign with UT, but then had to call the other coaches that had been recruiting them – coaches from all the major college baseball programs – Arizona State, Mississippi State, Oklahoma State, and others, and tell those team's coaches that the two players had signed. Most of the other coaches were polite, thanked José and Jamie for the call, and wished them luck in the future – except for Gary Ward at Oklahoma State. Ward had been instrumental in getting Doughty to first Murray State and then Seminole, and both schools were considered a pipeline for players headed to Stillwater and Oklahoma State. Ward was pretty upset with both players! He even told José that if José had signed with OSU, Ward had been prepared to give him a car!

One thing stood out quickly in the fall. The Texas pitching staff was doing an outstanding job. Of course, this is a zero-sum game. If the pitching is great, does that mean your team can't hit the ball? Or the other way around, if your team is pounding the ball, does that mean your pitching is suspect? Hard to know, until you get to face actual outside competition. Robert Gauntt, one of the newer guys on the team, singled off of Roger Clemens in Robert's first at bat this fall. He told a couple of guys on the team he just might be able to play some this year – but then Clemens struck Robert out the next 8 times Robert came to bat against Roger! Like Hodo, Robert said he had never seen a slider like the one Clemens was throwing and had no idea how to hit it.

Texas did scrimmage against a couple of good junior college teams during the fall of 1982 – and UT got beat by both teams. Gus always scheduled San Jacinto Junior College, where his buddy Wayne Graham was now coaching, but playing that usually lower level of competition doesn't always give you a true picture of your team's capabilities, either. "Usually lower level" doesn't always hold true, because a couple of years ago San Jac came into Austin and one of their pitchers went through the Texas lineup like UT was a Little League team. After the scrimmage, Coach Gustafson told that San Jacinto pitcher that Gus had a place for him at UT if he was interested. That pitcher was Roger Clemens, now one of Texas' best pitchers. He and

Capel had faced each other in high school in the Houston area and knew each other very well. Capel said that Roger had grown up since high school and a year in junior college, adding weight and muscle, and had added about 10 mph to his fast ball.

The regular umpires that called games in the spring were used in the fall intrasquad games, so they got to know the team, and the players got used to their strike zones. That made things interesting when UT scrimmaged another team, and Billy Bates would walk up to the plate to open the home half of the first inning and say, "Hi, Jon," to umpire Jon Bible. Bible would respond with something like "Afternoon, Bill. How are you today?" The opposing team's catcher would be dumbfounded, knowing that Texas already had an advantage.

Bible was also one of Gus's friends, and sometimes even helped scout for talent. He had umpired a series last year at Angelina Junior College, and Steve Labay had a great series that weekend – both hitting and pitching well. After the last game that weekend Labay ran into Bible, and the umpire told Steve, "I'm going to mention you to Coach Gustafson down at Texas." Two weeks later Steve was sitting in Gus's office in the Disch, being offered a scholarship.

Steve had multiple scholarship offers after having a good year at Angelina, so he was waffling about where to sign. Gus had Burt Hooton, the Los Angeles Dodgers all-star pitcher that had played at Texas, talk to Labay. Hooton told Steve, "You can come to Texas and play in the College World Series or go somewhere else and watch it on TV." And that was enough to convince Steve that he should be a Longhorn!

Mike "Froggie" Capel, one of the veterans on the team, led the team in the fall with a 1.19 ERA. Nearly all of the Texas pitchers have nicknames, bestowed by the team over the years. Capel is "Froggie," because of his voice. The nickname was a takeoff from the character in the "Little Rascals" TV show. Clements is "Goose," named after Goose Gossage and his blazing fastball. Roger is probably the hardest working guy on the team, always trying to get better. He is usually the first guy at the ballpark, and one of the last to leave. He runs so much you would think he was training for a marathon.

Kirk Killingsworth is, of course, "Killer." Not just for his name, but because last year he beaned Coach Gus with an errant throw. Kirk was originally recruited as an outfielder, and only because a player Gus was recruiting ended up signing with another team. Gus asked Doug Gassoway if he knew of any decent unsigned outfielders, and Doug told Gus about "the kid from Plano." Gus called Killingsworth and offered him a ¾ scholarship – everything but meals. Kirk told coach Gustafson, "Texas Tech just offered me a full ride." Gus told him, "Well, you can go to Tech, or A&M, but then we'll just beat you every year." So, Kirk agreed to come to UT. Early in the spring last year, in pre-game warmups prior to the Texas game against Lamar, Kirk was showing off his arm in the outfield. The cutoff man got distracted (easy to do, with both infield and outfield warmups going on at the same time), and the throw from Killingsworth nearly beaned the cutoff guy – and then bounced one time and hit Coach Gus, sitting in his usual folding chair by third base, right in the eye. Gus ended up in the hospital and broke his consecutive game coached streak. Kirk called Gus in the hospital, to not only check up on the coach but to assure him that the throw was not intentional. Gus told him, "If you are that accurate, maybe we should try you on the mound." When Cliff got home from the hospital, he was told to wear eye patches on both eyes for a week to protect his injured eye. When John

Turman, one of the team's managers, and Kelly Gruber found out about the patches, they went to Cliff's house and put patches on both eyes of the bust Gustafson kept in his study. If Cliff knew who did it, he never said!

Killingsworth had pitched in high school, but not since he got to UT. As he headed to the mound for his first pitch, a third of the way through the UT spring schedule in '82, he turned to Coach Gus and Clint Thomas, the pitching coach, and asked, "What if I do good?" Gus said, "Let me worry about that." Kirk ended '82 with a 9-0 record. He recorded 6 saves and led the entire country with a 0.80 ERA – not giving up an earned run for the first 36 innings he pitched. Not bad for a kid that had not pitched for a year and a half!

Gus was leaning towards turning Kirk into a starter for 1983, but Killingsworth did not have that good a fall in '82 – he ended up with one of the worst ERAs on the team. Kirk did hit .300 in the fall, the second-best batting average on the team (behind transfer Steve Labay). Kirk commented that he might have to go back to playing outfield if he couldn't figure out how to get the ball past people at the plate.

Coach Gustafson always said that the hardest three outs to get were numbers 25, 26, and 27 – the last three outs in the game. Pitchers were usually getting tired, batters had seen every pitch the pitcher could throw, and the people at the plate were concentrating just a little more, trying to get that tying (and then winning) run on base.

Gus has always tried to find a pitcher that could come in late in the game and get those final outs. That takes a different mindset. You must be comfortable pitching from the stretch, because you might be coming into the game with people on base. You have to be able to throw strikes, because walks late in the game can come back to bite you very quickly. And, most importantly, you need to have confidence in your ability to get people out – you can't let the situation overwhelm you. Killingsworth has those qualities, even if he didn't have a great fall – Gus said Kirk's arm might be a little tired from overuse. Gustafson said he will see how Killingsworth pitches in the spring.

Calvin Schiraldi is "Nibbler," for his ability to hit the corners of the plate consistently. The good news is that it looks like Calvin is back in the groove! He didn't have a good summer, not pitching well in his summer league after having beaned Kevin Penner from Wichita State last June in Omaha. But he has apparently regained his form from last spring and ended this fall with a 1.80 ERA.

Calvin had lost about 25 pounds during his senior year of high school after developing a serious infection and having to go on a liquid diet, while still trying to participate in sports. That weight loss cost him several miles per hour on his fastball, and forced him to improve his other pitches to stay competitive. But over this past summer Calvin finally got his weight back, and with that the increased velocity on his fastball returned – making him an even better pitcher.

Schiraldi is a slob, and the team teases him mercilessly for his habit of dropping his clothes in front of his locker (closest to the shower in the locker room). He does the same thing with his uniform after practice and then has to root through the clothes on the floor, putting on the same (now dirtier) outfit he was wearing before practice. He is rooming with Mike Capel and Steve Labay in an apartment off of Riverside, just on the south side of Town Lake, and when Capel's girlfriend comes over Mike says she just has to shake her head in amazement at the mess in the place. Dirty dishes, spit cups everywhere, clothes piled up – but instead of cleaning up all Schiraldi and Capel want to do is play video games.

Roger Clemens' fall record was right behind Schiraldi's, with an ERA of 1.84. One of the freshmen, Wade Phillips, also looked good in the fall with a 1.86.

José Tolentino tells the story that about a month into the fall season he was ready to quit the team. He had found the transfer to UT from junior college to be almost overwhelming. Much larger classes, longer practices, and José, being from Mexico, had learned English as a second language. He talked about how he had been facing a history exam, studied hard, thought he knew the material, but then suffered an anxiety attack when he sat down with his blue book in class, and couldn't put anything worthwhile on paper. He said he went back to the dining hall for lunch, feeling sorry for himself and ready to drop out of school and go ahead and sign a pro contract, when he heard two grad students in line in front of him who couldn't speak enough English to even get their lunch orders understood correctly. Then José sat down next to a guy in a wheelchair, who had to move the chair by breathing into a straw. José said he realized then that he really didn't have it that bad, and resolved to reach deeper and make it work at UT. He says that one lunch really turned his life around!

Another area where the team used to complain was when after a weight workout with strength and conditioning coach Dana Leduc, Dana would make everyone run "the ramps" at the stadium. All the way up one side to the top, back down and all the way up the other side – that was one lap. And the team would have to do 6 or 8 of the damn things after every workout. The players thought they had it bad, until they saw the swim team doing the ramps. They were on what the swimmers called their "wheels" - 2 x 6 boards with lawn mower wheels on each side, with the swimmers having to use their gloved or taped hands to paddle their way up the ramps! After the baseball team saw the swimmers, the baseball guys decided they didn't have it that bad, after all!

The baseball team had to lift weights with the football team, and the football guys would tease the baseball team about the 'light weight" workouts the baseball guys were doing, compared to the heavier weights the football team members were lifting. But the baseball team had José Tolentino, and he was just about as strong as the football linemen – and he got the football guys to leave the baseball team alone. Roger Clemens did drop a weight on Calvin Schiraldi's toe in one workout, and Calvin got out of lifting for a couple of weeks – Calvin was secretly thankful for the accident!

One fun thing in the fall is that the veterans on the team get to haze the freshmen. No, the team is not supposed to haze, but it is a tradition at Texas, mostly harmless, and the older guys on the team think it helps the team to bond. Boudreaux, Hodo, Bates, Phillips, Ruffin – the team got all the freshmen at one time or another. The older guys don't do anything really malicious – just silly stuff like making the new guys duck walk around campus, singing the "Eyes," while coeds laughed at them. And everyone had to know all the words to the David Allen Coe song, "You Never Even Called Me by My Name." Or the vets would blindfold the freshmen, put them in a car, take them someplace like Paleface Park up on Lake Travis or Mount Bonnell, and dump them, telling them they have to figure out how to get back to the dorm. Then, park a couple of miles down the road and wait to see if the guys that were dumped would show up.

The one vile thing done to the freshmen is the cracked egg game. Freshman number one must take a cracked egg and put it in his mouth – and then pass the egg yolk mouth-to-mouth to the other players down the line. The last guy in line has to swallow the mess! Mike Capel told about how when he was a freshman, he ended up being the last guy in line, and had to swallow the egg yolk. Not only that, but since the egg yolk had to be whole, his line of freshmen had to do it twice! Mike said that when he and Calvin Schiraldi were freshman, they did get the veterans once. The freshmen were ordered to be available at a certain time for a hazing session, but the freshman all went to the roof of Moore-Hill, the player's dorm. When the older players showed up, they got egged!

One fun hazing tradition was that on Monday nights in the fall the veterans on the team would make the freshmen go to Baskin Robbins and get ice cream for the older players, and then everyone would sit and watch Monday Night Football while they ate their ice cream.

Bruce Ruffin did get one back on Brumley late in the fall. Bruce could throw it hard, but was known for his lack of control. He was pitching batting practice, and Mike Brumley strolled to the plate. Ruffin threw the first pitch over Brumley's head, hitting the back of the cage. Brumley just dropped his bat and walked out – he said he wasn't going to stand in there against a flame-thrower who didn't know where the ball was going!

Finally, the Fall World Series, the intrasquad series of games that culminated fall practice in October were over, and the team had survived! Now, the players could all concentrate on finishing the semester's classes and finals, and get ready to defend the conference championship – but there was one more baseball event. The interview.

After the Fall World Series, Gus and the other coaches sit down with every player, and tell them where they think the player stands, whether or not the coaches feel that player can contribute in the spring, what they did well in the fall, and where they still need to show improvement. Unfortunately, some players are told in that interview that they will not be part of the team in the spring. Cuts had to be made to get down to the required NCAA team roster limits.

A good example of the "fall interview" is what Coach Gus told Steve Labay – "Yes, you hit well in the fall – but your pitching was not up to UT standards. You need better control if you are going to pitch for us. Keep working on that slider that Clint taught you, and maybe you will see some time on the mound in the spring." As one of the few left-handed pitchers on the squad, the coaches knew they needed Labay to be good – and this was Gus' way of motivating Steve to work a little harder.

CHAPTER 3

JANUARY 1983

January for a baseball player is like the time period after Thanksgiving for a five-year-old child. You know Christmas is coming in another month or so, and you can't wait – but you also know that something a few weeks away can seem like forever. You are squirming in your seat with excitement but frustrated at the same time. College baseball players practicing in January know that February and real games will eventually get here – but it does seem like it is taking months and months. One player made the comment that he really felt sorry for northern teams, who not only had to wait for the season to open, but for the snow to melt off their ballfield!

Unofficial team workouts started as soon as a few players got back to school after New Year's. In fact, if someone had walked by the baseball field off of Interstate 35 on Sunday, January 2nd, they probably would have heard the ping from an aluminum bat hitting the ball in the batting cage under the stands. Some people just couldn't wait! School started on Monday, January 16th, and the first official practice was on Friday, January 21st – approximately four weeks before the Longhorns were to start the season against Midwestern on February 18th.

And speaking of aluminum bats, the team had new ones this year, allegedly improved over the ones they have been using the last couple of years. UT first used aluminum bats in 1974, with Coach Gustafson a big believer in them, as an improvement over wooden bats. He commented back then that the use of aluminum bats would save his team over $1000 each year – the cost of broken wooden bats each season – and they helped to take the "sting" out of hitting the ball wrong with a wooden bat, especially in cold weather. And each year, the bat manufacturers have made the bats lighter and stronger, helping the batter to hit the ball harder and further. Now pitchers are taught to take a defensive position after throwing the ball – some were used to just falling off the mound after throwing a pitch – with the new defensive posture not just to defend their position, but to help keep them from being injured by a rocket coming back at them from the plate!

There are still a few position battles going on, with the coaches having to make some decisions before the team gets to the crux of the season. Jamie Doughty and David Denny will fight over the third base spot. Deron Loy, the junior college transfer that hit 16 home runs for his JC team last year, will push Jeff Hearon at catcher. Possible outfielders include Steve Labay, Bud Ray, Mike Simon, Johnny Sutton, and Mike Trent. Another pitcher to watch is freshman Wade Phillips. He has shown a good moving fastball so far and has a chance to start some games. And, knowing Coach Gus, he will move people around both the infield and outfield to see what combinations work well together. Bud Ray is new to the team, having transferred in between semesters. He will be a little behind having missed fall practice, so it will be interesting to see how quickly he finds a place on the team.

One thing the players get to do in the early spring is check arm speed on the JUGS gun – everybody gets tested. The pitchers were all up there, but Mike Brumley threw 93, and Bud Ray 91 – not bad for non-pitchers! Bud was as strong as an ox. He had grown up in a family in the construction business and had been building his body naturally since he was very young. He actually makes a lot of money going into bars and challenging everyone in the house to an arm-wrestling contest – and then beating everybody in the place. Once he even beat Gene Chilton, a 280-pound lineman on the UT football team!

Some of the preseason polls are starting to come out. Baseball America has UT ranked number 2, behind Miami (who won it all last year). Miami has Phil Lane returning, probably the best position player in the country this year since Spike has gone to the pros. Arizona State is ranked 3rd in that poll, followed by Oklahoma State. Wichita State, the team that knocked Texas out of the College World Series last June, is ranked 8th. Coach Gus is telling everyone that will listen that Texas is way overrated - with most of the team from last year gone, there will be a big learning curve this year, and UT will probably be inconsistent until the new starters can find their groove. Gus keeps bringing up the two scrimmages the Texas team lost against junior college teams – showing how far he thinks UT still has to go to be a good team. The pollsters seem to think that the Texas returning pitchers are enough to give the team an edge over just about everyone else – but UT still must prove it on the field.

One big surprise this January is who is working out with the team – Burt Hooton. The Los Angeles Dodger's star pitcher is driving up to Austin 3 times a week to start getting ready for his year, and to help with the current UT pitching staff. He is now living on a ranch he bought near Bourne, so it is not that far to Austin. He works out in San Antonio on the days he doesn't head north. He has tried to teach everyone here how to throw what he calls his "knuckle curve" – some of the pitchers can't handle it, because it requires big hands with long fingers to properly grip the ball for that pitch - but some of the Texas pitchers are getting it down to the point that they may use it in a game.

One Saturday in late January Burt actually pitched in one of the intrasquad scrimmages! It was a thrill for the Texas hitters to face off against a major league pitcher. Hooton is not the only pro making use of the artificial turf and mostly decent weather in Austin – there are probably half a dozen or so major and minor leaguers, all previous Longhorns, working out with the current team to get the pros ready for their spring training assignments. Gus uses them for motivation for his young team – "See where you can be if you keep working and developing your game?"

Bud Ray, a player joining the 'Horns for the first time this spring, made an interesting comment. He had played with Roger Clemens at San Jacinto Junior College a couple of years ago before Roger moved on to UT. Now Bud is here, too, and said that when they were at San Jac he faced Roger many times in practice and knew Roger's pitches. But Bud says now, facing Roger again in intrasquad games, getting a hit is nearly impossible. Bud agrees with what others have been saying - Roger must have added close to 10 MPH to his fastball since Bud last faced him! Everyone on the team knows that Roger is one of the hardest working guys around, and that he is always trying to improve.

This just shows what hard work can accomplish – if you have the raw material to start with and are willing to put in the work!

Last year, in the fall of '81, when Roger first joined the team, the first time Spike Owen walked up to the plate with Roger on the mound, Goose put one in the earhole of Spike's helmet. Roger was just announcing to everyone that he was here, and wasn't going to back down to anyone, even the stars on the team. He was just showing how competitive he is in everything he does!

CHAPTER 4

FEBRUARY

Real baseball. Finally. The beginning of something that will hopefully propel this team back to Omaha.

Every team wants a good winning percentage at the end of the year, plus hopefully a conference championship, to help convince the NCAA that their team is one of the top eight teams in the country and deserves to host one of the Regional Championships that determine the teams going to Omaha. Being a regional host gives a team some big advantages – home team crowd, being able to sleep in your own bed at night, regular routine going to the ballpark, and starting the tournament as the home team in your first game.

February 18th

Texas started the year with a double header against Midwestern State University, a small school located in Wichita Falls. Kirk Killingsworth pitched the first game, and Wade Phillips, one of the new freshmen, the second. Both pitched complete games, with the first game only going seven innings – the normal procedure for a college doubleheader. Midwestern led in both games, but then committed a bunch of errors (the wind was blowing hard from right to left, making it difficult to judge fly balls), allowing Texas to sweep. Kirk threw a three hitter in the first game, giving up a single walk. Phillips gave up 8 hits, but didn't give up a single walk, and struck out 5 MSU batters. Both pitchers looked good for their first game of the year.

UT's starting lineup for the first game was Mike Simon in center field, Mike Brumley at shortstop, Steve Labay in right field, José Tolentino at first, Jeff Hearron catching, Alan Brown at DH, David Denny in left field, Jamie Doughty at third, and Bill Bates at second.

The second game Coach Gustafson substituted a few players, with Deron Loy catching instead of Jeff, and Bryan Burrows and Deron Gustafson both playing at second. Jamie homered in the first game, barely over the fence, and David Denny was 6 for 8 on the day – and was upset that he wasn't hitting 1.000. Bill Bates stole his first base as a Longhorn – but the MSU catcher threw out 5 of Texas' other baserunners, which doesn't bode well for the season. The Longhorns had four newcomers on the team starting their first game – Labay, Tolentino, Doughty (all junior college transfers) and Bill Bates, the only freshman to start. For the new guys, this was their first introduction to the Wild Bunch, and for most of these guys this was the biggest crowd they had ever seen at a game where they were playing.

I'm not sure how to explain the Wild Bunch. Heckling has been around as long as baseball has been played – but these guys have taken it to a new level. The group apparently started as "The Law School Bunch" – wannabe lawyers wandering over to Clark

Field, the old UT baseball field with a hill in center field, because Clark was located right next to the Law School. They would sit together in the bleachers, tease players on the other team, insult the umpires, and even each other. Being law students, they were pretty quick witted, and they developed a reputation for outstanding insults. Even John Mazur, the old umpire that did a lot of UT games in those days, would play along with them. When the Law School Bunch would holler, "Hey, John, show us your teeth!" He would pull out his false teeth and wave the plate at the stands.

A lot of those students graduated, got attorney jobs here in Austin, and continued to come to the Texas games, even after UT moved to the new ballfield, Disch-Falk Field, across I-35 from the rest of the campus. They have been joined by other like-minded fans over the years, until now there is a group of 20 or so that come to just about every game. They have their own kazoo band, with quite a repertoire of songs that they play at the appropriate time – for example, the Big Top Circus Theme whenever someone on the other team makes an error. They are not profane, so the UT administration, for the most part, ignores their antics. Insults they use range from "You are so fat. How fat is he? When he sits around the house, he really sits AROUND the house," and "You are so ugly your momma must feed you with a slingshot" to things a little more subtle. After UT Board of Regents Chairman Frank Erwin was arrested on suspicion of driving while intoxicated (he got the case dismissed), the Wild Bunch would toast him at games with, "Hey Frank, it's the bottom of the fifth!"

They could sometimes really get under the skin of some player, and once a player loses focus on the game, he is basically out of commission – and the Wild Bunch would double down if they knew what they were doing was working. None of the transfers or freshmen had ever seen anything like the Wild Bunch. The Wild Bunch guys sit in Section 3, behind the opposing team's dugout on the first base side of the field, and raise hell the entire game. José Tolentino, the new Texas first baseman, saw them giving the "Hook 'Em" hand sign, and thought they were doing it for him – so he gave it right back, which only encouraged them that much more!

The Athletic Director, Deloss Dodds, asked Coach Gustafson what he thought, and Gus said he thought the Wild Bunch were basically harmless, and might even help give his team a little edge – so the administration let them continue with their antics. Players in the dugout had to hide grins every now and then when the Wild Bunch came out with a particular biting insult. The team thinks they are great! Sometimes they even pick on the UT players. Texas' Robert Gauntt got picked off of first base in a game last year, and the Wild Bunch gave him hell all the way back across the field to the home team dugout.

Gus didn't say much after the opening double header – he rarely does after wins, as he expects to win every game. Texas goes right back to work tomorrow, Saturday, with a double header against Texas Arlington.

One interesting thing is that Brumley is playing shortstop wearing a brace on his hand. He got hit on the fingers in one of the junior college scrimmages last fall, and the damage still hasn't healed. It will be interesting to see how well he can hit and field playing with that brace!

February 19th

Texas split today's twin bill. In the first game, Texas Arlington beat UT 10-6, giving the 'Horns their first loss of the year – the earliest first loss since 1978, when UT lost on opening day. Last year Texas won their first 33 games before losing one. UT gave up 12 hits in the opener, including at one point 3 consecutive doubles. Roger Clemens took the loss, but the team used 3 pitchers, none of whom were very successful. UT actually led 6-3 going into the 6th inning, but UTA scored 7 runs that inning and never looked back. Roger committed 2 errors and threw a wild pitch. He commented after the game that he blew it and knew that he didn't pitch like he was capable of doing.

There was also a dust up between Jeff Hearron, the Texas catcher, and Randy Christal, the home plate umpire, during the game. Apparently, Jeff said something to Christal, who told Jeff, "One more word and you're gone." Jeff said something else, and Christal ejected him. Gus yelled at Christal, defending Hearron, but all that did was make Christal madder. After the second game of the double header, he told Gus that he was quitting, and wouldn't ump any more games at UT after today. Christal has been an umpire at the college level for over 10 years, including working games at Omaha – he is well thought of throughout the baseball community. He is normally a pretty even-tempered ump, but today things went bad. Christal was umping in the UT game against Wichita State at the College World Series last year and called Spike Owen out at third base on a close play. Replays showed that Spike was probably safe. That memory might still have been on Jeff's mind and may be what started today's disagreement.

And Texas nearly lost the nightcap. Texas Arlington was leading 6-2 in the 8th, having scored 3 in the top of the 8th off of the UT starter, Calvin Schiraldi, and his replacement Bruce Ruffin. Bruce, one of the new freshmen, gave up a bases-loaded walk for that 3rd run in the 8th. But the 'Horns loaded the bases in the bottom of the 8th, the UTA pitcher hit a batter to force in a run, and then Steve Labay cleared the bases with a grand slam! Gus put Labay in to pitch the top of the 9th, giving Steve not only the winning hit, but making him the winning pitcher, too – a very unusual combination. Labay's 370 foot shot to left was a line drive that barely cleared the fence, but it was enough – followed by three quick outs as a pitcher in the 9th. Today, it was easy to see why he was recruited to Texas! UT has another double header against these same guys tomorrow, Sunday – no rest for the 'Horns!

February 20th

The Sunday games were deja vu all over again. Texas split the doubleheader, just like on Saturday. Mike Capel was the loser in the first game, giving up 5 runs in the 5th inning alone. The 'Horns were leading 3-1 up until that inning, but couldn't recover from the 5th, and it didn't help when the umps blew a call when UTA's Todd Cox tried to make a diving catch in the 4th, and Labay was called out – even though video replays showed Cox dropped the ball. Texas ended up losing that game 8-5. Labay ended up 2 for 4 for the day, even with the out that wasn't. No one else got more than one hit in that first game, as UT only had 5 total hits.

The second half of the double header was a Labay pitching masterpiece. He threw a 3-hit shutout, with only one batter even reaching second base. He retired 18 of the last 19 batters in the game, and the last 13 in a row. Texas won that game 6-0, with Mike Brumley going 2 for 5, David Denny 2 for 4 with 2 RBIs, and Deron Loy 2 for 3 with an RBI. The 'Horns are now 4-2 for the year, and sure to lose the top rating in the polls. Capel, Clemens and Schiraldi now have a combined 6.86 ERA after their first outings. Coach Gus said he was disappointed with the pitching, but that you couldn't judge a pitcher on just one outing, just like you can't bench a hitter that goes 0 for 4 in a single game. UT now has a mid-week double header with Texas Lutheran, a team Texas has beaten 46 straight times. Maybe that level of competition is what the "Horns need to help them get their act together!

February 23rd

Not good. For the first time in 24 years, Texas Lutheran – the small Division III school in Seguin with less than 1400 students enrolled, beat Texas. UT easily won the first game on Wednesday, 13-2 with Kirk Killingsworth throwing a 4-hitter, and José Tolentino driving in 5 runs, including a grand slam homer. Billy Bates also had a good game at the plate, with four RBI and a bases-loaded triple.

But in the second game, Coach Gus made several substitutions, and Texas didn't play well at all. Mike Trent went in to play left, Alan Brown was the new DH, Bud Ray played right, and Deron Gustafson played second. Those four newcomers combined to go 0 for 12, but the rest of the team didn't do much better – UT only had 4 hits for the game, with Bryan Burrows going 2 for 4. Roger Clemens gave up a 2-run homer to David Dahse, the Bulldog's center fielder and cleanup hitter, with two outs in the top of the 9th to give Texas Lutheran a 3-run rally that inning and the 3-2 lead in the game. In the bottom of the 9th, Burrows singled. He was sacrificed to second, but he was stranded there by two fly ball outs by pinch hitter David Denny and Mike Brumley. Ball game. Urban Seay, the freshman pitcher for TLC, pitched a great game (and a complete game), and deserved the win – but that doesn't mean anyone on the UT team liked the results. Coach Gus just stared hard at everyone as the players filed out of the dugout and back to the locker room, not saying a word – but he didn't have to say anything. The team knew how he felt. Now Texas has Louisiana Tech coming in for 3 games this next weekend – a double header on Saturday, and then a single game on Sunday. The 'Horns have a lot of things to work on to show they are a team worthy of an invite back to the playoffs!

Another advantage Texas has over a lot of other teams is that UT video tapes the games, and players and coaches can review the tapes to watch for issues with where players are playing in the field, batting stances, pitching motion, whatever. This was started in 1976 by Reed Rinn, a UT engineering student who was then employed at KLRN-TV on the University campus. An anonymous fan of the baseball team donated a new portable video camera and recorder to the team, but no one on the staff knew how to use it. Coach Gus talked to the baseball sports information director, Bill Little, to see if he was aware of anyone that could help. Bill knew Reed from his work as a video engineer at KLRN, and he also knew that Reed was a huge fan of Texas baseball. Bill contacted Reed and he gladly accepted the assignment as volunteer videographer for the baseball team. Reed initially recorded every game from his regular seat with the Wild Bunch, bringing a duffel bag full of extra batteries and tapes in order to record both games of a double header! After each game, Reed took the video recorder and tapes into Coach

Gus' office where Coach was eager to review them. Once the coaches saw how valuable those tapes were, Reed was moved up to a position behind home plate and up in front of the press box. Reed was also made a part of the team "traveling squad" and traveled with the team to road games to video tape them, as well. Reed continued as the team videographer for about 15 years, and Coach Gus felt that those Texas teams were the first in the country to have a professional videographer.

February 26th

Well, Texas finally won a double header, after splitting the last 3. Calvin Schiraldi threw a 6-hitter in the first game, but even that game was in doubt at one point, when Louisiana Tech scored 3 runs in the 4th with an error by Schiraldi, 2 hits and 3 walks giving Tech a lead in the game, 3-2. UT scored 4 in the 6th to retake the lead, and never looked back. Billy Bates and Jeff Hearron were both 2 for 3 for the game.

The second game was cut to 7 innings because it was so cold on the field some of the players said they could see their breath. Gus again juggled the lineup, putting Brumley back in center, where he played last year, and inserting Bryan Burrows at short. The coach said it was just to get Burrows some experience, in case he was ever needed at that position. The starting Tech pitcher in the second game, Jimmy Tuggle, was pretty wild, walking 5 in the first inning and giving up a wild pitch. Texas had a 6-1 lead through 4 innings, with Mike Capel throwing a one-hitter through the first 5. In the 6th, UT gave up two infield errors (not Burrows – errors were by Capel and Deron Gustafson) and 3 runs, so Kirk Killingsworth came in to close out the game (Kirk was also the designated hitter for the game, and was 2 for 3 at the plate). The 'Horns won the nightcap 9-4, and Texas is now 7-3 so far this year.

February 28th

Another game against Louisiana Tech, and this time Texas got the series sweep. It did take 11 innings today, but UT got the win! José Tolentino singled in the bottom of the 11th, and came all the way around when Mike Trent doubled. Trent's shot down the right field line was barely over Carl Boyd, the Tech first baseman, and then when Bill Pittman in right bobbled the ball José was able to come home from third. All this after Jeff Hearron had tied the game in the bottom of the 9th with a triple that brought home 2 runs, tying the game – or the 'Horns would have lost another one. David Denny's triple in the 5th scored 2, and Texas drew 7 walks during the game, but left 12 stranded on base. UT also had 3 errors in the game – not the typical UT defense – and the Texas starter, Wade Phillips, gave up 2 home runs in his 7 innings, including one by Tech pitcher Bob Van Vuren over the green monster, the tall fence in centerfield – only the second time since Disch-Falk Field opened that someone has cleared the monster. Eric Boudreaux pitched well in relief, holding Tech scoreless for 4 innings, and he got the win.

This 7-6 win puts UT at 8-3 for the year. Not a great record, but at least the 'Horns have won 3 in a row! Now Texas has two games against Oral Roberts on Monday and Tuesday, and then Cal-State Fullerton comes to town next weekend.

February 29ᵗʰ

A leap year game against Oral Roberts to end the first month of ball games seems only fitting. And Texas won. Roger Clemens pitched a great game, and more importantly, it seems as if Clint Thomas, the UT pitching coach, has fixed Roger's issues with his delivery. A pitcher's arm is supposed to accelerate through the entire motion, from the point behind his back to when he releases the ball. This not only adds speed to the pitch, but also helps to control the pitch location. What Clint noticed is that Roger was trying to throw 95 from the start of his motion, instead of just letting the speed build as his front leg hit the ground and the arm moved forward. That meant that a lot of Roger's pitches were staying up in the zone, and that made them more hittable. Not to get into the weeds on the biomechanics of a pitch, but you can think of the arm as a lever, being forced forward by the strength of a pitcher's legs and the torque of his body twisting as he starts his stride toward the plate and then hitting the ground with his front leg. By having Roger loosen his grip a little, and going back to a smoother arm acceleration, his pitches today were staying down more, and the results were outstanding. Roger did leave one pitch up, and ORU's Ron Henika made Clemens pay by putting it over the Green Monster in centerfield, the second one hit over that wall in the last two days. Other than that, Roger kept ORU scoreless, and showed the form that has him predicted to be an All-American and first round draft choice this spring. He dropped his ERA from 6.28 to 4.29 and struck out 9. Tolentino was the hitting star today, going 3 for 4, singling in 1 run and scoring the winning run in the 6ᵗʰ. Stacy Helms, the ORU pitcher, was a friend of José Tolentino's from Seminole Junior College. José said he took Helms out on Sunday night and tried to get him drunk, but that Helms wouldn't drink. This was Helm's first loss of the year. Texas played errorless ball, which the 'Horns haven't done much of this season. A good win!

CHAPTER 5

MARCH

March 1st

UT beat Oral Roberts again. But barely! Roger Lewis, who pitched for Texas' pitching coach Clint Thomas in summer ball, threw a 3-hitter against the 'Horns. Normally that would be good enough to win, but he also made a costly error that cost ORU the game. In the 5th, with Lewis throwing a no-hitter up to that point, Mike Simon singled. Bryan Burrows walked, and Billy Bates laid down a sacrifice bunt. Lewis fielded the bunt but threw the ball over the first baseman's head. Two runs scored, with Bates ending up on third. Mike Brumley hit a hard shot off of first baseman Keith Mucha's glove, and the ball caromed to Keith Miller at second. He threw Brumley out – but Bates scored on the play, giving UT the winning run in a 3-2 victory.

Steve Labay gave up 2 home runs as he tired in the 7th, but luckily no one was on base when they were hit. And Texas got another break when Mike Batesole tried to stretch a triple he hit off of reliever Calvin Schiraldi into an inside-the-park home run. He was thrown out at home plate in the 8th, with the throw from left-fielder Mike Trent and the relay by Mike Brumley to Jeff Hearron at the plate being one of the best plays of the year. Schiraldi did give up a single in the 9th, putting the tying run on base, but ended up striking out the side for his first save of the year.

ORU was ranked 9th in the country last week by Collegiate Baseball, and Texas just beat them twice – but UT slipped to 6th in the rankings after a not-so-stellar first couple of weeks of the season. The 'Horns are now 10-3 on the year but have won 5 straight. Texas plays ORU again later in the year, but next time up at their place in Tulsa. Now UT has Augie Garrido's Cal-State Fullerton squad coming to town. They are a perennial College World Series contender and will be the toughest competition the 'Horns have faced so far this year. Texas has a single game on Friday against CSF, and then a doubleheader on Saturday. A good litmus test on how the 'Horns are developing as a team!

March 3rd

A lot of the guys on the team dip snuff. The local American Tobacco Products distributor donates free rolls of both Skoal and Copenhagen, one of the perks the players get for being on the team. Every day when the players come into practice there are cans of the stuff on a stand in the locker room, replenished by one of the team managers. People were taking entire rolls (several cans) for themselves, until someone put up a sign, asking that the dippers only take a can or two, as the late arriving team members were finding the display empty by the time they got to the ballpark. It is a nice gesture from the ATP guy, as some guys on the team can't even afford the 25 cents it costs to buy a can of the stuff.

Mike Trent told a great story today. Yesterday, as he was leaving the locker room and heading to the field, sitting on the big trash can outside the locker room door was Earl Campbell! Earl said to Mike, "Hey, man." Mike, in awe, responded, "Hey!' Earl said, "You got any snuff?" Mike dug his can out of his back pocket, and handed it to Earl, expecting Earl to take a pinch out of the can. Instead, Earl took his finger, swirled it around the inside edge of the can, emptying it, and stuck an entire can of Skoal into his mouth! Mike was then handed the empty can. Today, as Mike was leaving the locker room, Earl was back on the trash can. But when Earl asked for snuff, Mike told him, "Not for you – you took my entire stash yesterday!"

March 4th

Another close, comeback win in extra innings. Texas won 8-7 with 3 runs in the bottom of the 10th, after Cal-State Fullerton scored twice in the top half of the inning. The game started off badly, with Cal-State scoring 4 quick runs off of the UT starter, Mike Capel. Wade Phillips, one of the new freshmen pitchers came in for relief. He gave up a run scoring single, but then pitched scoreless ball for the next 8 innings – one of Texas' best pitching performances so far this year.

UT scored 1 in the bottom of the 1st, and then 4 in the 6th, to take a 5-4 lead. But CSF scored 1 in the top of the 9th, tying the game, and giving the fans at DFF free baseball. In the 10th, Kirk Killingsworth (who had come in after Phillips tired in the 9th) gave up a bunt single, then issued an intentional walk to

CSF's hottest hitter. That backfired when the next batter, Bob Caffrey, laced a 2-run double off the wall in center, giving them a 7-5 lead. That didn't last long, as Deron Loy singled, Mike Trent doubled, and pinch hitter Alan Brown singled to center to tie the game again in the bottom of the 10th. Brown was out on a fielder's choice, but a throwing error on the play put Bryan Burrows at second. Billy Bates singled, moving Burrows to third. CSF intentionally walked Mike Brumley to set up a force play at home – but then their pitcher also walked Steve Labay, allowing Burrows to walk home with the winning run.

The Longhorns are now 11-3 and have won 6 straight games. CSF lost only their 3rd game of the year, and they were ranked #5 in the country coming into this game. Texas needs at least one win tomorrow out of the double header to win the series.

March 5th

And UT got both wins! That is 8 in a row, and 5 in a row over two teams ranked in the top 10 in the country, Oral Roberts and Cal-State Fullerton. Maybe Texas is not as bad as the early season critics made the team out to be! The 'Horns beat CSF 3-1 and 10-3 for the sweep.

In the first game, UT started off slowly, with Calvin Schiraldi loading the bases – but then he struck out the side, ending the threat. Jeff Hearron knocked in a run in the 2nd, giving Texas the lead, but CSF tied the game in the top of the 4th. But in the bottom of the 4th, Jeff hit a 2-run homer, giving UT the winning runs in a 7-inning game. Killingsworth came in to close it out in the 7th.

In the second game, Texas scored 5 in the 2nd inning after the Titans gave up 3 hits and kicked the ball around for 4 errors. Burrows had the big hit in the inning, a 2-run single. Tolentino followed with a home run the next inning (and was 3 for 5 for the day), giving the 'Horns a big lead. Roger Clemens pitched a complete game, giving up 3 runs, but getting the last six outs in a row to close out the game. Gus actually said some nice things about the team, and Augie Garrido was very complimentary – "Texas has a good ball club, the best facility we've ever played in and the best fans. They also have far and away the best pitching we've seen."

The team has Sunday, tomorrow, off, and then they have Lubbock Christian coming in here to play on Monday. LCC is the number one NAIA team in the country, and has won 15 out of 16 games this year – including a sweep of Texas Tech last weekend.

March 7th

And Texas got beat again. And this time it was by one of their former teammates. Bobby Hinson, who played for UT his first two years in college, outpitched Steve Labay and Kirk Killingsworth to go to 9-0 in his career. He had late inning help from a couple of relievers, but Hinson was outstanding. Coach Gus said that if Hinson had pitched like that when he was here, he would still be here. The game was scheduled for 7 innings, but the teams were tied at that point. Then, with a runner on second in the top of the 8th, Killingsworth was looking for a bunt, and put a pitch down the middle. The batter, Chet Feldman, wasn't bunting. He put the ball over the wall in left field, and that was the ball game. It was Kirk's first loss as a Longhorn. Jeff Hearron was 2 for 3 for the game and drove in 1 of the 'Horn's 2 runs, but that wasn't enough against Hinson.

Texas did win the nightcap, 8-0, with both Hearron and José Tolentino going 3 for 3 in that game, and Mike Capel and Killingsworth combining for the shutout. UT is now 14-4 for the year. Not exactly ready for prime time – and Texas starts conference play in a couple of weeks. And A&M swept Call-State Fullerton in a double header yesterday. Maybe the wins against CSF were not the great victories against a powerhouse team that Texas thought at the time. UT has Dallas Baptist coming in this weekend for back-to-back doubleheaders. Hopefully, they don't have any pitchers that transferred from Texas!

Gus was not a happy camper. After the second game, he told all the pitchers to come out to the bullpen, and he chewed on everybody. He told them they need to quit reading their press clippings and pitch like they had shown they could in the past. He didn't pick on any individuals, but everyone knew he was upset at the entire staff. And they probably deserved it. He said something about how UT didn't deserve to be highly ranked, because the team's play just ranked. He was right. Texas needed to play better, and there would be no repeat trip to Omaha if the 'Horns don't get their act together.

March 9th

The team had a funny thing happen today. It could have been a serious problem, but it turned out okay. David Denny has been taking both infield practice and outfield practice, but mostly playing outfield and serving as the designated hitter on occasion. Today, Bill Bethea sent Denny out to the outfield to shag fly balls.

As mentioned, a lot of the guys on the team dip snuff. When Denny got to the outfield, the rest of the outfielders asked him if he ever dipped. David said no, and they told him that if he was going to be an outfielder, he had to dip. He agreed to try a dip, and asked which brand was milder – Skoal or Copenhagen? Somebody told him Skoal, so he took a dip.

A few minutes later, when it was Denny's turn to catch a fungo, the ball came down and beaned David right in the forehead, knocking him cold! Eddie Day, the team's lead trainer, rushed out onto the field and got Denny back to the dugout. Once Eddie found the snuff (still in David's cheek), Day, and the coaches, were livid. No one would admit to giving the snuff to Denny. Everyone who was in the outfield that day ended up running extra lines for a few days! For those of you who have never played, "running lines" means to run from one foul line to the other across the outfield – the equivalent of taking a lap in some other sport.

The bad news was that Billy Bates has been diagnosed with torn ligaments in his left thumb. He injured it on a slide into second. He needs surgery but says he will postpone the surgery until "after we win the World Series." It is possible Gus will rest him some before Texas starts conference play. But knowing Bates, he will want to play, just taping up the thumb and putting up with the pain.

March 11th

UT won both games against Dallas Baptist today. The pitching was outstanding, with both Calvin Schiraldi and Roger Clemens throwing shutouts. Calvin only gave up 4 hits, and Roger only gave up 2 hits and 1 walk the entire second game. Calvin Schiraldi has been consistently good this year, but this was by far the best Roger Clemens has looked all year. He has won his last 3 starts and is up to 3-2 for the year. The tweak to Roger's pitching motion that Clint Thomas made has obviously made a difference!

Texas won the first game 6-0, with Mike Brumley, Deron Loy, and Jeff Hearron all going 2 for 3 in the game. Hearron drove in 2 runs – he is hitting over .500 in the last 7 games - and José Tolentino also had 2 RBIs with a sacrifice fly and a double. Also interesting was that Billy Bates was in his usual spot at second base and batting in his normal spot as the leadoff hitter, bad thumb and all.

UT won the nightcap 4-0, with José hitting 2 more doubles (giving him 10 so far this season). Deron Gustafson had a double in the 3rd, went to third on a ground out, and then caused the Dallas Baptist pitcher, Bill Elliot, to balk for the first run of the game. Deron also had a good game at second base, and it is nice to see him playing well so that Bates can get some time off when he needs to rest that hand. But no rest for the team– another double header against this same DBU team tomorrow, Saturday.

March 12th

The 'Horns swept Dallas Baptist again, but it wasn't as easy as the Friday games. UT scored 5 runs in the first couple of innings in the early game, with Billy Bates and Mike Trent both going 2 for 3. Trent, Jamie Doughty, and Bryan Burrows drove in 2 runs apiece. Trent, David Denny, and Doughty all hit doubles, and Bates a triple. Texas ended up winning 9-4. Killingsworth was the winner but gave up 4 earned runs in his 5 innings, unusual for him. The homer he gave up in the 3rd was the first run scored against UT in 25 innings. Eric Boudreaux pitched the 6th and 7th to close out the win.

Texas won the last game in this 4-game series 8-6. Steve Labay, José Tolentino, Bud Ray, Deron Loy, and Deron Gustafson (again filling in for Bates) had 2 hits apiece, including doubles by Tolentino, Ray, and Loy. The game was tied 4-4 in the bottom of the 4th, when UT scored 4 more runs on 6 consecutive 2-out hits. 2 of the 4 runs the 'Horn's pitchers gave up were homers by Richard Salaiz, who played his freshman year here at UT. What is it about former players coming back here and trying to beat this team? Wade Phillips was the starter and winner, relieved by Eric Boudreaux (again, who pitched in the 7th and 8th), and then Mike Capel came in to close – and he nearly blew the game. DBU got runners to second and third, only down 2 runs, but then Capel got the last batter to ground out to Tolentino at first to end the threat and the game.

Mike Brumley didn't play in either game. In the opener, Gus penciled Mike in to play centerfield instead of his usual position this year, shortstop. Mike got pretty upset, telling Coach Gus that he was a shortstop, and wasn't going to take a "demotion" back to the outfield. Gus got mad at a player questioning his moves and told Brumley he would play where he was told to play, or he wouldn't play at all. So Brumley was on the bench for the doubleheader.

What had occurred was a repeat scene from the 1967 movie Cool Hand Luke – "What we have here is a failure to communicate." Gus was just trying to get backup shortstop Bryan Burrows some experience, but still wanted Brumley's bat in the lineup – but Mike apparently thought the move was supposed to be permanent. Mike knew when he got to UT that he would be behind Spike Owen for a couple of years, but then would get his chance at short. So, he was surprised when Gus penciled him in for an outfield slot. They talked after they cooled off a bit, and

Gus agreed that Mike could play short in the second game – but the coaches decided during the first game of the double header that they couldn't let the rebellion stand. Both the player and coach got their backs up over a situation that neither really understood. Gus did say after the game that, "When he's ready to play under those circumstances, he'll probably play again." Texas needs Mike Brumley playing, so hopefully this mess gets straightened out quickly! UT has another busy week, and 17 ball games over the next 9 days – a doubleheader against St. Mary's on Monday, a doubleheader against Southwestern on Tuesday, 4 games against Emporia State on Wednesday and Thursday, and then single games against a ranked Arizona State team on Friday and Saturday. This is Gus's version of a college Spring Break – who needs a trip to the beach?

March 14th

Conference play opened this past weekend, but due to some strange scheduling quirk Texas doesn't play their conference opener for another couple of weeks. Arkansas and Baylor split their Saturday doubleheader, giving the Razorbacks a 2-1 conference record. Arkansas is who Texas opens with in their first conference series. The bigger news is that Houston swept Rice this weekend, to remain undefeated on the year at 17-0. When you combine the Houston baseball team with their Phi Slamma Jamma basketball monster, you start to wonder what is in the water down in Houston? The UH baseball team is currently ranked #4 in the country by Collegiate Baseball, behind Texas, Wichita State and Miami. It is beginning to look like they might be UT's toughest conference competition this year, but you can never count out Rice or Arkansas, either. Anyway, back to the Texas games.

Today UT played St. Mary's, and split another doubleheader, giving the 'Horns a 19-5 record this year. Texas only lost 6 games all of last year, with two of those losses in Omaha, so you can see how the team has been struggling early this season. Mark Bond, who pitched a 3-hitter against the Longhorns last year (as a freshman) but still lost that game, only gave up 4 hits in the opener today – and won the opening game today, 5-1. This was the first time Texas has been held under 2 runs since UT lost to Miami last June in the College World Series. Jamie Doughty had a rough game at third, with 3 errors in the game. Mike Trent went 2 for 2, and Steve Labay knocked in only Texas run of the game – but there weren't many UT hitting highlights to talk about in game one.

In the second game, the teams were tied 2-2 until the 4th, when UT scored 5 runs on 6 hits, including 4 in a row. Allan Brown had a 2-run double, and Kirk Killingsworth put a 2-run bomb over the wall to give Texas a comfortable lead. Brown added a 2-run home run off the scoreboard in left in the 5th. Steve Labay was the loser in game one, going the full 7 innings. Mike Capel won the nightcap, 12-2, going 7 innings. David Seitz, who was playing basketball for UT up until last week, came in for the last 2 innings, and looked like he was just getting into baseball shape. He gave up a hit and two walks in his 2 innings but struck out 3. Mike Brumley did not play in either game, apparently still in Gus's doghouse.

March 15th

Texas was supposed to play a doubleheader against Southwestern today, but both games were rained out. Most of the guys were happy to have a break from almost daily baseball. The day wasn't a total loss. A couple of the players got to go to a funeral in Tyler with one of the coaches. They were asked to represent the team at the funeral for Don Russell, who played baseball for UT in 1948 and 1949, with that team winning the national championship in '49.

They didn't know Mr. Russell, but did meet an interesting character at the funeral. J.L. Smith pitched for UT starting a couple of years after that '49 championship, and in his junior year, 1953, ended up pitching in 5 of the 6 games UT played in Omaha that year. He was named the Most Valuable Player at that CWS, even though UT finished second that year. He holds the College World Series record for most appearances and most games finished in one series. He went on to military service after his years at UT, and now works for the Post Office in Austin. He says he still comes to a lot of UT games, but no one recognizes him as a former Texas baseball star. Coach Gustafson was a teammate in 1952. J.L. told the current players a lot of interesting stories about that trip to Omaha – how the team took a bus to San Antonio, and then boarded a train for the trip north. Quite an experience!

In other news today, and more important than the funeral, Mike Brumley is back in Gus's good graces. Mike had actually started packing, and was determined to go back to Tulsa, but his parents came in for the weekend. Mike's dad suggested that they go talk to Gus, with Mike's dad just there for support. Mike and his dad met with Coach Gus for a little over 2 hours during the rainout and settled their issues. Mike has agreed to play wherever he is asked to play. Gus still wants Burrows to get some experience at short, just in case Brumley gets injured at some point, so Mike has agreed to play outfield when needed. But Gus also said that Brumley is, "Still our shortstop and always has been." The team is thrilled the two managed to make up – but probably didn't kiss! Tomorrow and Thursday, weather permitting (hopefully no more thunderstorms), Texas is scheduled to play doubleheaders against Emporia State. Back to the grind…

March 16th

God it was cold. All the team needed was a few snow flurries to make it a perfect day. The 'Horns swept the doubleheader against Emporia State, but the Kansas team brought their weather south with them – the wind chill was in the mid-30s the entire afternoon, with about a 20-mph wind blowing. There were only about 500 die-hard fans in the stands. Maybe people from up north who were used to that kind of weather?

Texas won the first (7 innings, as usual) game 4-0, with Roger Clemens and Calvin Schiraldi combining for the shutout. Schiraldi was perfect in his 3 innings. Bryan Burrows, playing short, was 2 for 3 in the game, including a double, and knocked in 1 of the 4 UT runs. Steve Labay had 1 hit, but also a sacrifice fly that drove in a run. Brumley did not play in the opener.

The second game was a laugher. UT won 14-1, scoring 6 in the first and 5 more in the fourth to wrap it up early. Wade Phillips added to the Texas 18-inning scoreless streak until the fifth and ran his season record to 3-0. JR Davenport pitched a couple of innings in relief, and Killingsworth came to pitch the ninth. Kirk was also one of the hitting stars for the game, going 4 for 5, with two 2-run singles and an RBI double. Labay blasted another home run. Burrows again played shortstop and was 2 for 5, and 4 for 8 for the doubleheader. Mike Brumley finally played, but in centerfield – and went 1 for 5 for the game. The Longhorns had 14 hits for the game, so there were a lot of batting averages getting padded. Texas is now at 21-5 for the year. And the team will do this again tomorrow, but hopefully with warmer weather!

March 17ᵗʰ

Another doubleheader sweep! UT won their games today 9-4 and 9-5, but it wasn't as easy as the final scores indicate. Emporia State hit a grand slam in the first game after Texas was leading 7-0 to make it a lot closer, but then the 'Horns pitching staff held them scoreless the rest of that game.

In the nightcap, Texas was losing 5-1 going into the 7ᵗʰ. Deron Gustafson reminded the team about Coach Gus's threat for "a little extra conditioning" the next time UT lost to a team that they should beat easily. Texas took that warning to heart and scored 8 runs in the 7ᵗʰ and 8ᵗʰ to win that game, too. Knowing Gus, "extra conditioning" means running lines and running the stairs here at the Disch, or running the ramps at the football stadium. And running until several people are puking. The players will tell you it is not fun.

Eric Boudreaux pitched a complete game in the opener, but was only leading 7-4 after the grand slam hit by ESU's Cliff Thompson in the 5th. Billy Bates added a 2-run homer in the 6ᵗʰ to end the scoring. Steve Labay went 3 for 4 in that first game, with 3 RBIs. He continues to be the team's most valuable offensive player, and his pitching is an added bonus – he will be starting against Arizona State.

In the second game, the team's newest addition, David Seitz, started. But he only made it into the 4th. He struck out 7, but walked 5, not showing great control at this point. He is basically just now going through spring training, after reporting late at the end of the UT basketball season, so issues like that are to be expected. The Hornets had scored 4 in the 2nd and loaded the bases in the 4th. José Tolentino made a great diving stop and started a double play in that inning that kept UT out of additional trouble.

Mike Poehl relieved Seitz and pitched 3 1/3, Bruce Ruffin did 1 1/3 (and was the winner when Deron Gustafson hit a 2 RBI triple to break a 5-5 tie in the 8th), and then Killingsworth came in to handle the 9th and close it out. Mike Brumley was back at shortstop for both games and went 3 for 7 for the day. Deron Loy was 2 for 3, and Bud Ray was 2 for 4 and scored twice in game 2. So, no extra running. At least until next week! But now the competition gets stiffer with Arizona State coming in tomorrow.

March 18th

Tonight's game was a cakewalk. Literally. Arizona State walked 13 Longhorn batters, something Bill Bates said he had not seen since Little League. Coach Gus said that Arizona State had ended up with a late flight, not arriving in Austin until around 4:00 this afternoon. They might not have had time to get settled in before the game.

And the Wild Bunch got to the freshman ASU starter, Gilbert Villanueva. He got the first 2 outs in the bottom of the first, and then walked 6 straight batters with the crowd screaming on every ball 3 pitch. UT was winning 3-0 when he exited, not even finishing the first inning. And all that without a single hit. Texas only got 6 hits the entire game, but the walks helped the 'Horns cruise to an 11-2 win. In the 3rd, the ASU catcher dropped Jeff Hearron's pop foul – and then Hearron homered for UT's first hit of the game. In the 8th, ASU walked 5 more. 3 of those were intentional walks to set up potential double plays, but Mike Trent lashed a 2-run single, and Billy Bates added an RBI single later in the inning.

Steve Labay only gave up 4 hits and 2 runs over 7 innings, and was relieved in the 8th (Killingsworth, again) after giving up a leadoff walk. Killer pitched 2 scoreless innings to end the game. Arizona State had been ranked number 1 in the country a couple of weeks ago, but had lost 4 of their last 6 PAC-10 games to drop in the rankings. Texas was still happy to beat them, and UT is now 6-0 against top 20 teams this year. It is the Division II bunch that have been giving the 'Horns problems! Texas has now won 6 in a row, and the team is now 24-5 for the year. Not anywhere near last year's 30-game winning streak that UT started with in '82, but not horrible, either. Except in Gus's eyes – he expects to win every game.

March 19th

Texas was supposed to play a doubleheader against Arizona State this evening, but the rain only allowed the teams to get one game in. Roger Clemens pitched his best game of the year, shutting out ASU 6-0 on just 6 hits. He has now thrown 27 consecutive scoreless innings, showing that the changes Clint Thomas made in his delivery are more than working. Roger is now 5-2, winning 5 straight games after having started the season with 2 losses. Roger has always had that blazing fastball – that's why his nickname is "Goose," named after Goose Gossage – but now with the change in grip his breaking balls have more bite, and he is not hanging anything up over the plate. He has been working on his changeup, and to a lot of hitters the changeup looks like a fastball from some other pitcher!

Billy Bates had a hit and a run scoring sacrifice fly (Texas also had sac flies by Deron Loy and Kirk Killingsworth), Mike Trent had an RBI double, and Jeff Hearron also doubled. Mike Brumley has settled back in at shortstop, and was 2 for 4 for the game.

ASU coach Jim Brock was hilarious, as usual, in his pregame and postgame interviews. He talked about how Coach Gus had agreed to come to Arizona to play – "some day." He said UT called the third game because they were scared to play a hot team. And he said he didn't think Roger was throwing a regulation-sized baseball. He said Cliff's idea of a College World Series would be for 7 teams to go to Omaha and play it off, with the winner having to come to Austin to face UT. The dichotomy of the loquacious Brock and the taciturn Gustafson was pretty apparent. You can tell the two guys really like each other and respect each other. But Gus was happy to have the sweep against his buddy!

And before the rains came, Bill Bates got a jolt. He had played in what was supposed to be the first game of the doubleheader, and pretty much up until now Gus had been playing Deron in the nightcap games. But as Bill Bates was sitting at his locker, thinking he would be on the bench for this game, Bill Bethea came by and just casually mentioned, "Have you looked at the lineup for the second game?" Bates was penciled in to start and bat leading off. It was Bates' first inkling that he might have won the season's starter's job at second base!

March 20th

Again, no rest for the weary. A Sunday doubleheader today against Texas Wesleyan, another double header tomorrow, Monday, against the same team, and then two games on Tuesday against SE Oklahoma. That's 7 straight days of baseball. That's hard on a pitching staff, and the aches and pains from that many games in a row start to add up for the people playing every day. But Cliff is determined to get the team settled in before they start conference play, so UT plays on. And on. And on…

Texas swept the doubleheader today. UT won 4-3 in the first game, with the game going a full 9 innings. It was supposed to be a 7-inning game, but Wesleyan scored 3 in the top of the 7th to tie the game, and the 'Horns didn't put it away until the 9th when Jeff Hearron hit a sacrifice fly after the TW pitcher walked the bases loaded with no outs. Calvin Schiraldi pitched the first 7, and looked great until he gave up the tying runs on a 2-run single and a double. Kirk Killingsworth came in and got a strikeout to end the 7th, and then pitched a scoreless 2 innings to get UT the win. He hasn't given up a run in over 7 innings and is now 5-1 for the year.

Mike Trent went 2 for 2 for the game, with 2 walks. Bryan Burrows was 2 for 4, including a triple. Brumley was 1 for 4 with a double and an RBI. Texas only had 9 hits for the game, but they got them at the right time to give them the lead going into that bad 7th inning. Texas was a little lucky to end up with the victory, but a win is a win!

The big news of the day was Mike Capel throwing a 1-hitter in game 2. UT won that one 7-0 and the 'Horns have now won 9 straight. The team seems to be rolling, and maybe Texas deserves their ranking as the number one team in the country this week. Capel gave up a single in the 4th to slightly spoil what was otherwise a great day on the mound. Froggie is now 4-1 for the year.

UT scored all 7 runs in the 4th, with Mike Trent and Doug Hodo getting RBI singles, and Mike Brumley hitting a sacrifice fly. The other runs came on 5 straight walks, with 3 of them bases loaded affairs. The Wild Bunch was again getting into the head of the Texas Wesleyan pitcher, even causing him to balk in a run. Texas is now 27-5 on the year, and even Gus cracked a smile!

March 21st

What a difference a day makes. Texas lost both games of the doubleheader today. And after the second game Gus let the team know what he thought about the losses. Texas Wesleyan had not beaten UT since 1913. And they did it twice today. Rusty Ford, the Wesleyan pitcher, threw a 7 inning 6-hit shutout against the 'Horns in the first game, winning 3-0. And he finished the game after a line drive shot from Jeff Hearron hit him in the face in the bottom of the 6th. After getting knocked down, he was able to get up, find the ball, and throw Hearron out at first. After treatment to stop the bleeding (he ended up with a fracture in his mouth and a broken nose), he came back out and pitched the 7th. It was the first time Texas had been shut out in 130 games, going back over 2 years.

Wesleyan scored their 3 runs in the 1st off freshman Wade Phillips. Wade kept them scoreless the rest of the game, but UT couldn't generate any offense against Ford. Bryan Burrows went 2 for 3 with a double, and was the only guy on the UT team to make it as far as third base. Bates, Brumley, and Tolentino hit singles, and Texas left 6 runners on base in the game. Ford had been a teammate of Steve Labay at Angelina Junior College before transferring to TWC. If Gus had known he could pitch like this, he would have recruited Ford, too!

The UT team may have been in shock after the first game, but they looked terrible in the double header game. About the only good news is that there were maybe 500 fans there to see UT's embarrassing performance. Texas lost game two 6-5, after leading 4-3 going into the 7th. Eric Boudreaux was the starter and gave up a leadoff single in the 7th. He was relieved by Kirk Killingsworth, and Killer gave up a couple of hits to end up as the losing pitcher in this one. It was the first time in 4 years Texas had lost a doubleheader. Doug Hodo went 4 for 4 in the nightcap, but no one else had more than a single hit. Texas got one run back in the 8th when Mike Brumley tripled and then Hodo brought him home, but it wasn't enough.

Coach Gus' comments to the press after the game were pretty mild compared to what he said to the team in the locker room. He said, in public, "The first game we got beat by a superb pitching performance, and that'll happen. The second shouldn't have happened. I thought we looked pathetic with the bat all day. I'll have to think long and hard to think of a worse performance."

He kept the 'Horns in the locker room for over 30 minutes following game 2. He was as mad as some of the guys on the team have ever seen him. He started with a comment about how "we couldn't even knock a pitcher out of the game that had lost to Arkansas and TCU." He then went around the room, talking to each player individually. He concentrated on the junior college transfers, challenging them as to whether they had really bought in to what it takes to be a winner at UT. He had everyone in the room hanging their heads. The only funny incident was that he was so mad that when he got around to Bud Ray, he couldn't remember Bud's name! He looked at Bud for a long, silent minute, and the team wondered what was coming. Bud didn't play in either game today, so the players couldn't figure out why the long stare – until Gus finally said, "And what's your name?" The guys on the team had a hard time keeping from smiling, much less laughing! Bud just said, "Bud Ray, coach." And he got chewed on just like everyone else.

March 22nd

UT has another doubleheader today, against SE Oklahoma – another team the 'Horns should beat fairly easily. But before the game, Roger Clemens called a team meeting – just the team, no coaches. Roger started off about how Gus was right – it appeared that some people were not willing to make the sacrifices necessary for this team to win consistently. The team's other well-respected pitcher, Calvin Schiraldi, echoed what Roger had said. But then, surprisingly, they turned the meeting over to newcomer José Tolentino! People respected Roger and Calvin for their work ethic, and respected José for him overcoming the things he had beaten to turn into a decent student and great ballplayer. So, the team was willing to listen to all three of them.

José talked about how those sacrifices meant little things, like not staying out late on a Friday or Saturday night after the game, knowing that the team had a game or doubleheader the next day. He said that the players needed to hold each other accountable, too, and that too many people were going out on their own, instead of with teammates that could make sure everyone got to bed at a reasonable hour. He said, "We really don't know each other, because we never hang out together outside of the Disch. We need to be more than teammates. We need to be friends!" Someone said, "Well, why don't we go out together?" Mike Capel made a couple of comments – he said, "We all need to be pulling on the same rope," and "Let's go have fun – I never had any fun losing!" The meeting helped to relax the team. They were all a little frustrated, and maybe pressing, after losing so many games to teams they should have stomped. After that meeting, everyone could feel a little more pep during batting practice and pregame warmups.

And UT ended up blowing away SE Oklahoma State in both games that day. The 14-2, 15-3 sweep is the way Texas should have been playing all year! Steve Labay threw a complete game 5-hitter in the opener, and the 'Horns sent 13 people to the plate in the 3rd for 8 runs and UT's biggest inning of the year to date. Bryan Burrows had a 2-run double, and Mike Brumley even stole home! Mike Simon was 2 for 3 for the game, Billy Bates drove in 3 runs, and David Denny was 2 for 4 with a double. But the hitting hero for the game was freshman Doug Hodo. He went 3 for 4, with 2 RBIs, a double, and a triple. He was 5 for 8 in the doubleheader and assured himself a trip to Arkansas next weekend. Before today, he wasn't sure he would be on the traveling squad – he had only played in 3 of the first 36 games - and he had gotten a date for Friday night to a sorority dance in San Marcos with a girl going to Southwest Texas. Looks like he will have to break his date!

Our newcomer, David Seitz, started the second game and pitched well for 3 innings. He gave up a run in the 1st, but then retired 11 in a row before loading the bases in the 4th, when Gus had seen enough and pulled him. Calvin Schiraldi pitched 3 1/3, and the scorekeeper gave him the win. Roger Clemens came in and closed the game, pitching the last 2 innings. David Denny went 5 for 5, drove in 2, and then after the game told a reporter that he was going to be Hodo's agent for pro negotiations. David was 7 for 9 for the doubleheader, and Texas needs his hot bat going into conference play, too. Now, the team gets a couple of days off before heading to Arkansas – and they all need the break!

Texas has played 18 games over the last 12 days, and that was with 3 rainouts. They have played through thunderstorms, lightning (with some long delays), freezing cold days and a few hot days. UT is 15-3 over that span and are back ranked as the number 1 team in the country, mostly as a result of the wins over some other decent teams during the marathon. No one wants to talk about the doubleheader with Texas Wesleyan! José Tolentino played in every game. Doug Hodo went from a non-entity to a possible starter. Coach Gus probably ate 50 peanut butter sandwiches and drank 20 gallons of iced tea. A tough schedule, but the team thinks they are a much better team than they were two weeks ago. People are tired, but it was worth it!

CHAPTER 6

THE CONFERENCE

March 24th

The Southwest Conference battles actually started two weeks ago, but due to the mentioned scheduling quirk Texas doesn't have their first conference games until this coming weekend. Baylor and Rice have already played 2 series, and everyone else has played 1. UT is the last team to start conference play. The Longhorns were the preseason conference favorite in the coaches' poll, but that was before Houston got off to such a hot start. The Cougars are now 26-2 for the season, and 3-0 in the conference, having swept Tech last weekend. The Aggies are also having a good year, at 20-5 for the year and 2-1 in conference play. Winning this conference is not going to be a walk in the park!

Texas is 29-7 for the year, with every one of those wins and losses having occurred at home in Disch-Falk Field. UT starts their conference schedule with Arkansas, and the first Texas road trip. The Razorbacks have moved the series to the Arkansas Travelers' field in Little Rock, where the minor league team plays, to allow more fans to attend and to showcase the venue – the Arkansas coach wants to hold the conference tournament up there next year. This year the conference tournament will again be in Austin, and the Texas team is happy they get to stay home for that, too!

Little Rock's Ray Winder Field, the home of the Travelers, has natural grass – which Texas hasn't played on all year, since all their games have been in Austin. So, UT went north a day early and practiced on that field on Thursday. The 'Horns haven't been a great fielding team so far this year – they have made 40 errors over the 36 games played. And that is on a field where you rarely get a bad bounce! So, Gus was worried about the team not being comfortable on the real stuff and had everyone fielding ground balls for a couple of hours. The coaches are actually thrilled Texas is playing in Little Rock instead of the Razorback's bandbox stadium in Fayetteville. They don't think the crowd noise here will be anywhere near as bad as what they heard a couple of years back, the last time UT visited Fayettenam and George Cole Field. It may not really matter – with the Texas pitching staff, the 'Horns should do well wherever they play.

March 25th

The weather is a factor. It is so cold Gus said he was surprised there are no icicles hanging from the edge of the dugout. With the wind blowing the way it is, the wind chill factor must be below freezing! And Texas has had some games where they didn't play well in cold weather. About the only good news is that it is equally cold for both teams. Gus, as usual, took his huge space heaters with him up to Little Rock. He hates to be cold! It was almost hot in the dugout, and with those huge heaters taking up so much room, there was barely space for all the players. The dugouts there are a little below ground level, with steps leading up to the field – so that did help keep a little heat in the dugout.

Arkansas was hitting .326 coming into the series with UT, standing 22-6 for the year and a with a 3-3 conference record. Gus wanted to quiet those bats, so he put Roger Clemens on the mound for the opener on Friday afternoon. Goose was outstanding, as he has been since Clint Thomas made the mechanical change to his grip and motion. UT won 9-4, with Roger only giving up 1 unearned run over the first 7 innings. He struck out 11 and retired 10 in a row at one point in the game. He did seem to tire in the 8th, giving up 5 hits and 3 more runs, but by that time Texas had such a huge lead it didn't matter.

The cold weather helped to hold down the crowd, with only about a 1,000 people rattling around a ballpark that will hold over 10,000. Texas had their share of fans there, too, and with the small crowd the UT team could hear the Longhorn fans cheering every time Texas scored. Jeff Hearron had a couple of doubles to lead the hitting, and Mike Trent drove in a couple of runs with two singles. Arkansas helped out with 12 walks, the most they have given up in a single game all year. Gus said he thought the cold contributed to that number, too. And the cold may have contributed to the 3 errors Texas had in the game – but they didn't cost UT. A good way to start conference play!

March 26th

The rain and cold caused the scheduled doubleheader in Little Rock to be postponed until Sunday. The bad news is that the Texas team has to stay another day in Arkansas, and they don't get their usual Sunday off day. But at least UT gets to go home after Sunday – to paraphrase Abe Lemons, the 'Horns get to go home, but the poor Razorbacks have to live here!

March 27th

Jeff Hearron said this afternoon was "colder than a tin toilet in a Yukon blizzard." Temperatures for both games were in the low 40s, and the wind was blowing over 20 mph. Everybody was volunteering to be the designated hitter today, so as not to have to go out and play in the field for the bottom half of each inning. Cliff Thomas said he was freezing just pitching batting practice! There were only about 350 people at the double header, and probably a third of that number were diehard Texas fans. But even with the cold, Texas managed a sweep!

UT won the 7-inning opener 6-1, behind Calvin Schiraldi's 3-hitter. He was on fire the entire game and is now 5-0 for the year. Billy Bates was 3 for 5 for the game with a double, José Tolentino was 2 for 3 with a double, and Kirk Killingsworth (who was the DH for this game) hit a solo home run. Killer's home run was hit so far that it actually went through a window in a building behind the outfield fence! Jeff Hearron drove in 2 of the 'Horn's 6 runs. But Calvin was the star. He said he didn't mind pitching in the cold but felt the Razorback hitters were a little uncomfortable trying to hit the ball in this weather. He struck out 7 in this 7-inning game, and only gave up a single earned run.

UT did have one injury before the game started. Deron Loy was helping to hit infield, and a return throw got him when he wasn't paying attention, hitting him in the eye. It reminded the players that were on the team last year of the injury to Coach Gus. Hope it is not serious!

Bud Ray had been pounding the ball in practice and looked great during pregame batting practice, so Gus put him in late in the game to pinch hit. Bud struck out, and when he got back to the dugout Gus asked him what happened. Bud told Gus that he had forgotten to bring a coat, and that he had gotten so cold in the dugout that he was shivering – and that is why he couldn't get around on the Arkansas pitcher's fastball.

The second game was a slugfest. The Texas pitching wasn't sharp for most of the game, to say the least. UT was leading 3-0 going into the bottom of the 4th, but Arkansas scored 4 runs off of starter Mike Capel and reliever Steve Labay to take the lead. Killingsworth came in to get the last out in the 4th, and UT retook the lead with 3 runs in the top of the 5th. Kirk gave up a run in the bottom of the 5th to make it a 6-5 game. The Killer held the Razorbacks scoreless for the next 3 innings, and Texas scored 4 in the top of the 8th to take a 10-5 lead, which you would think would be safe with the usually outstanding UT pitching staff. But Kirk gave up 4 runs in the bottom of the 8th, to make it a 1 run game going into the 9th.

In the top of the 9th, Jeff Hearron hit one of the longest homeruns Gus said he had ever seen – hitting the top of a 50-foot-high screen at the 380-foot mark in left field. Coach Gustafson said after the game that the home run ball would have gone 500 feet! That gave UT an extra insurance run, making it an 11-9 game, but to make sure Texas held the lead Gus brought Roger Clemens in to finish the game. He had pitched 7 innings on Friday, but the coach felt he still had a little left in his tank – and he shut Arkansas down in the bottom of the 9th, striking out 1 and just giving up 1 single to earn his first save as a Longhorn.

Freshman Doug Hodo had 3 hits in the game, including 2 doubles, and Bryan Burrows was 3 for 4, including a double, and scored twice. He did have to leave the game in the 9th after bruising his shoulder after a scary collision on a popup. Hope he is OK!

The Texas 3-0 conference record puts UT second in the conference, behind Houston's 6-0 record. At least now Texas gets a few days off, with no midweek game this week. Next weekend the 'Horns have TCU coming in for the conference home opener. Houston hosts Texas Tech, and the Texas team is hoping Tech can take a game or two from the Cougars, but that may be difficult with Houston playing as well as they are and being at home for the weekend. And Tech seems to be down this year, with conference and overall records below .500 for the season. On the other hand, the Cougars are at 30-2 for the year, one of the best overall records in the country. But at least Texas is now in the conference race! In the rankings, UT has dropped to number 2 in the country according to Baseball America, behind Miami's 38-8 record (they have won 27 of their last 29). But Collegiate Baseball still has Texas number 1. The Houston Cougars are currently number 3 in both polls. Those polls only matter at the end of the year, as the NCAA considers them when seeding teams for the regional playoffs. As the Oakland Raider's Al Davis puts it, "Just win, baby!"

March 29th

Some terrible news. Billy Bates says he is quitting the team. Bates was having some family problems at home, and wanted a second opinion on his injured thumb – the Austin doctors were saying he needed surgery now, but Bill wanted to check with the Houston Oiler's ortho guy. So, Bill asked Gus for a day off – just skipping practice for one day – so that he could go home to Houston. Gus said no, and Bates left for Houston anyway. Bill's friends, especially Mike Brumley and Mike Trent, had tried to talk Bates out of leaving, but it didn't work. Bates called Wayne Graham, asking about a chance to transfer to San Jacinto Junior College, and apparently Wayne called Gus, asking what was going on with Bates.

March 31st

It wasn't an April Fool's joke. Bates is back! And, just in time. Texas starts their second conference series with TCU tomorrow night, and UT needs Bill in the lineup! Apparently when he left, he had just jumped in the car and took off, leaving all his stuff in Austin. When he came back to get his clothes, he agreed to sit down and talk to Gus about the situation, and they worked out their differences.

A couple of funny notes this week – while the team was in Arkansas, several of the players got buzz cuts to honor balding Coach Gustafson. The 3 Texas catchers, Jeff Hearron, Alan Brown, and Deron Loy, plus Gus's son Deron, all got shorn. They look like they are ready for boot camp with the Marines. Deron said that when his girlfriend saw his haircut, she told him, "I'll see you in six weeks." Deron Loy said the barber originally left him a tail on the back of his head, and offered to dye it burnt orange – but Darron decided on the all over cut. The rest of the team says they are not planning on joining that trend!

And Jeff Hearron and a couple of co-conspirators got into the rooms in Arkansas where first baseman José Tolentino and trainers Eddie Day and Tommy Allen were staying, filled their telephone earpieces with shaving cream, and then called their rooms to give the victims an earful. Jeff is well known for his hijinks, but if someone tries to get him back, he'll pull stuff on that teammate all year. John Turman, one of the team managers, walked into Roger Clemens room to find a bunch of guys playing cards. The phone rang, and Roger told John to answer it – and John got an earful of shaving cream.

Last fall, while the team was in the locker room, Hearron took a big hunk of Vaseline and smeared it all around under his nose, so that it looked like he had the biggest booger of all time hanging from a nostril. Then he grabbed a bat, and told Gus he was having trouble with his stance, and could the coach take a look at how he was standing? Gus watched him take his stance and never said a word about Hearron's nose – so Jeff's joke got turned back on him a little – that time! And every time he would pull something, he would apologize, like it was an accident – but there were too many instances for them to not be on purpose! You can always tell when Hearron is around because he has a bad shoulder, and loves to apply DMSO on that shoulder. DMSO, dimethyl sulfoxide, is an anti-inflammatory drug usually used on horses. It smells terrible, so you can smell Jeff coming!

April 1st

The Longhorns beat TCU tonight, but barely, with Roger Clemens striking out the last two batters in the 9th after a home run had shrunk the Texas lead to just one run. UT won 6-5, with Roger going the distance (which saves the bullpen for tomorrow's doubleheader, if needed). Roger didn't have that great a game, with all 5 TCU runs earned. That didn't help his ERA, but a win is a win, and it raised his record on the year to 7-2. UT was leading 2-0 in the 3rd, when Roger gave up 4 runs, including a 3-run homer to TCU's Jimmy Twardowski.

Roger is suffering from an inflamed elbow. He had the same tendonitis problem last year, and Gus even left him at home from one road trip to help him heal. This year, Roger is determined to pitch through the pain – it will be interesting to see how well he can handle the discomfort.

David Denny in left field and José Tolentino at first made spectacular fielding plays to keep Texas in the game, and UT scored 1 in the bottom of the 3rd to get the 'Horns back to within 1 run. José homered in the 5th to tie the game, and then UT scored 2 in the 6th to finally retake the lead. Doug Hodo, the freshman who has turned into a hitting machine over the last half dozen games, was again 3 for 5 for the night, including a triple in the 6th that scored Mike Brumley. Hodo then scored that vital insurance run when the TCU third baseman let the relay throw skip by him into the dugout.

The Texas team had heard before their game started that Texas Tech had swept a doubleheader from UH down in Houston, and the Houston losses plus the UT win tonight puts Texas in first place in the conference! Gus said that he was worried after the team heard about Houston losing that his team might not take TCU seriously – the Frogs have lost 22 straight here in Austin – but UH finally getting beat just fired up the 'Horns! The conference race is just getting started, and there are some good teams out there. But it is nice to be looking down on everyone else in the standings! But UT can't let up – a doubleheader tomorrow, and TCU has already shown the 'Horns they can be dangerous.

April 2nd

And dangerous they were. Texas nearly lost both games today. UT did lose the first one, even though Calvin Schiraldi threw a 1-hit gem. Unfortunately, that 1 hit was a wind-blown home run in the top of the 7th, by TCU's Jeff Shafer, and Texas lost the opener 1-0. It was Calvin's first loss of the year. UT only had 4 hits against the TCU pitcher, freshman Brian Ohnoufka, one of which was a double by José Tolentino, and the 'Horns left 6 on base during the game. Texas got shut out for only the second time all season.

In the second game, UT got pounded early. Starter Mike Capel couldn't get anyone out, giving up 3 hits and 3 runs in the 1st before he was relieved by Steve Labay. Steve didn't fare any better. He did get UT out of the 1st without any additional damage, but in the 2nd, he gave up 6 more runs on 6 hits, putting Texas into a 9-0 hole after just 2 innings! But Wade Phillips came in and pitched 4 scoreless innings. Then Kirk Killingsworth pitched the last 3 1/3, giving up just 1 hit in the latter part of the game.

Texas somehow found a way to come back and win the game. Coach Gus said he couldn't ever remember coming back from being down 9 runs. UT scored 1 in the bottom of the 3rd, but the big inning was the 4th. TCU pitchers gave up 7 walks in that inning, and Mike Brumley hit a grand slam home run – the 'Horn's first hit of the game – to make the score 9-8 after the 4th, and UT was suddenly back in it. In the bottom of the 8th, Texas scored 3 to finally take the lead. José Tolentino hit a solo homer to tie the game, Alan Brown (short haircut and all) hit a pinch-hit sacrifice fly that gave UT the lead, and then Bryan Burrows surprised TCU with a bunt single that scored David Denny with the final run. David was 2 for 3 for the game, including a double. Texas' only other player with multiple hits was José, who was 2 for 4, including his 4th homer of the year. But it was a team effort to get the comeback win, with 8 different players scoring during the game.

The conference standings are convoluted at the top. Texas' 5-1 record puts the 'Horns in first place in the standings by percentage points over Houston (who beat Tech today), but UT is ½ game back of them on win-loss record, because Houston is 7-2, having played one more conference series than Texas has. That will balance out at the end of the year, unless UT has a bunch of rainouts. Next weekend Texas goes to Baylor, and Houston goes to Arkansas, so both teams have road series against teams in the middle of the standings. But before the next UT conference series, there is another midweek doubleheader against Hardin-Simmons, to give some of the younger players and pitchers a chance to get some additional game experience before UT gets to the playoffs at the end of the year.

April 5th

If you just look at the final scores, Texas did what they were supposed to do, which is blow Hardin-Simmons away in the doubleheader. The little private college from Abilene has never beaten UT. But the actual first game was in doubt for a while. UT was only leading 3-1 through the first 5 innings, but then the 'Horns scored 4 in the sixth to beat HSU 7-1 in the 7-inning opener. Mike Brumley had 2 hits in the opener, and was 3 for 8 in the doubleheader. Doug Hodo doubled and scored 1 of the 2 UT runs in the bottom of the first. Texas had 9 hits in the game, with only David Denny and Bud Ray not putting a ball in play. In the bottom of the sixth the 'Horns had 5 hits in a row, something Texas has rarely done this year, to give UT that final cushion.

Steve Labay was the winner, going 5 1/3, with Eric Boudreaux coming in to finish the game after Labay tired. Steve has been suffering from a little bursitis, and this was the first game in several weeks he has been able to just rear back and throw. This was Labay's first win (he is now 6-1) since he beat SE Oklahoma on March 22nd. Steve only gave up 3 hits and 1 run in his 5 innings, which is a good sign going into the rest of conference play and the playoffs – even if it was against less than stellar competition.

In the nightcap, Texas won 10-2. UT scored 1 in the first, and 4 in the 3rd for a pretty comfortable 5-0 lead early in this one. Gus used several different players in this game, with Mike Simon replacing Mike Trent in center, Deron Loy catching after Jeff Hearron played the first game, Jamie Doughty playing third instead of Bryan Burrows, and Deron Gustafson at second with Billy Bates sitting out game 2. Steve Labay, who pitched the first 5 innings in game 1, played right, replacing Bud Ray. Mike Simon went 2 for 4, and Labay was 2 for 5. Deron Loy was 2 for 4, with 2 doubles. But the hitting star in game 2 was José Tolentino, who was 4 for 5, and pounding the ball all over the field.

Mike Capel was the winner, throwing 5 scoreless innings. Roger Clemens relieved him and added 2 more goose eggs. Calvin Schiraldi and Kirk Killingsworth pitched an inning each, and each gave up a run to give the game the final 10-2 score. Froggie hadn't had a win in over a month, too, so it was nice to see him pitching well.

Texas now gets into the heart of their conference competition, so no more mid-week games until May 2nd and 3rd, when the team heads up to Tulsa to play Oral Roberts. Tuesdays will now just be intrasquad games, which are a lot less stressful. Gus does like to put a little extra pressure on those games, too, just to keep the players focused. For example, he might announce that the losing team gets to stay and run a few lines after the game, while the winners get to shower and head for dinner. Keeps things interesting!

UT heads north to Baylor this weekend for their second conference road trip. Ferrell Field is not that big, so hopefully good pitching will help the 'Horns keep the Bears from hitting car windshields in the parking lot. The team has heard that broken windshields have happened a couple of times in earlier games!

April 8th

Roger may have been a little nervous. When he went to the mound for the bottom of the first against Baylor, there were more than a dozen major league scouts, and 5 radar guns, facing him from behind home plate. There may have been more scouts than fans in the stands – it was another very chilly day. He gave up singles to the first two batters, who then pulled off a double steal. Roger then uncorked a couple of wild pitches, and both runners scored. Not exactly an auspicious start in front of all those scouts!

But then he settled down, only giving up 3 more hits the rest of the game – all singles, and shutting Baylor out after that rocky first inning. His complete game victory raised his record for the year to 8-2 and gives him 8 straight wins since Clint Thomas tweaked Roger's motion. As Jeff Hearron said in the dugout about the 6th or 7th inning, "Goose is cooking today!" Roger walked 2, struck out 4, and this was also his 8th complete game, again keeping the bullpen fresh for the doubleheader tomorrow. Bud Ray helped Roger out with a couple of great grabs in right field. A good defense is a pitcher's best friend!

Texas won the game 9-2, with every starter getting at least one hit except for José Tolentino – and he was robbed on a couple of hard shots. Steve Labay was 2 for 3, and Jeff Hearron, Kirk Killingsworth (DH), and Bud Ray all went 2 for 4 for the game. Kirk drove in 3 runs. Mike Brumley was 2 for 5, with a double. UT scored 4 runs in the top of the 4th, and added insurance runs in the 6th, 7th, and 9th for what turned out to be a pretty easy victory.

The Houston/Arkansas series doesn't start until tomorrow, so the Texas win today puts UT tied with Houston in the conference win/loss standings, and the Longhorns are still in first place on percentage points. The Texas 6-1 record is slightly better, percentage wise, than the Cougars at 7-2. Texas would love to see the Pigs take a game or two from Houston, which would give the 'Horns a little breathing room in the race for the conference championship.

April 9th

Texas had a couple of players break curfew last night, and they got caught when the coaches pulled a bed check. Deron Loy and Bud Ray had snuck out to attend a party, and at 10:10 they got a call that they had missed curfew and had better get back to the team hotel. On Saturday morning, on the bus on the way to the ballpark, Gus announced, "We had two people miss curfew last night. When we get back to Austin, they will have to do 30 laps to get back on the team." Bud did end up playing in both games of the doubleheader, and had a great day at the plate!

UT swept the doubleheader today. In the 7-inning opener, Texas won 8-0, with Calvin Schiraldi getting the shutout. He only gave up 4 hits, and only 2 Bears were able to reach second during the game. Calvin actually faced more radar guns today than Roger did yesterday, with 8 guys looking like gun toting hoodlums behind home plate. One scout said after the game that Calvin hit 89 at one point – but it was his control that was impressive. He didn't walk anyone in his 7 innings.

Steve Smith, the Baylor pitcher, was injured in the 2nd in a collision with the Bear's third baseman as they chased a popup in foul territory. Steve suffered a chipped tooth and a cut on his chin, but stayed in the game until the 4th. In that inning Baylor started reminding people of the Bad News Bears. Mickey Sullivan, the

Baylor coach, even looks a little like Walter Matthau, who starred in that movie. The Wild Bunch, with their kazoos, were going crazy in the stands playing the "circus" theme – as Baylor spent the inning juggling balls. Baylor's catcher dropped a popup, and their right fielder misplayed what should have been an ordinary sacrifice fly from Kirk Killingsworth. Jeff Hearron also had a sac fly in the 4th, Bud Ray had a 2-run triple, and David Denny scored Bud with a single. When the dust settled after the top of the 4th UT was leading 5-0, and with the way Calvin was pitching, there wasn't much doubt about the eventual outcome. Texas scored 3 more in the top of the 7th as icing on the cake.

The Longhorns won the 2nd game 7-2, with Mike Capel pitching 6 more scoreless innings before giving way to Killingsworth for the last 3 Baylor at bats. Kirk did give up 2 runs in the bottom of the 9th, with Alan Koonce, a pitcher who hadn't had a turn at bat all year, hitting a 2-run single to spoil what would have been Texas' first twin shutouts of the year. The team did give Kirk a rough time about that on the bus ride home!

The game was scoreless through the first 5 innings, but UT scored 3 in the 6th to take the lead, and then added additional runs the next 3 innings. Tolentino drove in 1 in the 6th with a double and went 3 for 4 for the game. Jeff Hearron hit a sacrifice fly, and Texas scored another run in the 6th on the 5th Baylor error of the day to give the 'Horns their 3-0 lead. Hearron also had a double later in the game and scored on Bud Ray's single. Bud drove in 2 more in this game, giving him 4 RBIs for the day. There were a couple of unusual situations during this game. At one point, the sprinklers came on in the outfield, chasing the Texas team off the field. Some kids had found the sprinkler system control valve and managed to turn it on. Later, one of the umpires, Murray Strey, had to temporarily leave the game with chest pains. It wasn't that hot out there, but chest pains are not something to ignore. Hope he is OK!

The scheduled doubleheader up in Fayetteville between Houston and Arkansas got postponed due to bad weather in the Ozarks, which means the teams will try and play tomorrow, Sunday. With the Texas sweep and those teams not playing UT now has a 1-game lead in the conference standings, with UT at 8-1 and Houston at 7-2. This was the first Texas sweep over Baylor in 3 years, and the team had a fun bus ride back to Austin! Next weekend the 'Horns get Rice, and they should be tougher competition. Rice is in third place in the conference with an 8-6 record, but they are 30-8-1 for the year. Don't ask how they managed to tie a baseball game!

At least Texas gets the Owls in Austin, which gives UT that advantage. In fact, the 'Horns don't leave home again until they go to Tulsa in May, and then UT has their last conference series down in College Station after that trip to play Oral Roberts. So, just one more conference road trip. It will be nice for the guys to mostly be in Austin through the end of the semester, with papers due, finals to take, and all the stress that goes with trying to be a student-athlete. Gus says he doesn't know who set up this conference schedule, but it does help to be able to stay home for a while!

April 11th

On Sunday, Houston and Arkansas split their doubleheader, leaving UT with a one game lead in the conference standings. Today, Monday, the Razorbacks did it again! Texas now has a 1 ½ game lead towards the conference championship. But there are still a lot of series left to play, and UT still has to face the

Cougars head-to-head. But Texas can't complain about the conference standings at the moment!

April 14th

UT signed six ballplayers this week during the recruitment open season, so it looks like Coach Gustafson will continue to have great teams for the next few years. While there is no guarantee these guys will ever hit campus – they could all end up going to the pros straight out of high school – UT should be able to get at least some of them in the Texas dugout next year. A San Marcos outfielder, Daryl Derryberry, and an Austin Travis catcher, Chuck Oertli, were from this area. Gus signed two shortstops, Ty Harrington from Waco Midway, and Jeff Herrington from Dallas White. Rusty Richards is the younger sibling of former UT outfielder Randy Richards. And Texas got a pitcher, Greg Swindell, whose brother is the current second baseman for the Houston Cougars. No one knows how Gus got Swindell away from his brother's team, but he looks like he could pitch for UT next year – he hasn't lost a game in 3 years in high school! Baylor tried to recruit the two new UT shortstops to play football for them, but both prefer baseball – and Texas has by far the better baseball program.

And, speaking of the Cougars, yesterday they dropped a doubleheader to Dallas Baptist. They have now lost 4 of their last 5 games and seem to be coming back to earth a little. It would be nice if UT was going to face them while they were in their slump, but they are not on the Texas schedule until the end of the month.

Tomorrow starts the series against Rice. David Hall, who led the Southwest Conference in hitting when he played for

Texas back in 1970, is now the coach for the Owls – and they are hitting .329 in conference play. They blasted 48 hits in their 3-game series against TCU, and 41 in their series against Tech. And their top pitchers have been blowing teams away, too. Tim Englund is undefeated on the year, with a 7-0 record, and a 2.25 ERA. David Hinnrichs is 8-2, with a 2.87 ERA. Texas has their work cut out for them!

April 15th

UT won, but it was close, 4-3, and down to the wire. Roger Clemens started for the Longhorns and didn't have his best stuff tonight. His fastball was still blazing by everybody, but his control, and his breaking balls weren't up to his usual standards. He is trying to pitch through the pain in his elbow, and the coaches think it is affecting his delivery a little. He gave up 9 hits in his 8 plus innings and was charged with all 3 Rice runs.

Texas scored 2 in the first, when Billy Bates beat out a drag bunt for a single, and then scored when Doug Hodo, the best hitting freshman in the conference, tripled. Doug then scored on an error by the Owl's third baseman on a hard-hit ball by Jeff Hearron. Rice tied the game in the 4th when they got a bases-loaded single to score 2.

UT regained the lead in the bottom of the 4th on a suicide squeeze bunt by Bryan Burrows after singles by David Denny and Steve Labay. In the 5th, Rice nearly scored again, but Labay, playing right field tonight, threw out the runner at home. In the top of the 8th, Rice got a double, a sacrifice bunt, and a sacrifice fly to tie the game 3-3.

Roger was relieved in the 9th by Kirk Killingsworth after Roger gave up another single, and the Killer also gave up a single, followed by a ground out on a hit-and-run play that got the leading run to third. But Billy Bates was able to corral a short hop ball and got the last out in the top of the 9th. In the bottom of the inning. Rice pitcher Tim Englund gave up his first walk of the game, to Steve Labay. Mike Trent sacrificed Steve to second, and he scored on Bryan Burrows' bloop single to centerfield to win the game.

This was the Longhorn's 40th win of the year, their 5th straight win, and Texas has won 11 of the last 12, losing only that road game to TCU. This is the 8th time this year UT has won a game in their last at bat, which shows just how cardiac this season has been for Coach Gus and the team. The 'Horns are now 9-1 in the conference race, with a 2-game lead over Houston, with the Cougars not starting their series against TCU until tomorrow.

Hodo had a double and a triple in the game, going 2 for 4, but Burrows had the key hits with his sacrifice bunt and single in the bottom of the 9th. It was a team win, and it gave the Rice pitcher his first loss of the year. And now the teams get to do it again tomorrow!

April 16th

Texas swept, but it was again a couple of 1-run games. UT won 7-6 in the first short game, and then 3-2 in the 9-inning affair. Calvin Schiraldi has been pitching well, but he gave up 10 hits and 5 runs in his 4 2/3 innings before Kirk Killingsworth came in to finish the first game and get the save. Rice is a good team, and their hitters force tough outs – they don't swing at bad pitches and wait for something they think they can drive. Luckily, the 'Horns had scored 7 in the bottom of the second and were able to hold onto that lead, even after the Killer gave up a 6th run on a wild pitch.

In that second inning, after Rice had scored in the top half to take a 1-run lead, Rice pitcher David Pavias got 2 quick outs and had a 0-2 count on the 3rd batter, Steve Labay. Steve, playing right field in the first game, worked his way back to a walk (Steve was also 2 for 2 in the game, the only Texas player with more than 1 hit). Pavias then walked the next 2 batters, loading the bases. Rice coach David Hall then pulled Pavias, and his replacement, Derek Hoelscher, only added fuel to the fire. He walked Billy Bates, allowing Labay to stroll home from third base, and then gave up a bases-clearing triple to Mike Brumley. Hoelscher was yanked after not retiring anyone. That gave UT a 4-1 lead, all with 2 outs. But the party wasn't over. Killingsworth, who had also been slotted in as designated hitter (replacing Doug Hodo) when Killer came into the game in the 5th, hit a 2-run homer against Rice's 3rd pitcher of the inning. Kirk was followed to the plate by José Tolentino, who quickly made it back-to-back home runs. José's shot was about 390 feet, landing just under the scoreboard. It was 7-1 by the time Rice finally got Jeff Hearron out to end the inning. Rice clawed back into the game, but those 7 runs turned out to be just enough to give Texas the win. In the top of the 7th, Rice's Scott Johnson doubled, and then took third on a sacrifice bunt by cleanup hitter Bryan Foxx. But Rice tried a squeeze play with #5 hitter Mike Fox, attempting to score Johnson, trying to tie the game. Fox missed the pitch, and Johnson was tagged out in a run down to end Rice's last scoring opportunity. Unusual strategy by David Hall, using his middle of the lineup guys as bunters – but if it had worked, he would have looked like a genius. He probably learned that small ball strategy when he was an assistant coach here in Austin, after he had used up his eligibility as a player. Gus said after the game that if he had been in the same situation, he would have contemplated a squeeze, too.

In the second game, Mike Capel pitched a gem. He only gave up 5 hits and 2 runs in his 8 innings, with Killingsworth then coming in to pitch a perfect 9th and get his second save of the day. Froggie gave up a run in the top of the 1st, but then held Rice scoreless until the 8th. In that inning Capel gave up a triple to Rice's Bryan Foxx, allowing Rice to get within 1 run, and then Mike Trent made a great diving catch in center to keep Rice from tying the game. In the 9th, Rice's James Thompson almost knocked Killingsworth down with a line drive to the Killer's chest – but Kirk was able to recover and throw Thompson out at first. The next two batters went quietly, and Texas had their 7th straight win.

José Tolentino was the hitting star in this game, doubling in Doug Hodo in the 3rd inning, and then scoring himself in the 6th. In that inning José tripled, and then scored on a wild pitch. In the 7th, Mike Brumley tripled in Bryan Burrows (playing third in this game) for what turned out to be the winning run. Mike had triples in both games, which is pretty rare. But UT needed those runs! Billy Bates was also 2 for 4 in the game, but no one batting behind him was able to bring him home. Texas swept, but Gus said after the game that he wasn't sure the 'Horns would have gotten the same results in Houston. Rice is a good team. Coach Gus added that they deserve a regional slot, and that Rice is "just as good as Texas."

April 18th

Houston swept a doubleheader from TCU on Saturday and beat the Horned Frogs again yesterday (Sunday), so with the 3 Texas wins this weekend UT maintains their 1 1/2-game lead in the conference standings win-loss column. The conference championship is beginning to look like it will come down to Texas or Houston. Rice is still in 3rd place in the conference, but their 9-9 record puts them 5 full games behind UT. Arkansas, at 10-7, is only 3 ½ games back in the standings, so they have a remote shot at taking the trophy, too. But UT and Houston seem to have risen to the top, and the Texas series with the Cougars may decide the championship. UT gets Texas Tech and their league-leading offense in Austin next weekend, and Houston goes to Waco to play Baylor. The following weekend is when the Cougars come to town, and that might get interesting!

April 22nd

UT finally got a relatively easy win, beating Texas Tech 12-3. The coaches said they felt the team relax a little as the game got into the later innings, compared to the stress last weekend against Rice. Roger Clemens was his usual self, pitching a complete game and seeming to be in control through most of it. He did give up a couple of home runs in the top of the 4th, when Tech got the game to within 1 run at 4-3, but Roger shut the Red Raiders down for the rest of the game. This was Clemens' 9th straight win. He only walked one batter and struck out 7. He did give up 9 hits in the game, but kept Tech from scoring except in that one inning.

The Texas hitters were pounding the ball tonight. Billy Bates and José Tolentino were both 3 for 5, and all 3 of Tolentino's hits were doubles. Doug Hodo (who drove in 3 runs), Bryan Burrows, and Jeff Hearron were all 2 for 4, and all 3 had a double, too. Overall, UT blasted 18 hits against 3 different Tech pitchers – more hits than the Longhorns had in both games combined last Saturday against Rice. And, as icing on the cake, Baylor upset Houston! Baylor won 14-5, stretching the Texas conference lead to 2 ½ games. A good night all around!

April 23rd

A Texas sweep! And Baylor swept Houston! That gives Texas at least a share of the conference title, and one more UT win or Houston loss will give the 'Horns the outright regular season crown. UT won today 9-1 and 8-2, with Texas enjoying a 6-run inning in both games.

In the 7-inning opener, UT scored 2 in the bottom of the 2nd to grab the lead, but then Tech got an unearned run off of Calvin Schiraldi in the top of the 3rd to cut the lead in half. But in the bottom of the 3rd, Texas scored 6 to give the home team a comfortable cushion. UT did it on just 2 hits, 4 walks, and a big error by the Tech third baseman. With the bases loaded, he grabbed a ball a few feet behind third, decided not to try and get the force by going to the bag, and then threw the ball over the first baseman's head. All 3 runners scored, pushing the Texas lead from 5-1 to 8-1. You could see the Tech team deflate after that play. Mike Brumley was the key batter for the game, going 3 for 4 and scoring twice.

Calvin Schiraldi threw a 2-hitter against what had been the hottest hitting team in the league. He is now 8-1 on the year.

He gave up a leadoff single in the 2nd, and then an RBI single in the 3rd – but that was it. He retired the last 13 Tech batters in a row. He was mostly using his forkball, and hitting the corners consistently. No wonder they call him Nibbler! He said after the game that he was just trying to get back into the groove, after not having that great a game last week against Rice. He said, "Today, I was more a pitcher than a thrower, putting my pitches where I wanted them, and making them hit my pitch."

In the second game of the day, Mike Capel tried to match Calvin's outing. He only gave up 2 hits through the first 5 innings, before tiring a little in the 6th. He gave up 2 more hits, with Tech scoring 2, and Gus put Killingsworth on the mound to put out the fire. The Killer pitched 3 1/3 scoreless innings for his 6th save of the year.

Bryan Burrows was the only batter to have more than 1 hit in this game, but UT bunched enough together to have another big inning in the bottom of the 4th. Texas scored 1 in the 3rd, and then in the 4th Jeff Hearron's double started a hit parade. It was 7-0 by the time Tech got the 3rd out that inning. David Denny, Mike Trent, Billy Bates (with a double) and Mike Brumley all had an RBI in that inning, and Burrows had 2. Over the weekend Texas raised their conference team batting average from .260 to .287, and left a lot of Tech pitchers wondering if anyone had gotten the license plate off the truck that had flattened them. UT is 45-8 overall for the year, and now 14-1 in the Southwest Conference.

Baylor won a couple of pitcher's duels today against Houston, winning 3-0 and 2-1 to get the sweep in Waco. Brumley said that Baylor had always been his 2nd favorite team in the conference, behind only UT, and that he was going to vote for every Baylor player on his All-Conference ballot. Texas gets the still second place Houston Cougars in Austin next weekend, so it will be interesting to see their team mood after the crushing defeats against Baylor. The Texas team is not celebrating a conference championship just yet – teams that tie for the championship both get a trophy – but the 'Horns are celebrating today, because Gus told the team they could have tomorrow off, Monday! No practice!

April 29th

Well, Texas found out what kind of mood Houston would be in – mad as hell. Part of that was probably from what happened to the Cougars last weekend up in Waco, and part was probably that they are still fuming over the incident 4 years ago, in 1979, when there was a riot here in the stands. UT was in the process of sweeping Houston that weekend, and the Wild Bunch had been giving the Cougar players grief every game over their poor play. Finally, one of the players' girlfriends had heard enough, and walked down to the front row of the stands and threw her drink in the face of one of the Wild Bunch guys. The guy reacted by grabbing a drink off the top of the dugout in front of the stands and throwing it back at the girl. Unfortunately, that cup was the spit cup from a guy that had been dipping snuff for the entire doubleheader that afternoon. The girl screamed, some of her friends jumped on the guy from the Wild Bunch, and several Houston players piled out of the dugout and climbed over the railing into the stands. It took the coaches and a couple of campus cops about 15 minutes to restore order. The guy from the Wild Bunch that threw the cup shall remain anonymous – he was a law student at the time and is now a full-fledged attorney – but for the rest of his days at UT he was known as "Spit Cup." On the

Monday after that incident, Deloss Dodds, the Athletic Director, told Coach Gustafson to "counsel" Scott Wilson, and for Scott to warn the rest of the Wild Bunch that the administration would not tolerate such incidents in the future. Gus passed on the warning, but as Scott was about to leave, Coach grinned, and said, "I'll bet it will be a long time before that girl throws another cup of water!"

Houston beat UT 4-3 today in this first game of a 3-game series. Doug Drabek, the starting Cougar pitcher, raised his record to 12-2 on the year, and Rayner Noble only gave up 1 hit over the last 2 innings for the save. Roger Clemens was the losing pitcher for the first time since February 23rd, ending his 9-game winning streak.

Texas was winning going into the 8th, leading 3-1 at that point, with Mike Brumley and David Denny driving in runs in the 4th and 6th, and then José Tolentino hitting his 6th homer of the year in the bottom of the 7th. At that point, Roger had retired 12 consecutive batters, UT had 2 outs in the top of the 8th, and they thought they were cruising to their 56th conference championship. But Rayner Noble singled, Corky Swindell hit a Texas Leaguer into left, and the tying runs were on base. Don Larson then hit what should have been an ordinary RBI single, but center fielder Mike Trent and right fielder Steve Labay both thought the other guy was going to field the ball, and it ended up skipping all the way to the wall for a triple. Riley Epps then singled Larson in from third, and suddenly Houston had the lead. Killingsworth then relieved Clemens, but the damage was already done.

Now, Texas has to win one of the Saturday games to clinch the championship, or else the race gets tight again. Houston's win did help one other team, with the Houston win eliminating

Baylor from the conference tournament and cementing Rice's place in that tourney. Gus told the press people after the game that he wouldn't be surprised if Houston swept Texas – that the 'Horns had made some mistakes you just can't make in a close game, and that Houston had gotten the clutch hits and pitching they needed to beat UT. He let the team know after the game, behind closed doors, just what he thought of their performance. He was not a happy camper, to say the least!

April 30th

Today was Senior Day. The Seniors, including the student trainers. managers, and support staff, are announced and get to walk out on the field with their parents. The moms get a hug from Coach Gus, and everybody gets pictures. A couple of players were almost in tears when they realized that today they would be playing their last home regular season game of their career. Yes, Texas still has the Conference Tournament, and probably a Regional here, but this is still the end of an era. For some of these guys, it seems like they have been at Texas forever! A lot of the good players are juniors, and sure to be drafted in June, and so this is probably their last year on the team, too - but you don't get to walk unless you are graduating. John Turman, one of the team's managers, told the team that "Since this is my last year, you damn well better get me a ring!"

Well, Texas is again Southwest Conference champions. That was pretty much a foregone conclusion after last weekend – UT only needed to win 1 of their last 6 conference games – but Houston did beat the Longhorns once today, to win 2 out of 3 in the series, and build some confidence for the conference tournament. The Texas team did get to throw Coach Gus into the shower, but not until after the second game today. Houston won the opener by the same 4-3 score they had won by last night, but this time in extra innings. Jeff Hearron went 3 for 3 in the game, and doubled in Kirk Killingsworth in the 6th to tie the game 3-3. David Denny was given an intentional walk to load the bases, but then Johnny Sutton, pinch hitting for Mike Trent, came to bat for the first time all year. Johnny had been pounding the ball in practice, and Gus thought he might have a chance to get a hit off of Rayner Noble, who had been tough up to that point. Unfortunately, Johnny grounded into a pitcher to catcher to first double play to end the inning. That pretty much took the wind out of Texas' sails, and then Killingsworth walked in the winning run in the top of the 8th, giving up a bases-loaded walk to Corky Swindell. The Killer had come in to relieve Calvin Schiraldi in the 6th. Killingsworth and Steve Labay actually traded places a couple of times in this game, with Steve coming in to pitch and Killingsworth going to right field, and then back to their original places. Noble did not give up another hit after Hearron's double in the 6th, raising Rayner's record to 11-3 on the year. After a save last night and a win today, Texas is sure to see him again in the conference tournament!

This weekend UT held a reunion for former baseball players, and the current players got to see some old teammates from earlier teams. There were over 400 players at the reception, and lots of great stories. More players got to meet J.L. Smith, the pitcher from the early '50s that some had met at the funeral earlier this year. Bibb Falk was there at the reunion, and there were 9 former players over 80 years old! Those 9 octogenarians were honored today in between games at the ballpark.

One funny thing today – UT Vice President Shirley Byrd Perry was presenting commemorative plaques to Coach

Gustafson, Coach Falk, and representatives of Billy Disch's family, in honor of the UT Centennial. Her comment was, "I give these to honor these three great former coaches of the University of Texas." When Coach Gus took the microphone, he grinned and said, "I didn't know two losses could get you fired."

Texas won the second game going away, and it looks like Coach Gus may be able to keep his job. UT won 12-2, scoring in every inning except the 6th. The game was shortened to 7 innings since the first game went into extras. Hearron continued his hot hitting, going 2 for 4, with a double and a home run. His homer cleared the centerfield wall, making him the first Longhorn to put one over the monster. José Tolentino also homered, Steve Labay was 2 for 3, and David Denny had 2 doubles. Houston tried 5 different pitchers, but the Texas batters found holes against each of them.

Mike Capel started, and only gave up 1 hit through 3 ½ innings, but walked 3 and gave up 2 earned runs. Wade Phillips came in to relieve Capel and gave up a double that scored the 2 guys Mike had put on base. Phillips, who hadn't pitched since April 2nd, then shut down the Cougars the rest of the game, retiring 10 in a row. Texas had been winning 6-0 going into that 4th inning, and then they got those 2 runs back in the bottom of the 4th, building the lead to 8-2. UT scored 4 more in the 5th to salt the game away and start the celebration.

With the regular season title assured, the press was already asking Coach Gustafson (after he dried off from getting pushed into the shower) about the conference tournament. Gus said that obviously pitching was the key, and the ability to win the first two games of the tourney. He mentioned that Houston obviously has two good pitchers, but he also talked about Rice. He said the Owls might be the tournament favorite, with both good pitching and great hitting. He didn't mention the Texas staff, which has been fantastic all year. Now UT travels to Tulsa for a midweek series against Oral Roberts, the team the 'Horns beat twice back in early March. Then Texas heads to College Station for the last conference series next weekend. Two road trips in one week – not the best scenario, but the players don't get to make the schedule! This is the last week of classes at UT, so some players will have to make up exams, and missing the final review in class before you take the final exam is never a good thing. For some people trying to make grades to stay eligible, it can be a problem. The team does have tutors to help, but the end of a semester is always a stressful time.

May 2nd

For a road game, Texas played pretty well, but UT still got beat today. Oral Roberts is ranked number 6 in the country for a reason – they are good. While the competition was going to be tough, Gus decided to not start the normal weekend starters – Gus is probably saving those guys for A&M – but the 'Horns still felt pretty good putting Steve Labay on the mound to start the game. But he gave up solo homers in both the 1st and 2nd innings, back-to-back doubles in that inning scored a 3rd run, and then he gave up a single and a walk. He was replaced by Eric Boudreaux, who hadn't pitched in a real game since April 5th. Eric threw what looked like a perfect double play ball, which would have gotten UT out of the inning, but it went right between normally slick fielding Billy Bates' legs. Jamie Doughty, playing right field, did manage to throw out an ORU runner at the plate on the play, so Texas did get a second out. They got the 3rd out when the runner from first was hit by a sharp single from Keith Murcha – a fitting end to a bad inning. Suddenly Texas was down 4-0. UT got back into it in the 4th, when José Tolentino and David Denny hit doubles, and Jamie Doughty crushed a long homer. It was his first homer since Opening Day! But ORU scored 2 more in the 6th and 1 in the 7th to give them the win. The 'Horns came close again in the 9th, when Mike Brumley singled in a run and then Tolentino brought him in with his 3rd hit of the night. But then the Oral Roberts reliever, Todd Burns, got Jeff Hearron to fly out to end the threat. Texas had 3 errors in the game, the early 1 by Bates and 2 by Tolentino. Those kept innings alive for ORU, and eventually cost the 'Horns the game. This was UT's first non-conference road loss in 12 years. More importantly, as Coach Gustafson said after the game, if UT keeps losing Texas could lose their chance to host a Regional. Texas gets a shot at revenge tomorrow night.

May 3rd

They did it to Texas again. Oral Roberts beat UT 6-1, evening the record against the Longhorns at 2-2 for the year. It looked like the 'Horns were just not focused for this series after capturing the conference title on Saturday, or maybe these were just "trap games" in between the two more important conference weekend series with Houston and A&M. Texas' defense was terrible again. UT had 2 errors, and 2 misplays in the outfield that were generously called hits by the ORU scorekeeper. ORU second baseman Keith Miller led off the bottom of the 1st with a routine fly ball that was lost in the sun between left fielder David Denny and center fielder Steve Labay. Right fielder Jamie Doughty then let a ball drop at his feet for a triple, scoring Miller for ORU's first run. In Jamie's defense, he is normally a third baseman, and this was only his second game in right field all year. The team was surprised when Gus had Roger Clemens starting, and he was the loser for his second loss in a row, dropping his season record to 9-4. He gave up 10 hits, but his defense didn't help him much. They game got out of hand in the 6th when ORU designated hitter Mike Batesole put one over the fence in left, a 2-run homer, giving Oral Roberts a 5-1 lead.

Texas got their only run in the 5th when Mike Brumley singled, and then scored on Kirk Killingsworth's double. Brumley was 2 for 3 for the game, but no one else got more than a single hit, and the 3 ORU pitchers held UT to 6 hits for the game. Texas definitely don't look like the number 1 team in the country, and the 'Horns have now lost 4 out of their last 5 games. Calvin Schiraldi and Killingsworth also pitched in the game, and Calvin was the only one who had a decent outing. But by that time the cow was out of the barn, as they say up here in Oklahoma.

When Gus went out to pull Roger from the game, he was pretty upset. It was just frustration that he hadn't been able to recapture the magic he had at mid-season, and the fact that he had been pitching with pain for half the year with an inflamed elbow tendon – but Roger never said anything about it. Roger went down to the locker room, and when he hadn't returned a few minutes later Gus sent John Turman, one of the student managers, in to find Roger. John found Roger in his street clothes, so frustrated with himself that he was about to quit the team and walk out! John told Roger to hang on a minute, went back to the dugout and got Gus, and Gus talked Roger into staying.

Those two losses might have actually helped Texas a little, getting the team to realize that they can't just roll the ball out to the mound and expect to win. A team has got to stay focused every minute, or good (or even not-so-good) teams can make anyone look bad. Time for UT to move on from this series, and go watch the train going by the outfield fence down in College Station.

Texas did get a little good news today. The Associated Press All-Conference Team was announced, based on a poll of the Southwest Conference coaches. Calvin Schiraldi was named the conference pitcher of the year. José Tolentino also made the first team. The team was a little disappointed that Coach Gus didn't win coach of the year – they gave it to Norm DeBriyn up in Arkansas – but since Texas was the preseason favorite to win the conference all the 'Horns did was meet expectations. Arkansas and Houston are currently tied for second in the conference. Texas Tech's Todd Howey won freshman of the year, over Billy Bates. Howey is hitting about .400, but the other conference coaches didn't give Bates enough credit for the runs he has saved Texas this year with his great play at second base. Rayner Noble from Houston was the player of the year, and that award is well deserved – he is probably the best combo hitter and pitcher in college ball this year. Killingsworth isn't bad, but Noble is in a whole different league – at least when he is playing against UT!

When the team got back to Austin Jeff Hearron struck again. He nailed a flyswatter to the wall in the locker room, with a sign calling it the "Jamie Doughty Professional Model" – this was after Doughty had his issues in the outfield up in Tulsa. Everybody got a good laugh out of it, including Jamie – but Coach Bethea took it down when he saw it. "Sweets" - Coach Bethea - was probably just trying to keep Gus from seeing it and blowing his top again about how badly Texas played against Oral Roberts.

May 6th

Last conference series of the year. And Texas needs some wins to solidify their shot at one of the top 8 seeds in the country so that they host a Regional when the playoffs start in a couple of weeks. Arkansas swept a double header from Oral Roberts this afternoon, which makes the UT losses up there look even worse. That does help the Razorbacks look better in the standings – they might get a shot at hosting a Regional, too.

UT got the first game win tonight, beating A&M 13-4. That puts the 'Horns at 47-12 for the year, and 16-3 in the conference. Texas scored first, in the top of the 1st, with José Tolentino slapping another double that scored Mike Brumley, who had singled. But A&M came back and took the lead in the bottom of the 1st. Calvin Schiraldi, the UT starter, gave up a single, put the runner on second after a bad pickoff throw, and then Calvin gave up back-to-back doubles. Players and fans were starting to wonder what was up with this team, and why had the UT pitching suddenly gone south?

But Deron Loy homered in the top of the 2nd to tie the game, and the Longhorns took the lead in the top of the 3rd when A&M starter Robert Slavens gave up 2 walks, threw a wild pitch, and then balked home the go-ahead run. In the 4th, Steve Labay drove in a run with a triple (he drove in 3 in the game, on 3 hits), and Bryan Burrows drove in another with a perfectly executed suicide squeeze bunt. The Aggies got a run off of Schiraldi in the 5th, to make it a 5-3 game, but they never got any closer. Jeff Hearron hit two late solo home runs, including a long one over the scoreboard in the 6th, and UT scored 5 more in the 8th to put the game away. In that inning Burrows had a 2-run single, and Kirk Killingsworth singled in another run.

Loy finished the onslaught with another single for his 2nd RBI of the day. Every player scored in the game except for Burrows, who did drive in 3. Calvin scattered 8 hits, but did give up 4 doubles in the game. This was his first 9-inning complete game of the year! The Aggies are in last place in the conference, and after tonight they are 24-19 for the year, so this may not be the toughest competition Texas has faced this year – but UT is still playing A&M, and the 'Horns want bragging rights over their rival for the next year. So, Texas needs to at least win the series, and Gus told the team he really wants a sweep! He doesn't much like the Aggies, and over the years he has made his feelings about the Aggies well known to the Texas team.

May 7th

Last 2 regular season games of the year. And UT won them both, but in different ways. The first game was a 14-11 slugfest. Roger Clemens had one of his worst starts of the year, giving up 8 hits and 7 runs in the first 2 innings. Wade Phillips came in and relieved Roger with no outs in the 2nd and gave up 2 more runs before getting out of the jam. Texas was down 9-2 before the game barely got started! But UT scored 4 runs in the 3rd, and 2 each in the 5th and 6th to retake the lead, 10-9. A&M came back with 2 runs in the bottom of the 6th to take the lead at 11-10 (and this was going to be a 7-inning game), but the 'Horns came through with 4 in the top of the 7th to give the UT the win. Wade pitched until he got in trouble in the 6th, and then was relieved by Kirk Killingsworth, who gave up a 2-run homer to give A&M their lead in the 6th, but then Killer pitched a scoreless 7th for the win. It was back-and-forth all afternoon, and UT happened to get the runs they needed at the right time.

Texas had 12 hits in the game (A&M had 15) with Deron Loy and David Denny both going 3 for 4. One of David's hits was a double, and he drove in 4 of UT's runs in the game. In the 7th, Killingsworth singled in a run, David Denny singled in 2 more, and then Steve Labay finished it off with another RBI single.

The second game was a pitching gem by both teams, until UT broke it open in the 9th. Mike Capel threw a complete game shutout, only giving up 2 hits, and Texas won the game 3-0. Rick Luecken, who was the loser in game 1, shut out UT through 8 innings in game 2 on only 3 hits. In the top of the 9th, Mike Brumley hit a liner that skipped between outfielders for a double, Doug Hodo singled, and José Tolentino broke the scoreless tie with a double, scoring Brumley. Deron Loy laid down a perfect suicide squeeze to score Hodo, and then David Denny singled, scoring Tolentino. With Capel flashing his stuff, those 3 runs were plenty. Mike has probably moved up to 2nd in the pitching rotation since Roger has been a little off lately – Clemens was lucky not to get the loss in game 1. Capel is now 9-1 on the year, and only faced 30 batters today.

Texas needed this sweep badly. UT had dropped to number 6 in the polls after dropping several games in the past week. Another couple of losses this weekend, or a bad conference tournament showing, and the 'Horns might not be one of the eight teams selected to host a Regional – a key to making it back to Omaha. A lot of guys are a little sad at this being their last regular season game of their career, but excited to start the playoffs!

One funny incident today. Last week Jeff Hearron was seeing his girlfriend while she was painting her toenails. As a lark, he painted his, too – figuring no one would ever know. But after he started showing symptoms of possible heat stroke during the second game of the double header today, the trainers took him into the A&M locker room for treatment - and immediately took off his shoes and socks. Talk about being embarrassed!

Now that the regular season is over, it is time to look at the team's final stats. UT had 7 regulars hit over .300 for the year, led by freshman Doug Hodo's .392 average. José Tolentino had the most hits, with 72, the most RBIs, with 51, and he led the team with 7 home runs and 25 doubles. Mike Brumley led the team with 23 stolen bases, and Billy Bates and Mike Trent each had 13. Jeff Hearron was clutch with 6 game-winning RBIs, followed by José with 5. Hearron was an Iron Man, catching 417 out of the team's 491 innings this year, and led the team with a .357 average in conference play.

The top UT pitchers for the year were Calvin Schiraldi, with a 1.95 ERA, and Mike Capel at 2.80. Both were 9-1 on the year. Kirk Killingsworth had 6 saves, and ended up with a 9-3 record. Roger Clemens was the workhorse of the group, throwing 117 2/3 innings, and 9 complete games. Steve Labay was another good 2-way player, going 6-2 on the mound with a 2.82 ERA, and batting .288 on the year. Overall, the team hit .294 for the year, with Texas' opponents only batting .230 – showing the strength of the UT pitching staff. Here are the numbers for the regular season:

TEXAS BASEBALL STATISTICS
FINAL REGULAR SEASON TOTALS
RECORD 49-12

Player, Position	G	AB	R	H	BI	Avg.	2B	3B	HR	TB	S	SF	SB	BB	SO
Doug Hodo, of	25	79	16	31	18	.392	8	3	0	45	0	3	5	5	12
Deron Loy, c	29	82	17	28	18	.341	5	0	1	36	1	2	0	17	9
José Tolentino, 1b	61	214	53	72	51	.336	25	2	7	122	2	3	0	43	9
Jeff Hearron, c	52	160	32	52	43	.325	13	3	6	89	1	7	0	30	23
Bryan Burrows, 3b	53	157	31	48	32	.306	10	2	0	62	3	1	4	27	16
David Denny, of	49	157	36	48	31	.306	13	2	0	65	2	1	3	26	26
Mike Trent, of	44	103	28	31	14	.301	7	0	0	38	5	0	13	29	18
Bill Bates, 2b	53	168	42	48	22	.289	9	2	1	65	11	2	13	38	19
Steve Labay, of	51	160	39	46	42	.288	4	3	3	65	6	5	9	43	10
Mike Brumley, ss	55	197	54	54	31	.274	7	4	1	70	2	7	23	47	26
Kirk Killingsworth, of	27	88	16	21	31	.239	2	1	3	34	2	6	1	16	13
Others (less than 70 at-bats)															
Deron Gustafson, 2b	14	32	11	10	10	.313	2	1	0	14	1	3	0	13	3
Mike Simon, of	38	47	23	13	10	.277	2	1	0	17	0	1	10	17	13
Joe Bob Cooper, of	7	14	2	3	1	.214	0	0	0	3	0	0	0	2	1
Bud Ray, rf	19	48	8	9	9	.200	3	1	0	14	0	1	5	11	15
Jamie Doughty, 3b	22	55	15	11	9	.200	3	0	2	20	1	1	1	16	7
Alan Brown, dh	20	44	9	7	10	.159	1	0	1	11	1	1	0	6	5
J Sutton, of, pr	13	1	9	0	0	.000	0	0	0	0	0	0	2	0	0
Robert Gauntt, 1b	1	0	0	0	0	.000	0	0	0	0	0	0	0	0	0
TOTALS	61	1815	441	533	384	.294	114	25	25	772	38	44	88	388	227
OPPONENTS	61	1840	203	423	182	.230	92	12	25	614	21	11	22	155	373

Double plays: Texas 47, Opponents 38. Left on base: Texas 463, Opponents 340. Game-winning RBI: Hearron 6, Tolentino 5, Hodo 4, Labay 4, Burrows 3, Denny 3, Loy 3, Bates 2, Brumley 2, Killingsworth 2, Cooper 1, Doughty 1, Gustafson 1, Simon 1, Trent 1.

Pitcher	W	L	ERA	G	GS	CG	IP	H	R	ER	BB	SO	HB	WP	HR
J.R. Davenport	0	0	0.00	1	0	0	2	2	1	0	1	2	0	0	0
Mike Poehl	0	0	0.00	1	0	0	3 1/3	1	0	0	0	3	1	0	0
Calvin Schiraldi	9	1	1.95	17	12	7	92 1/3	74	29	20	32	75	0	3	1
Mike Capel	9	1	2.80	15	14	3	74	57	31	23	34	43	5	6	1
Steve Labay	6	2	2.82	12	8	3	54 1/3	54	24	17	12	33	3	0	6
Bruce Ruffin	1	0	2.84	4	0	0	6 1/3	4	3	2	7	6	0	0	0
Wade Phillips	4	1	2.92	9	5	2	52 1/3	43	19	17	6	36	0	1	4
Kirk Killingsworth	9	3	3.13	25	3	2	60 1/3	42	24	21	28	42	0	3	3
Roger Clemens	9	4	3.37	18	15	9	117 2/3	105	48	44	15	102	3	6	7
Eric Boudreaux	2	0	3.38	7	2	1	29 1/3	33	15	11	10	20	0	1	3
David Seitz	0	0	6.00	3	2	0	9	6	8	6	10	14	0	1	0
TOTALS	49	12	2.95	61	61	27	501	423	203	164	155	373	13	21	25

Other totals: Saves, 10 (Killingsworth 6, Schiraldi 2, Capel 1, Clemens 1;
Shutouts, 6 (Clemens 2, Schiraldi 2, Labay 1, Capel 1

CHAPTER 7

THE SOUTHWEST CONFERENCE TOURNAMENT

After winning the regular season conference title and 49 games this year, an argument can be made that this tournament doesn't mean that much to UT. Coach Gus is not putting some pitcher out there to throw 120 pitches just to keep UT in a game this weekend. Arkansas is also ranked, so they are pretty much assured of making a Regional, too. But for the other two teams in this tournament – Rice and Houston – winning everything this weekend is the ticket to more baseball. The tournament winner gets the conference's automatic berth into the playoffs.

The final conference standings had UT in first place, Arkansas and Houston tied for second, and Rice in fourth. So, the Razorbacks and Cougars will play the first game Friday afternoon, and then Texas gets Rice (1 vs. 4) Friday night. Two years ago, when UT played Rice in the tournament, the game went 20 innings and ended up being played over 2 days since the game went so late into the evening. Both coaches say that will not happen again! Texas did end up winning that game, 7-6, and they are hoping for a similar outcome this year. All four teams are pretty equally balanced in ability – decent pitching and hitting. All the teams have two good pitchers. UT might have a slight advantage when the tournament gets further into the weekend, with the Texas pitching depth – but that assumes the 'Horns win one or both of those first two games!

Texas caught Arkansas early in the year, but they have improved quite a bit since then. One interesting stat about Arkansas is that they have been in every tournament since its inception but have yet to win one. Four out of the last six tournaments were won by one of the visiting teams (UT was one of those teams, winning last year in College Station). Any of these 4 teams could get hot and win the tournament. UT played 3 one-run games against Rice, and then Houston beat Texas 2 out of 3. Yes, the Longhorns want to win the tournament – but anything can happen in a baseball game. The Athletics Department is not selling tournament seating packages – the thought is that most fans just want to see the games where their favorite team is playing. Reserved seats in the main grandstand are $4, with the bleacher general admission seats going for $3, and $2 for kids. Texas expects a sellout or close to it for their game with Rice.

Rice has the best team batting average going into the tournament, at .309, followed by Arkansas at .304. Houston's pitching ERA is actually a little better than UT's – 2.91 against Texas' 2.95. Rice has hit more home runs than any of the other teams, and UT is dead last in that category – but that is largely a factor of how big your ballpark is compared to the others. Corky

Swindell is the top hitter for average in the tournament, at .419, followed by Doug Hodo at .392. Arkansas has 50 more stolen bases than the 2nd place team, Texas – those Piggies like to run! But statistics are only good for helping predict outcomes – everyone still has to play the games. And win!

May 13th

Charlie Corbell did it to Houston one more time. In the opening game of the tournament this afternoon, Arkansas' top pitcher beat the Cougars for the 4th time in two years, this time 4-3. But Houston did make it interesting in the 9th. Last year, in the tournament down in College Station, Arkansas pitcher Lester Lancaster was leading Houston 8-4 in the bottom of the 9th, but Houston got a 3-run homer to win the game and end the Razorback's season.

This year, Corbell had a 4-1 lead in the top of the 9th, thanks partly to Mike Robinson's 2-run homer in the 8th, but 3 Arkansas errors led to 2 runs, and suddenly the game was 4-3, and Houston had runners at the corners with 2 outs. Enter Lancaster to relieve Corbell. He had to be thinking about last year, when he threw a slider to Jeff Jacobson and it got hammered. This year he stuck with his fastball. The 1st one was a called strike on the outside corner. He missed with his 2nd pitch, for a 1-1 count. His 3rd pitch was fouled down the third base line to make it 1-2. His 4th was grounded to shortstop Jim Ward, and the 6-3 out ended the game in Arkansas' favor. So, the Razorbacks go into the winner's bracket, and will play tomorrow night against the winner of the Rice – Texas game tonight.

Before the late game started it was announced that UT had signed 5 more recruits for next year – maintaining the player pipeline is a second full-time job for the coaches. UT signed a pitcher from Everman, Jackie Davidson, and a shortstop from Houston Bellaire, Elanis Westbrook. Both are likely to go pro, but there is always a chance Texas will get them on campus. Other pickups included Mike Colpitt, the player of the year in Oklahoma, a pitcher from Angelina Junior College, Dennis Cook, and a pitcher from Bay City, Daniel Pena. Cook also plays outfield and hits well – Gus said Cook looks a lot like this year's great pickup, Steve Labay. Billy Bates has told the coaches that he will be back next year – there was a chance that he might transfer – and UT will also get Mike Simon back. Mike had knee surgery a couple of weeks ago but is expected to fully recover in time for next year's season.

Texas won tonight – but barely, as close as all the games against Rice have been. Once again, José Tolentino kept UT in the game until a Rice error in the bottom of the 9th gave the Longhorns the win, 4-3. Rice scored first, in the top of the 1st off of Calvin Schiraldi. Calvin walked Clinton Welch, who immediately stole second, barely beating Jeff Hearron's throw. Bryan Foxx then doubled, scoring Welch. That was it until the 4th, when José tied the game with an opposite field home run. But Rice came right back in the top of the 5th with 2 more runs. Mike Fox walked, was sacrificed to second, and scored on Jay Bluthardt's double that kissed the line in right field. Clinton Welch lifted a fly to right that Deron Loy misplayed, allowing Bluthardt to score.

In the bottom of the 7th, Tolentino came through again with a leadoff double off the wall in right. Hearron singled, moving José to third. Loy hit into a double play, with Tolentino staying at third. But then Steve Labay beat out an infield single, scoring José. David Denny hit a grounder to short that should have ended the inning, but Rice first baseman Dave Edwards dropped the throw from Welch at short. Alan Brown came in to pinch hit for Bryan Burrows, and Brown hit a clean single over the head of Rice pitcher Tim Englund, scoring Labay. Tie game at 3-3!

Calvin kept Rice scoreless in the 8th and 9th, and Texas got lucky in the 9th. With 1 out, Jamie Doughty doubled, and then went to third on a wild pitch. Billy Bates struck out for the second out of the inning, and it was beginning to look like the game might be heading to extra innings against Rice one more time. But Mike Brumley hit a ball right at the Rice replacement first baseman, Curtis Fox, who misplayed it. That allowed Brumley to score the winning run, and the 'Horns are moving into the winner's bracket game against Arkansas on Saturday night.

Rice has to be devastated. They keep playing UT close, but giving Texas extra chances to score can be deadly. Having to continually play the 'Horns here in Austin is not helping them, as there were 3700 people in the stands, mostly cheering for UT. Schiraldi only gave up 5 hits over his 9 sparkling innings and struck out 7. He goes to 10-1 on the year and shows why he is the Texas Friday night guy. UT only had 8 hits against Englund, with Tolentino the only batter to get more than one – and his were a home run and a double. Now Rice has to come back on Saturday afternoon and play Houston, with both teams having a chip on their shoulder after the way they played in their first games on Friday. It should be an interesting game! Houston is probably a slight favorite, because they will have Rayner Noble on the mound – and he has been great all year. Texas will have Mike Capel pitching Saturday night, facing Arkansas' Tim Dietz, who is 6-2 on the year.

May 14ᵗʰ

Houston beat Rice in 13 innings! Normally that would be a good thing for the other teams in the tournament, with the two schools going extra innings using up a lot of their pitching arms. But in this case, both starting pitchers pitched complete games! It wasn't that hot this afternoon, which helped, but both Rayner Noble from Houston and David Hinnrichs from Rice pitched outstanding games. Houston scored 2 in the top of the 13ᵗʰ to win 4-2.

Corky Swindell was the star at the plate for Houston. In the 4ᵗʰ, Steve Seberger doubled, and Swindell singled to drive in Seberger. Corky went to second on the throw home, and scored himself on Don Larson's single. Houston led 2-0, but that lead didn't last long. In the bottom of the 4ᵗʰ, Scott Johnson walked, and scored on a 3-base error by Houston's right fielder Billy Savarino. Bryan Foxx then scored on Mike Fox's suicide squeeze bunt, tying the game at 2.

That was all the scoring until the top of the 13ᵗʰ. In that inning Seberger drew a walk and went to second on Swindell's single to right. Don Larson flew out to left for the 2ⁿᵈ out in the inning, but then Riley Epps singled, scoring Seberger. When the Rice centerfielder mishandled Epp's single, Swindell was also able to score. Noble got that 4-2 lead to hold up in the bottom of the 13ᵗʰ, and that was the game. Rayner was also the DH for the game, going 1 for 4 at the plate. He only gave up 6 hits over his 13 innings and struck out 9 Rice batters. What a player! Hopefully after throwing that many pitches today, he is done as a pitcher for the next few days, and the UT team doesn't have to face him later in this tournament!

And Texas blasted Arkansas Saturday night! UT won 9-2 on a cool evening, with Mike Capel throwing a complete game 5-hitter. He is now 10-1 on the year, and showing why he has been moved up to number 2 in the pitching rotation. He did give up 2 solo home runs, in the 4th and the 9th, but by the time the teams got to the 9th the game had already been decided.

At the plate, Texas pretty much did their damage 1 or 2 runs per inning, taking advantage of whatever opportunities the Hogs gave them. José Tolentino did have another monster home run, his second of the tournament, but other than that it was pretty much the little stuff. UT didn't have more than 1 hit in an inning until the 8th, when they got 3 of their 8 total base knocks. Texas scored 3 runs on ground outs. Doug Hodo got one of those, and 2 more RBIs on a single. UT scored 3 in the 8th, 2 of those on David Denny's double down the left field line. Hodo and Tolentino were both 2 for 4, and the only 2 Horns to get more than 1 hit. A typical inning was the bottom of the 1st, when Billy Bates hit a leadoff single, stole second, was sacrificed to third by Mike Brumley, and scored on Hodo's 6-3 groundout. There was one unusual event in the 4th, when the Razorbacks pulled off a triple play. Gus had put the hit-and-run on with 2 runners going. Steve Labay hit a low liner that was gloved by Arkansas's second baseman Brett Harrison with a shoestring catch. The runners were easily doubled off of second and first to complete the trifecta. First triple play around here in years, and UT wasn't the team to pull it off!

Now the 'Horns wait on either Arkansas or Houston to come out of the loser's bracket to play Texas Sunday evening. UT only has to beat whichever team survives once to win the tournament. It is nice to be in that position!

An interesting thing happened tonight after the Texas game with Arkansas. After the stands had cleared, Roger Clemens went to the mound to try and figure out why he is not pitching well right now. It was just him, Deron Loy (as catcher), and Clint Thomas, the UT pitching coach. It was nearly dark in the ballpark – the big lights had been turned off– but Roger was showing one more time how dedicated he is to his craft. His fastball has fallen off by several mph over the last few games, and he is determined to get it back. He thinks he has found the problem and fixed it. After looking at tapes of his performance last summer in Omaha, the coaches think he has been landing a little too stiffly on his front leg, which causes his arm to drag and takes some velocity off his fastball. He says his elbow feels better, so that may help, too. Texas will see the results of this late-night practice session Sunday night...

May 15th

The tournament is down to Arkansas and Texas. The Razorbacks beat Houston this afternoon, 9-7, to eliminate the Cougars. And this win probably guarantees a regional berth for Arkansas, even if they don't win the tournament and get the Conference's automatic bid into the playoffs. The game was back and forth for the first 6 innings. Arkansas scored 2 in the top of the 1st, but Houston came back with 3 in the 2nd to take the lead. The Hogs tied it in the 4th, but then Houston came back in the 5th with 2 more runs to retake the lead, 5-3.

But then came the 6th. Arkansas got 2 quick singles, and then loaded the bases on a surprise 2-strike bunt by Jim Ward. Then right fielder Scott Loseke hit a hard grounder to Houston's second baseman Corky Swindell, who threw the ball away trying to go to second to start a double play. 2 runs scored, and then a 3rd run when Houston's left fielder Mike Boaz misplayed the bad throw from Swindell. Suddenly Arkansas was up, 6-5. Norm Roberts then got an infield single to score another run.

Arkansas got 2 more runs in the 7th to make it 9-5, and then hung on as Houston scored 1 each in the 8th and 9th. Charlie Corbell pitched the final 4 innings for the Razorbacks, allowing 4 hits and the last 2 runs, but he got the save, the first of his career. But now they have to turn right around and play UT this evening, after having used 2 of their best pitchers this afternoon.

As it turned out, they did have one decent pitcher left in their bullpen. Arkansas beat Texas tonight 5-4. UT jumped all over them early, scoring 3 in the 3rd. Bryan Burrows and Billy Bates drew walks, and then Mike Brumley, trying to sacrifice, beat out the bunt to load the bases. José Tolentino laced a double to left center, scoring everybody on base. In the bottom of the 4th, Texas scored another run when David Denny doubled, and was then sacrificed to third by Burrows. Billy Bates walked, and then stole second. After a 2nd out, Denny broke for home, and was caught in a rundown – but was awarded home plate on catcher interference after running into the Arkansas catcher, Tom Pagnozzi. Suddenly it was 4-0, and Texas was coasting with Roger Clemens throwing darts on the mound.

Unfortunately, that was the last UT run of the evening. Back in the 3rd, after José cleared the bases, Arkansas coach Norm DeBriyn brought in reliever Lester Lancaster for his 3rd appearance this weekend. He got the save on Friday against Houston, and pitched again against Texas on Saturday night. Except for that unearned run in the 4th, Lancaster shut UT down on 6 hits over the last 6 2/3 innings, striking out 7.

Things fell apart for the 'Horns in the 6th. The Hog's Jim Ward walked, and then went to second on a passed ball. Brett Harrison hit a Texas League single down the right field line, scoring Ward. Clemens then hit Norm Roberts, followed by a single to left from Mike Loggins. Suddenly Arkansas had the tying runs on base. Roger then struck out Tom Pagnozzi for the 2nd out in the inning, and enticed Mark Berry to hit a high fly ball to right, which should have ended the rally. But, unfortunately, right fielder Alan Brown – playing only his 8th game in right field all year – dropped the fly ball, allowing all 3 runners to score since they were running with 2 outs. Suddenly there was a tie game. Ralph Kraus then hit a fly to center which Steve Labay should have been able to handle, but he misjudged the carry, the ball went over his head, and Kraus had a run-scoring triple. Arkansas had that final 5-4 lead. Roger threw a 4-hitter complete game, but his outfielders let him down at critical moments, and he lost his 3rd straight game, dropping his record to 9-5 on the year.

Texas had beaten the Razorbacks 7 straight times before today, and this was UT's first loss in the conference tournament since 1980, and their first loss in the tournament here at home since 1977. As Gus put it after the game, Texas has continued to show their inconsistency all year. He was furious. Now UT has to play the Hogs again on Monday evening, this time in a winner-take-all game. Gus has already announced that he will be starting Calvin Schiraldi, who pitched Friday night.

May 16th

Texas finally did run Arkansas out of pitching. UT beat them tonight 14-0, winning the tournament and the automatic bid into the NCAA playoffs. Calvin Schiraldi threw another complete game, his second of the weekend, and limited the Hogs to just 5 hits. This is Texas' 5th consecutive Southwest Conference Tournament championship. UT is now 52-13 on the year, and just about guaranteed to be the site of one of the Regionals in a couple of weeks.

This game was over quickly. UT scored 4 in the top of the 2nd, and then a tournament record 8 runs in the 3rd to take a 12-0 lead. Arkansas ran through 5 different pitchers in the game, and collectively they gave up 12 hits and 9 walks. In the 2nd, Jeff Hearron and David Denny started the 'Horns off with singles. Steve Labay walked, loading the bases, and moving the other 2 runners up a base. Mike Trent grounded out 4-3, but Hearron scored, and Denny went to third. David then scored on a nice safety squeeze bunt by Bryan Burrows. Bill Bates doubled in Labay, and then Mike Brumley singled, allowing Bates to score from second. And suddenly it was 4-0, and UT was rolling.

Texas batted around in the 3rd. José Tolentino singled, followed by another by David Denny. Jeff Hearron got hit by a pitch – something he has made into an art form – loading the bases. Steve Labay hit a sacrifice fly for the first out of the inning, with Tolentino tagging and scoring from third. Mike Trent walked, loading the bases, and then a series of Hog pitchers walked 3 more in a row with a run scoring each time. That made it 8-0, and brought José Tolentino up for the 2nd time that inning. He bombed one over the left field fence for a grand slam, and UT had their 12-0 lead. This was José's 2nd grand slam of the year, and his 3rd home run of the tournament.

In the 7th, with the score still 12-0, Gus gave Bill Bates the bunt sign, with Bryan Burrows running from first. Bill missed the sacrifice bunt attempt for a strike, and that led to a brush back pitch from Fred Faust. After Bates flied out, Burrows was thrown out at second on an attempted steal attempt. The Razorbacks took umbrage at UT appearing to try and run up the score even more, and when Bates came back to the plate in the 9th Tim Dietz, who had relieved Faust, again threw at Bates. The benches cleared, but nothing happened except for some yelling back-and-forth. The coaches restored order pretty quickly, and no one was ejected. Gus was unapologetic. He said he is always skeptical until the last out. He said he has seen several late inning rallies, and rattled off 3 from his memory. "You see some of these, and you don't know when enough is enough." He also said if it was his team on the receiving end of that situation, he wouldn't mind the other team trying to continue to score. "If you're that bad that they can beat you 30-0, let 'em have at it." Arkansas will probably make a Regional somewhere after making it to the finals of the conference tournament, and Gus said he wouldn't be surprised if Texas sees them again in Omaha. But both teams have to win a few more games to get there!

Four of the Texas guys made the All-Conference Tournament Team. Calvin Schiraldi, Jeff Hearron, José Tolentino, and Bryan Burrows were all named to the team. Calvin and José were unanimous selections. Calvin pitched 2 complete games, winning both, and José hit .529 in the tournament, with 2 doubles and 3 home runs, including the grand slam tonight against Arkansas. He had 9 RBIs and scored himself 6 times – a one-man wrecking crew at the plate. Hope he stays that hot!

The rest of the team did feel a little sorry for him. José's family comes up to Austin as often as they can, but it is an expensive trip from Mexico. They are planning on being here for the Regional, and then hopefully going on to Omaha, so they decided to skip the conference tournament. So, Monday after the final conference tournament game, when everyone was leaving the ballpark and meeting with family and girlfriends, getting hugs and congratulations, José, the tournament's most valuable player, didn't have anyone outside the gate waiting on him. It was pretty sad. Everyone could tell he was missing his family. People did congratulate him, but the team knew that he wished his parents and sister had been there to see him playing so well.

CHAPTER 8

LUBBOCK CHRISTIAN

May 19th

Normally the Regional Tournament is the following weekend after the Conference Tournament, but for some reason the NCAA put an extra week in between the two tournaments this year. So, Gus scheduled a 4-game series against Lubbock Christian to try and keep the Texas team sharp before they get into regional action. LCC is 50-22 and will host the NAIA World Series starting May 30th. They needed some warmup games, too. The two teams have a single game scheduled for this afternoon, a doubleheader tomorrow (Friday), and a single game scheduled for Sunday afternoon. There are no games scheduled for Saturday, as that is graduation day here at UT.

This will be the Chaparral's 17th straight game away from home, so maybe Texas can catch them a little tired. They did win 3 of 7 from Pan American down in the Valley, with that series ending on Tuesday. Texas will be pitching Mike Capel today, Kirk Killingsworth and Roger Clemens tomorrow, and on Sunday the 'Horns will have Calvin Schiraldi going against Bobby Hinson, who beat Texas here on March 7th, 4-2.

Doug Gassoway discovered an arcane agreement between Major League Baseball and the Mexican League. The two leagues had agreed that the United States Major Leagues would not draft citizens of Mexico – like José Tolentino – so he might be considered to be ineligible for the Major League draft coming up in a couple of weeks. So, José, with help from a couple of Wild Bunch attorneys, went down to Houston this week to get his American citizenship papers. José's mother was born in Ft Worth, and therefore she (and therefore José) are both, by law, American citizens. José, having been born in Mexico City, could claim citizenship in either country – but he wanted to be a United States citizen. Robert Gauntt, who hasn't played much this year, was penciled in to start at first in this evening's game in place of José. Gus was thinking that José wouldn't get back from Houston in time for the game. But after warmups, José comes flying out of the dugout, still buttoning his uniform shirt, shoes untied, and announcing he is now a U.S. citizen and ready to play! He got his citizenship papers at noon, and made it back to Austin in record time. Scott Wilson, in the Wild Bunch, said the DPS troopers patrolling Highway 290 between Houston and Austin must have taken the afternoon off!

Texas didn't play well tonight, but UT won, 8-5. The Longhorns had to score 6 runs in their last 3 innings to get the win. Gus chewed everyone out after the game for about 15 minutes, accusing the entire team of sleepwalking, being lackadaisical, and playing down to the level of their competition. The team had been given 2 days off after the conference tournament, and it looked like the entire bunch thought they were all still on vacation. There wasn't much of a crowd on hand – less than 300 people at the game – and that might have been a factor, too.

Some people did have a good game. Mike Brumley had 4 RBIs and hit a 2-run home run. Kirk Killingsworth and Steve Labay went 2 for 3. Probably the biggest surprise of the night was that Johnny Sutton started in center field. He had not played much all year, with only 1 official at bat this entire season before tonight. But he went 2 for 3, scored twice, and played a great center field. Johnny also stole a base. This is probably Gus's 47th different outfield iteration, as he has tried to find the answer all year to who should be playing and where. It may be late in the season, but maybe he has found something (or someone) in Sutton!

Johnny transferred to UT after his freshman year at SMU, where he had been a starter at second base, after SMU gave up baseball (probably to balance scholarships under Title IX). Johnny was another Doug Gassoway recommendation to Gus. Sutton played a little his sophomore year, and more last year, and thought he might have a chance to start this year. But he ended up as 3rd string second baseman and didn't really get a chance to play all year – until now. He was actually pretty upset after the long string of consecutive games during spring break, when he didn't get a chance during that marathon. But he kept a great attitude, and kept working on his arm strength after being asked to try the outfield (Mike Brumley taught Sutton how to throw from the outfield, a four-seamer to get more on the throw than what Johnny needed from second base). Sutton kept bugging the coaches for an opportunity, and looks like he is finally getting his chance!

In the mid-week practice games, it is usually the starters against what the rest of the team call themselves – "the scrubs." But the scrubs themselves would probably be ranked somewhere around #10 in the country – there is that much talent on this team. And the scrubs are just as competitive as the starters and win their share of those practice games. The scrubs also get another advantage – more time in the batting cage, as they can go in and hit in the cage during the real games. They play a game called "cage ball" where you get 3 points for a line drive off the back wall of the cage, 1 point for something at an angle, and negative points for a strike or a foul ball. Sutton has been pounding the ball in practice, and in the cage, and Bill Bethea took notice. Bill at times even had to go down to the batting cage and tell the players not in the game to get back in the dugout – they were that dedicated to improving their swings.

In this first game against Lubbock Christian Mike Capel gave up 10 hits but survived to pitch his 3rd consecutive complete 9-inning game. LCC scored first in the second inning to take a 1-0 lead. In the bottom of the 3rd, Sutton led off with a single, and Bryan Burrows and Bill Bates walked to load the bases. After Mike Brumley struck out, Killingsworth hit a sacrifice fly that scored Sutton and tied the score.

The Chaps scored 2 more in the top of the 4th to go back ahead. Texas picked up a run in the bottom of the 4th to get back to within 1 run, 3-2. LCC picked up another run in the 5th to go up 4-2. They nearly chased Capel that inning, as they had the bases loaded with no outs, but Mike got 3 consecutive popups to get out of the inning with just 1 run allowed.

UT tied it up in the 6th. An error, a walk, and Sutton's bunt single (he is nearly as fast as Bates) loaded the bases. With 2 outs, Mike Brumley singled in Labay and Sutton. And then the

Longhorns picked up 2 more runs in the 7th. The Killer singled, José Tolentino sacrificed him to second, and then Killingsworth scored on Jeff Hearron's triple. Mike Trent, pinch running for Hearron, scored on a balk for the 6th Texas run of the evening.

LCC got back within 1 in the top of the 8th, when replacement second baseman Deron Gustafson threw the ball away trying to complete a 1-4-3 double play, allowing a run to score. But in the bottom of the inning Mike Brumley hit his 2-run homer to right, with Bryan Burrows scoring in front of Mike, to give Texas a little insurance and finalize that 8-5 score.

May 20th

The two teams were supposed to play a doubleheader today, but torrential rain meant no baseball. The twin bill, scheduled to start at 5:00, was at first changed to a single game at 7 tonight – but the rain never let up, so now there is a single game scheduled for 1:00 on Saturday and a double header on Sunday afternoon. Gus really wants to get in all 4 games!

Texas did get some news today – Pan American and the Southland Conference champ, either Northeast Louisiana or Lamar, will be coming to Austin for the Regional next weekend. UT still doesn't know if this will be one of the 6-team Regionals or a 4-team Regional. Bill Little, who is taking over as Sports Information Director for the retiring Jones Ramsey, says he thinks Texas will get 6 teams here. He probably knows, but can't announce anything until the NCAA makes it official. Some wildcard invites have gone out, but Arkansas has yet to hear whether or not they will make the field. There are only 4 at-large bids remaining, so the Razorbacks are starting to get a little antsy. 2 at-large bids were announced yesterday, Mississippi

State and Cal-State Fullerton. Texas may get one of those teams here next week.

May 21st

Roger looked like the old Roger this afternoon. Clemens threw a 6-hitter against Lubbock Christian and won 4-3. He gave up a home run in the top of the 2nd to Chet Feldman, but then retired 11 in a row. He did give up single runs in the 7th and 8th but looked to be in command the entire game. His breaking balls were very sharp today, according to Cliff Gustafson. Coach Gus said this was the best Roger has looked in a long time, and that Roger might be the UT starting pitcher in the Regional, if the 'Horns end up starting on Thursday. Calvin Schiraldi, who would normally pitch the first game in a series, is scheduled to pitch tomorrow, Sunday, and so might not have enough recovery time to be ready to go by Thursday. Roger is now 10-5 for the year, and this is his first win since beating Texas Tech on April 22nd. Nice to see him getting sharp again right before Texas starts the NCAA playoffs!

Johnny Sutton started again in center field, going 1 for 3 and driving in 2 runs – the go ahead runs in the 2nd. Gus says he might be starting in the Regional over David Denny, who Gus feels is in a slump. Mike Brumley and José Tolentino were both 2 for 4 in the game – José continues to pound the ball to all fields.

After the solo homer by Lubbock Christian in the top of the second, UT got on the board in the bottom half of the inning on singles by José and Jeff Hearron, and then an error by the LCC shortstop loaded the bases. Sutton's single scored Tolentino and pinch runner Mike Trent. Texas picked up another run in the 5th when Bryan Burrows tripled and then scored on Bill Bates' single to center. That gave the 'Horns a 3-1 lead. UT got their last run in the 6th when Hearron walked, and then Jeff was again replaced by pinch runner Mike Trent. Trent went to third on David Denny's single, and then scored on Steve Labay's fielder's choice ground ball. It was 4-1 at that point, and Texas held on for the win.

UT won, but Gus was still not happy with the team's focus, and blasted the team again after the game in a closed-door meeting. He told the press that it wasn't a tongue-lashing, but "constructive criticism."

May 22nd

Texas won both games of the doubleheader, 5-0 and 9-2. Of course, this was after Gus had threatened the team last night with 50 sprints after the 2nd game today if they didn't play better than they had the previous games against Lubbock Christian. That is a lot of motivation!

Calvin Schiraldi was his usual self in the first game, pitching his 3rd 5-hitter and 4th complete game in a row. He struck out 9 in the shutout, has now thrown 20 consecutive scoreless innings, and raised his record to 12-1 for the year. He has got to be in the running for the best college pitcher in the country!

Bill Bates and Steve Labay both had 2 hits in the game, and Johnny Sutton had another hit. Mike Brumley stole his 26th base of the year. UT scored in the 1st and 2nd, and then more runs in the 4th and 5th to put the game away.

In the second game, Kirk Killingsworth showed a little rust, not having pitched in the last two weeks. He gave up 2 runs in the top of the 1st, but then found his groove and pitched a shutout the rest of the way. He, too, pitched a complete game, and struck out 10, his career high. The Texas relievers are probably playing dominoes out in the bullpen – they haven't been called on to pitch for so long that Clint Thomas may have forgotten the number he needs to ring the bullpen phone.

Kirk issued a walk in the 1st, followed by a single, a sacrifice bunt, and 2 more singles, allowing LCC to take the lead, 2-0. But Texas came right back in the bottom of the 1st with 3 runs of their own. Johnny Sutton was moved to leadoff for this game, and he started the rally with a clean single. Mike Brumley and Doug Hodo walked, and the bases were loaded with no outs recorded. José Tolentino hit a long sacrifice fly, with Sutton tagging and scoring from third. Brumley stole third and scored when the Chap catcher's throw went into left field. Two more walks to Deron Loy and Jamie Doughty reloaded the bases, and Hodo scored on a wild pitch.

The 'Horns scored again in the 2nd with a double from Brumley and a single from Hodo, and then in the 3rd José and Deron Loy hit back-to-back home runs to pretty much ice the game. UT was leading 6-2 at that point. After that, the biggest news was the 2 additional singles from Johnny Sutton. The team doesn't know why Gus decided to give him a chance, but he has been raking since he got his first start on Thursday. Today, in the 5th, Johnny hit his 3rd single of the game, scoring Mike Trent from third. Deron Gustafson moved to third on Sutton's single. Then Johnny and Deron pulled off the fake double steal, where the runner going to second gets himself in a rundown but distracts the fielders enough to allow the runner from third to score. They did it perfectly, a shining example of Gus Ball at its finest. Johnny also stole second earlier, his 4th stolen base in his short career. Brumley got his 27th. Sutton was 3 for 4 for the game, and José Tolentino was 2 for 2, with another home run – he is still hot as a firecracker at the plate.

Texas has won 5 in a row, and the Longhorns are 56-13 for the year. But UT had a better record last year and didn't get to dogpile in Omaha. There is still work to do. Now the team waits to see who they will draw in the Regional, and when it will start. UT is pushing for a Thursday start, if this is to be a 6-team Regional, so as to be able to handle any weather delays over this next weekend. Showers are common this time of year in central Texas, and the administration wants to make sure they have a team ready to move on to Omaha by the NCAA's deadline. UT should find out tomorrow who is coming to town and the opening game schedule. They are ready!

CHAPTER 9

THE AUSTIN REGIONAL

May 23rd

Texas found out today who will be coming to town for the Regional Tournament – mostly. UT will be playing Thursday night against the winner of the Southland Conference championship, with Lamar and Northeast Louisiana playing this afternoon to decide who gets to come face the 'Horns. The other teams in the Regional are set – Pan American will open the tournament Thursday afternoon against Grambling, and Mississippi State will play Tulane following that first game.

Coach Gustafson said that UT and Pan American should be favored, because those two teams have the deepest pitching staffs, and that pitching is the key in a six-team tournament. He also said he felt this was a strong Regional lineup – "Putting Mississippi State and Tulane in here really beefs it up. But I don't have any complaints."

Texas also found out that they have gone back up in the polls – UT is back to the top spot according to Collegiate Baseball, and #2 behind San Diego State in the Baseball America poll. What matters is that there are 36 teams in the playoffs, and Texas wants to be the last one standing on June 11th in Omaha. Other Regional hosts include North Carolina, Oklahoma State, Michigan, Maine, Stanford, Arizona State, and Florida State. Hosting gives a team a distinct advantage in a Regional, so if UT makes it to Omaha, they will probably see a lot of these teams in Rosenblatt. Arkansas did make it into the tournament as one of the last few wildcard teams to be invited – but they got sent to a tough Regional at Oklahoma State, where the other teams are Oral Roberts and Wichita State – with all 3 ranked in the top 20 in the polls.

May 24th

Texas found out last night that Northeast Louisiana beat Lamar, so now they know who they face Thursday night. On Friday, the loser of the Thursday Pan American – Grambling game will play the loser of Tulane – Mississippi State game in the opener. The middle game will be the Texas – NE Louisiana loser against the Pan American – Grambling winner, and the late game will be the UT – Northeast Louisiana winner against the winner of the game between Mississippi State and Tulane. Hopefully, UT will be in that game! Gus says Roger Clemens will start on Thursday, since Calvin Schiraldi pitched on Sunday and probably needs another day of rest. And everyone in the bullpen says they are ready if needed, since they haven't had to pitch in a couple of weeks!

There are talented players on each of the teams the fans will see in Austin. Pan American has Mitch Moran, their center fielder, with a school record 19 home runs – and he has also stolen 26 bases this year! He will be facing Martin Foley, the top Grambling pitcher, in Thursday's game. Foley is 9-2 on the year, and has struck out 49 batters this spring. Tulane's second baseman is John Zelenka, an All-American last year, who is batting .355 with 8 home runs and 40 RBIs. Mississippi State is led by Brad Winkler, their center fielder, who holds the SEC record with 194 runs scored. He is hitting .343, with 15 home runs and 70 RBIs for the year. But he hasn't been hitting that well since getting married on May 7th. He was 2 for 18 in the SE Conference tournament. They also have Rafael Palmeiro, hitting .419 - by far the best batting average in the Regional. UT will be facing Mitch Thomas, Northeast Louisiana's top pitcher. He was 4-0 in the Southland Conference, but is a freshman, and his ERA is a little up at 5.03. And, of course, Texas has José Tolentino, now hitting .354. He has 11 home runs on the year, and 27 doubles – both are only 2 under the UT records in those categories, and José has a chance to hold both records before the year is done.

Grambling has the best team batting average, hitting .329 for the year. Both Tulane and Mississippi State are also over .300, and Tulane has 8 starters hitting over .300. Texas will try and counter that with UT's Regional-leading ERA of 2.80, a full run lower than anyone else in the tourney. Does good pitching really nullify good hitting? This will be a good test of that old cliché!

May 26th

Things followed the form sheets today, with all 3 favorites winning. Pan American opened the tournament by beating Grambling 5-0, Mississippi State beat Tulane 4-2, and then Texas crushed Northeast Louisiana 15-0.

Jim Hickey, the Pan American pitcher, pitched a complete game 3-hitter to put the Broncos in the winner's bracket. He is now 16-2 on the year, struck out 8, and retired 13 of the last 14 Grambling batters. Pan American scored 3 in the 1st on 3 walks, a double by Mark Reissener, and a second double by Rafael Barbosa. Mitch Moran hit a 2-run homer in the 4th. If Pan American sticks around for most of the weekend, someone will probably see Hickey on the mound again.

Mississippi State usually pounds teams into submission, but this afternoon's game was a pitching gem by Jeff Brantley. He threw a 4-hitter, pitched a complete game, and didn't give up any earned runs. Brad Winkler went 3 for 3 with 2 RBIs, including adding 2 more to his school record 40 doubles, and DH Dan Van Cleve was 3 for 5. Third Baseman Mike Bradford made several outstanding plays to help keep Tulane from scoring more. Tulane got their 2 runs in the bottom of the 8th when Mississippi State first baseman Will Clark's error put runners on second and third with no outs, and Tulane got both runs home – but that was it for the Green Wave. Now Tulane and Grambling face off at 1:00 on Friday, with the loser being eliminated from the tournament.

Roger Clemens was outstanding. He was actually pitching a no-hitter until the 6th, when a shot ricocheted off of Roger's leg. He was pulled after 7 innings, not because he was hurt or tired, but so that Gus could save him for use later in the tournament if needed. Wade Phillips and Kirk Killingsworth pitched an inning each of no-hit ball to finish the game. Texas tied their season's high at 18 hits for the game, with Jeff Hearron leading the way, going 5 for 6 for the game, including 2 doubles and a triple. Steve Labay was 3 for 4, and José Tolentino, Bill Bates, Bryan Burrows, Johnny Sutton, and Deron Loy had 2 hits apiece. One of Loy's hits was a home run, and the other a triple. Sutton continues to hit the ball well and is playing great defense in the outfield.

The Texas – Northeast Louisiana game was scoreless for the first 3 innings, but UT scored 2 in the bottom of the 4th to take the lead. Hearron led off with his triple, but was thrown out at the plate after a comebacker to Indian's pitcher Mitch Thomas. David Denny did reach base on the fielder's choice, and Steve Labay singled, moving Denny to second. The relay throw got away from the second baseman, allowing Denny to score and Steve to reach second base. Johnny Sutton reached on an error, with Labay going to third. Bryan Burrows singled, scoring Steve Labay, and giving the 'Horns that 2-0 lead.

That was it until the bottom of the 6th. In that inning Labay coaxed a leadoff walk, and Sutton singled. Burrows hit a nice sacrifice bunt to move both runners up a base. Bates walked, loading the bases with 1 out. Mike Brumley hit a long sacrifice fly to left (off reliever Joey Jacola), allowing Labay to score. Then Deron Loy hit his triple, scoring Sutton and Bates. Jeff Hearron followed with another single, scoring Loy, and UT was up 6-0.

Texas batted around in the 7th. Labay started the inning with a single to left, and Sutton followed with a single right over second base. Burrows hit another good sacrifice bunt, putting runners on second and third. Bates singled, allowing Labay to score. Brumley hit another sacrifice fly, scoring Sutton. Loy follows with his homer off the scoreboard in left. José Tolentino singled, followed by a Jeff Hearron double. Denny tripled, scoring Tolentino and Hearron. Labay ended the onslaught with another single, scoring Denny. By the time the inning was over UT was up 13-0 and starting to think about Mississippi State.

But it wasn't over. Texas picked up 2 more in the 8th. Jamie Doughty started the 'Horns off with another walk and went to second on a wild pitch. Deron Gustafson, subbing for Bates, drew a walk. Brumley hit a fielder's choice ground ball that got the force out on Deron at second, but the shortstop's relay throw to first was over the first baseman's head, allowing Doughty to score. José hit another single, and then Hearron got his 5th hit, a single that scored Brumley. 15-0 ball game. Bill Bates did make an error in the game, one of his few this year – and he got some ribbing over that after the game. Now Texas gets down to serious business with much better competition. And Coach Bethea told the team after the game that Mississippi State had actually saved their best pitcher to face UT, instead of starting him this afternoon. Now both teams will find out how well that strategy works!

May 27th

A dreadful day for UT. First, the team found out that David Denny has strained ligaments in his elbow, and is probably out for the rest of the season. Then on Friday night Calvin Schiraldi couldn't find his control, and Texas lost to Mississippi State. That means they now have to win four straight games to win the Regional – a tough row, considering how good the competition is right now here in Austin.

In the first game Friday afternoon Tulane beat Grambling 8-7, but it took Tulane 10 innings to do so. Grambling becomes the first team to be eliminated in the Regional. The Tigers were winning 6-3 going into the 8th, but Tulane scored 3 runs in that inning without a hit – 5 walks, including 1 with the bases loaded, a wild pitch, and a sacrifice fly – and suddenly Tulane had tied the game. The Green Wave got an RBI double in the top of the 10th, and then held on for the win. They did use their best relief pitcher, Brian Migliore, for several innings, so he will probably not be available tomorrow when Tulane will have to play Texas.

In the second afternoon game Pan American hit 3 9th inning home runs to come back and beat Louisiana Tech, eliminating Tech and keeping Pan American undefeated in the tournament. After Tech had scored 3 in the bottom of the 8th to take a 6-5 lead, they got 2 quick outs, sandwiched around a walk, and looked ready to take the game. But Pam American's Rafael Barbosa hit a 2-run shot to give the Broncos the lead, 7-6. That was followed by solo shots from Luie Chavez and Gilbert Beason to give Pan American some insurance runs. Louisiana Tech got within 1 in the bottom of the 9th, but a baserunning mistake led to the final out when a popup was caught, and a runner doubled off second base. He apparently thought there were 2 outs, and took off when the ball was hit, even with the third base coach trying to get him to tag at second.

Ever wonder what the umpires, catcher, and batter are saying at the plate? After the first two 9th inning Pan American homers, home plate umpire Jim Garman told Gilbert Beason, "I bet you can't do that, too." Beason said he told the ump, "What do you mean? I've done it 8 times this year. I'll do it again." And he did, providing what turned out to be the winning run.

The Texas game tonight against Mississippi State was ugly. Calvin looked sharp in the bottom of the 1st (State was the home team tonight), but then after coming back out in the 2nd couldn't find the plate. In his 6 innings (and Gus could have pulled him earlier) Schiraldi walked 8, gave up 6 hits, and even had an error. UT did score first, but State tied the game in the 2nd, and got 1 more in the 4th and then 2 in the 6th before Calvin was lifted for Wade Phillips. Wade gave up 2 more runs to make the final score 6-2. Deron Loy played left, replacing the injured David Denny. Johnny Sutton was back in center. José Tolentino and Kirk Killingsworth, the Texas DH, were both 2 for 4, but overall the Longhorns looked bad at the plate against Mississippi State's Hans Herzog and then reliever Robin Jeter. UT actually out hit MSU 10-9, but those hits were scattered effectively by the Mississippi State pitchers, keeping the Texas runners from scoring.

In the top of the 1st, Bill Bates earned a leadoff walk, stole second, and was sacrificed to third by Mike Brumley. Deron Loy grounded out 6-3, with Bates scoring.

In the bottom of the 2nd Will Clark walked, but then Calvin picked him off of first. Pete White then hit a solo homer to left, tying the game at 1-1.

In the 4th, MSU's White hit another long shot that bounced off the bottom of the centerfield wall for a double. A ground out got him to third. Mike Bradford hit a sacrifice fly that scored White, giving MSU the lead.

The 6th was the clincher for Mississippi State. After an out, Chris Maloney walked. He was forced at second when Dave Van Cleve grounded to José Tolentino at first. Calvin tried to pick Van Cleve off of first, but his throw sailed and the MSU left fielder ended up at third on the 2-base error. Brad Winkler then hit the ball just to the base of the centerfield wall. The ball took a crazy bounce high in the air, and by the time it came down and Johnny Sutton had gotten it back to the infield Winkler had a 2-run inside-the-park home run. At that point MSU led 4-1.

They got another run in the 7th, when Brumley's throw to first went into the dugout, allowing Chuck Bartlett to take second (UT had 3 errors in the game). Will Clark's single made it 5-1.

Texas got 1 back in the top of the 8th, when Killingsworth singled, advanced to third on a couple of ground outs, and scored on an opposite field single by Bill Bates. But 5-2 was as close as the 'Horns would get.

In the bottom of the 8th, Mike Bradford singled, was sacrificed to second, and scored on Van Cleve's double off of Wade Phillips. The final was 6-2, but it didn't seem like it was that close. Texas got beat. They got outplayed. And as Gus told the team after the game, if they don't play better the next couple of days they will be going home for the summer.

Texas starts their comeback at 1:00 on Saturday against Tulane, who is also 1-1 in the tournament. They call that an elimination game. For UT, it is the first step towards redemption. After the Texas loss Friday night, Gus called Steve Labay and Kirk Killingsworth into his office, and told them they would both be starting games this weekend, and that he needed great games from both of them if the team was going to have a chance to make it back to Omaha. Both just nodded. They know what is at stake.

May 28th

Another 3-game day – and hopefully Texas is in 2 of them. UT starts off against Tulane, followed by Mississippi State playing Pan American, and then in the nightcap (assuming Texas beats Tulane) the 'Horns will play the loser of game 2. If UT wins both games today Texas will have played one more game than the remaining undefeated team – either MSU or Pan Am – and

Texas will have to beat that team twice tomorrow (Sunday). But UT has the pitching depth to handle that many games, and they just need to execute to keep winning. UT will have a slight advantage tonight if they make it that far, in that the loser of the afternoon game, in the heat, will have to turn right around and play Texas – and the Longhorns will have been resting for 3 or 4 hours between games. And the Texas team is starting to finally focus. The team knows what they have to do, and what it will take to win four straight games.

The first game against Tulane was another strange one, where the Texas starting pitching wasn't that great, but UT knocked the cover off the ball – just the opposite of what the 'Horns looked like over the last 3 months. UT hung on to win, 7-5, with Kirk Killingsworth shutting down the last Green Wave rally in the 8th, and then managed to get through the 9th for the save.

The starting pitcher, Mike Capel, had one of his worst games of the season, giving up 8 hits and 5 runs over his 7 2/3 innings. But Bill Bates and Steve Labay both went 3 for 4 in the game, and Johnny Sutton was 2 for 3 to help Texas score enough for the win.

Tulane scored first, in the top of the 1st. John Zalenka reached on a fielder's choice and scored when Tommy Mathews doubled. Mathew's hit bounced off of Sutton's glove in centerfield, and probably should have been caught. But Texas came right back in the bottom of the 1st. Bill Bates singled, and then scored when Mike Brumley tripled off the wall in center, barely missing a home run. José Tolentino then singled to right, scoring Brumley, and UT had a 2-1 lead.

The Longhorns added a couple of additional runs in the 2nd. Johnny Sutton drew a leadoff walk. Bryan Burrows got on when the Tulane shortstop bounced his throw to first and the first baseman couldn't handle it, and Sutton went to third on the play. Bill Bates bounced a ball over the wall in left for a ground-rule double, scoring Sutton, and moving Burrows to third. Deron Loy hit a long sacrifice fly to right, allowing Burrows to score. Texas was up 4-1 at that point.

Tulane got a run back in the 3rd, starting with a leadoff double by Glen Fourmax. Two fly balls got him to third and then home, making it a 4-2 game. And then in the 4th, Capel walked Steve Riley, and then Froggie gave up a 2-run homer to Dan Wagner. Suddenly Texas was in a tie game!

UT came back in the bottom of the 4th to retake the lead. Johnny Sutton started things off with an infield single (speed can kill!), followed by a walk to Bryan Burrows. Bill Bates tried to sacrifice to move the two runners up a base but ended up beating out a great bunt – so Texas had the bases loaded with no outs! Mike Brumley walked, with Sutton scoring from third as everyone moved up a base. Deron Loy hit into a double play, but Burrows was able to score on the play. UT was back on top, 6-4.

The Longhorns added another insurance run in the 5th. Steve Labay started things with a 1-out single. Reliever Keith Burdine, who had come in during the 2nd inning, then hit Kirk Killingsworth with an inside pitch. Gus called for a hit-and-run, and Johnny Sutton hit one of his patented singles right back up the middle to score Labay. Texas was up by 3 at that point, 7-4.

In the 7th, Tulane's Reggie Reginelli tripled past a diving Johnny Sutton in left center. Zelenka grounded out to short, with Reginelli scoring. The game was 7-5 at that point. And Tulane nearly scored more in the 8th. They started with a leadoff line drive to the wall in left center, but Sutton tracked this one down on the track and made a great catch for the first out in the inning. The Green Wave got 2 on with 2 outs, but Killingsworth came in to coax a ground ball out from pinch hitter Joe Scheuermann to finally end the inning.

In the top of the 9th, Glen Formax started another rally with a sharp single off of Killingsworth, but he was erased on a 4-6-3 double play. John Zalenka singled to keep Tulane's hopes alive, but Kirk got a game-ending ground out from Gregg Barrios to end Tulane's season and give UT at least one more game.

The second game today between the two undefeated tourney teams, Mississippi State and Pan American, was a back-and-forth affair that ended with MSU winning 7-5, sending Pan American into tonight's game against the 'Horns. That leaves Mississippi State as the last undefeated team in the tournament, and UT will have to beat them twice tomorrow to make it back to Omaha. That is, if Texas beats Pan Am tonight!

In the game against Mississippi State, Pan American scored first in the bottom of the 1st, with a single, an error, a sacrifice, and then a 2-run single by Mark Reissener. Then Rafael Barbosa put one further than Gus said he had ever seen a home run hit here, close to 450 feet, straight over the centerfield wall. And suddenly it was 4-0 Pan Am. They picked up another run in the 2nd on 2 doubles, the second a ground-rule double by Pat Marshall.

But in the top of the 5th Mississippi State started a comeback. MSU scored 4 runs on 4 straight singles, a ground out, an error, and then another ground out RBI. Suddenly there was a close ball game at 5-4. And then in the 6th MSU got 3 more. A walk and a 2-base error by the Pan Am centerfielder put runners on second and third. Brad Winkler showed why he is a star with a triple off the centerfield wall that scored both runners and gave Mississippi State their first lead of the game. Rafael Palmeiro singled, scoring Winkler, and that was the ball game.

Neither team showed much pitching in the game, with Pan American getting 13 hits and Mississippi State 15. One highlight was Mississippi State's freshman Will McRaney, who came in as a reliever in the 1st, and pitched 1-run ball for 5 1/3 innings. Ron Polk, the MSU coach, said after the game that McRaney's pitching was the key to winning, because he kept MSU in the game until the hits started falling. Robin Jeter pitched the last 3 innings for MSU and got the save.

The Saturday night game was the Kirk Killingsworth show. The same Killingsworth that saved the first game today came back tonight and pitched a complete game 4-hit gem. Texas beat Pan American 6-1, eliminating the Broncos, and putting UT into the tournament finals against Mississippi State tomorrow. Kirk actually pitched over 10 innings today, throwing 13 pitches this afternoon against Tulane for the save in that game, and then 125 pitches tonight for the first 9-inning complete game of his career. The Killer also set a UT record with his 28th appearance of the year. He said after the game that it was by far his best outing of the year. Gus said it couldn't have come at a better time, because he felt the team needed to rest some of the other UT pitchers, and added that Killingsworth had really pitched a shutout, since Texas gave Pan American their run. Kirk walked 1 and struck out 8. Not bad for a guy recruited to play outfield!

And matching Kirk's performance on the mound was another great hitting night by José Tolentino. He went 2 for 4, scored twice, and hit a monster 3-run home run.

Pan American actually scored first in the game, in the top of the 3rd. Bobby Joe Williams doubled, and Mitchell Moran walked, putting 2 on with 1 out. Bryan Burrows, playing third, then fielded a grounder from Mark Reissener and proceeded to throw it into right field, trying to get the ball to Bill Bates at second to start a double play. Williams scored on Burrows' error.

But Texas came back big time in the bottom of the 3rd. Johnny Sutton worked a leadoff walk from Pan Am pitcher Scott Cannon after about a 9 pitch at bat. Bryan Burrows and Bill Bates followed with walks, too, loading the bases. Mike Brumley struck out, and then Doug Hodo hit the ball on the ground to the first baseman, scoring Sutton. With 2 outs, José Tolentino unleashed his home run over the wall in right, over Comal Street, giving UT a 4-1 lead.

Pan American tried to come back in the top of the 8th. Pat Marshall flied out deep to the wall in centerfield to Mike Trent, who had moved to center to replace Johnny Sutton. Mark Reissener drew a walk, and Rafael Barbosa singled for the Bronco's first hit since the 3rd. But Kirk got out of it, getting Luie Chavez to ground out to end the inning.

Hearron pulled another one this inning. With two on, and Killer struggling a little, Jeff walked to the mound. He pulled off his mask, showing a cigarette butt dangling from his lips, and casually asked Killingsworth, "So, what do you want to throw here?" Kirk had to turn his back on Hearron and walk off the mound to keep from falling down, as he was laughing so hard. The Texas groundskeeper, George, was a smoker – and occasionally the team would find one of his discarded butts on the field. Hearron had apparently picked one up and saved it for the right moment. Sitting in the dugout, the other players didn't know what was going on – no one had ever seen Killer turn his back on his catcher – but once they figured it out the entire team was cracking up. Even Gus smiled. And it worked – Killingsworth relaxed and got out of the jam. Of course, Gus chewed out Hearron when he got back to the dugout, but it was worth it!

The 'Horns picked up a couple of insurance runs in their half of the 8th. Tolentino beat out an infield single hit between second and first when no one bothered to cover first base. Jeff Hearron singled to left, putting 2 on. Steve Labay tried to sacrifice the runners up a base, but ended up beating out the bunt single, loading the bases. Mike Trent followed with a single to center, bringing Tolentino and Hearron home. That gave the game the final 6-1 score. There were 5200 people here tonight, the biggest crowd of the year, and Bill Little said they are expecting a sellout tomorrow.

And now Texas has to beat Mississippi State twice. The Bulldogs haven't lost 2 games in a row all year long. Mississippi State is looking for their own 3rd trip in the last 5 years to Omaha. In their 3 victories here this weekend, they have pounded out 37 hits and scored 17 runs. But the fat lady hasn't sung just yet! As Gus put it, "We're halfway back. The opposition will get tougher tomorrow, but having to win 2 out of 2 is not nearly as long a shot as having to win 4 out of 4." He has already announced that Steve Labay will start the first game tomorrow afternoon.

May 29th
Memorial Day

We're headed to Omaha. It may be hard to believe, but Texas did it. UT came back after their loss on Friday to Mississippi State and won 4 straight games, including beating Mississippi State twice today. Steve Labay pitched the game of his life in the first game today, shutting out MSU 7-0. And then, with the Bulldogs out of pitching, UT pummeled them in the winner-take-all final game 12-3. It is beginning to look like the Texas team has finally gotten their act together!

Steve hadn't pitched in a game in nearly a month. A lot of complete games from the usual weekend starters had kept him in the outfield or serving as DH. But when Gus called on him, he was ready, and he delivered big time. It was MSU's first shutout in 66 games. He only gave up 5 hits, and after the 2nd Mississippi State couldn't even get a runner into scoring position. Brad Winkler, the MSU star right fielder, had been 10 for 11 coming into this afternoon's game – but Labay shut him down with a strike out and 2 ground outs. Gus made another great call putting Steve on the mound, since Mississippi State was starting 5 left-handed batters, and Gus thought that Steve was the best bet to keep them off the basepaths.

In his last outing, up in Tulsa against Oral Roberts, Steve didn't last through the 2nd inning, giving up 6 hits and 4 earned runs in his short stint on the mound. But today, he was just about perfect. Jeff Hearron, the UT catcher, said it was the best he had seen Steve throw all year. He said, "This is nothing against Steve, but he doesn't throw hard at all. But he has a good slider, and his fastball was in the black all day. I know he hasn't pitched in a long time, but the guy's a fighter." Between innings, Killingsworth would sit with Steve, and talk to him about how Steve was throwing, what might work against the upcoming batters, and what Killer would throw to those same hitters if he was pitching. That helped keep Steve calm and focused.

Johnny Sutton had another great day at the plate, going 2 for 3 and knocking in 3 runs. Doug Hodo was 3 for 5 with a double. Mike Brumley was 2 for 3 with a double. Jeff Hearron was 2 for 4 and scored twice. And all that was just in the first game of the day!

Texas started the scoring in the top of the 3rd (UT was the visiting team in the first game today) with MSU pitcher Jeff

Brantley walking Sutton and Mike Trent. Bryan Burrows laid down a nice bunt to move both runners up a base. Bill Bates hit a sacrifice fly to left, deep enough to score the speedy Sutton. Mike Brumley followed with a double down the left field line, scoring Trent. The 'Horns had a quick 2-0 lead, but they knew they needed more runs to make sure MSU and their powerful lineup couldn't come back one more time.

In the 4th, UT again started the inning with 2 walks – and walks have a tendency to come back and bite you. This time it was José Tolentino and Jeff Hearron getting free bases. Deron Loy pushed out the traditional Gusball sacrifice bunt, advancing the runners. Johnny Sutton, who has a knack for hitting the ball right back over second base, did it again with a long single, scoring both Tolentino and Hearron. That put Texas up 4-0, and they were starting to breathe a little easier.

Texas finished their scoring in the 5th. Brumley hit another double - this time just under the glove of the MSU second baseman – but it rolled almost to the wall before the right fielder could get to it. Doug Hodo followed with a ground-rule double over the wall in right center, scoring Brumley. José Tolentino followed with the 3rd straight UT double, scoring Hodo. This was José's 28th double of the year, a team record. Jeff Hearron walked, and then went to second on Deron Loy's fielder's choice out, with Tolentino being forced out at third. Johnny Sutton followed with another single right up the middle, scoring Hearron. And suddenly Texas had a 7-0 lead!

But as mentioned, Mississippi State hadn't lost 2 games in a row all year long – and they know what it takes to get to Omaha, too. The Texas team expected a dogfight in the nightcap.

But it wasn't. UT blew Mississippi State away, 12-3. Roger Clemens showed once again what a great fighter he is when the chips are down. He pitched 6 2/3 innings, giving up 10 hits, and was in trouble in several different innings – but managed to get the outs he needed at critical times to keep MSU off the scoreboard. MSU left 2 on base in the 3rd, 4th, and 5th innings against Roger. In the 4th, it was a great curve to strike out Mike Bradford for the 3rd out. In the 5th, after a single and throwing error by Mike Brumley put runners on second and third, Jay Porter took a called 3rd strike. MSU did break through in the 7th, with 4 straight hits scoring 2 before Calvin Schiraldi came in to put out the fire and finish the game. By the last inning, the 7,000 fans on hand were all chanting "O-Ma-Ha" – with the chant starting with the Wild Bunch behind the first base dugout, the people behind home plate doing the "Ma," and the third base side fans finishing the chant. It was cool!

The Texas hitters killed it tonight, with 16 hits against 3 MSU pitchers. Mike Brumley and José Tolentino were 3 for 4. Johnny Sutton and Bryan Burrows were 3 for 5. Tolentino and Burrows both scored 3 times. José and Brumley both had 3 RBIs. It was a total team victory, and Mike Brumley even gave credit to the scrubs, summing up the win: "It's the greatest comeback I've ever been involved with. The guys on the bench were unbelievable because they picked us up. I've never seen guys get so pumped up. It was like we just decided to win."

Once again, the game started slowly. But in the top of the 3rd (UT lost the coin flip to see who would be the home team) Texas drew first blood. Johnny Sutton started the inning off with a single and was then sacrificed to second by Mike Trent. After Bryan Burrows made the 2nd out in the inning, Bill Bates laced a single to left, scoring Sutton. 1-0, UT.

Mississippi State came right back in the bottom of the 3rd to tie the game. Steve Labay, playing right field tonight after his great performance on the mound in game one, just missed a diving catch, allowing Mike Bradford to reach. Two more singles followed, loading the bases. The second hit of the inning was a Chris Maloney single to right, and then Sutton just missed another diving catch on a low liner by Van Cleve for MSU's 3rd straight hit. Brad Winkler hit a sacrifice fly to left, scoring Bradford. And quickly it was a 1-1 game.

But UT started to separate in the 5th. Johnny Sutton (the Regional MVP) started the 'Horns off again with a single, this time down the third base line. Bradford misplayed the ball, and Sutton took second. Mike Trent drew a walk, putting 2 on. Bryan Burrows, again just trying to sacrifice, put down a perfect bunt to the left of the mound and beat the throw to first, loading the bases. Bill Bates grounded out 4-3, but Sutton scored. Mike Brumley also hit the ball toward the second baseman, but this time the ball scooted under his glove, scoring Trent and Burrows. Brumley stole second on the first pitch to Doug Hodo. Doug then singled, scoring Brumley. José Tolentino then shot a liner down the first base line, scoring Hodo, but José was thrown out at second trying to stretch the hit into another double. Suddenly Texas was up 6-1 and gaining confidence.

The Longhorns picked up 2 more in the 7th. Bryan Burrows started things off with a single up the middle. Bill Bates bunted, the pitcher tried to go to second, but Burrows beat the throw. Mike Brumley then sacrificed to put runners on second and third. Pinch hitter Kirk Killingsworth then singled, scoring both Burrows and Bates. Texas was up 8-1 at that point!

MSU did get 2 runs back in the bottom of the 7th. With 2 outs, Van Cleve doubled. Brad Winkler beat out an infield single, putting 2 on base. Rafael Palmeiro doubled off the right field wall, scoring Van Cleve. Jay Porter followed with another single, scoring Porter. That's when Schiraldi came in to finish the game. It was 8-3, and UT just needed 7 more outs to get back to Omaha. Calvin got the Longhorns out of the 7th, and then held MSU scoreless for the last 2 innings.

Texas got more insurance runs in the 8th. Johnny Sutton and Bryan Burrows both got on with infield singles, and then Bill Bates drew a walk to load the bases. Mike Brumley followed with a single to right, scoring Sutton. José Tolentino singled to center, scoring Burrows and Bates. Jeff Hearron singled to right, allowing Brumley to come home. After that great inning the Texas lead had ballooned to 12-3, and the fans started celebrating.

The 'Horns already know who they will be playing Friday in their opening game in Rosenblatt. James Madison swept through their 6-team Regional undefeated, so they will be well rested for their game against Texas. The College World Series is another double elimination tournament, but this time with 8 teams playing. And Texas plans on being there all week!

CHAPTER 10

THE COLLEGE WORLD SERIES

Eight teams. 14 or 15 games, 9 or 10 days, depending on if someone goes through undefeated. And that is the secret to getting through this tournament easily – remain undefeated. If a team continues to win, they get days off in the first part of the week, plus that team only has to win 1 game when they get to the finals. Texas has another advantage in that they are in the top half of the bracket, which means they start play on Friday night. Teams that don't start until Saturday miss that day of rest that the Friday bracket team might get later in the week. If Texas wins their first 3 games, they will be playing Friday/Monday/ Thursday. That allows their Friday starter to come back again in the semifinal game (with a full week's rest) next Friday if Gus wants him back on the mound. That's going to work for one of the teams here – why not UT?

Realistically, there are six teams here that could get to that semifinal game, and even the finals, undefeated – Texas, Stanford, Oklahoma State, Arizona State, Michigan, or red-hot Alabama, the team that upset Miami in their Regional. The other teams and fans are not giving James Madison or Maine much of a chance, although Maine did make it to the semifinal round last year. Usually, the teams from the Northeast are the most likely to go 0-2 and BBQ. It may not be fair, but those teams can't even practice outside in some cases until April, unless they take a spring break trip through the south to get in some early season games where the weather is more conducive to baseball, so they are always behind the curve on practice time, game experience, and usually talent – good players want to come south to play for the most part. The anomaly there is the Michigan team – they are also a "northern" team, but they have accumulated a bunch of great players. There are six teams that have a legitimate chance to take home the trophy – a team just has to get hot at the right time. The Texas team is upbeat and pretty confident after coming back in the Regional, and likes their chances, but they liked them last year, too, and UT went home empty handed. Maybe this is their year! The 'Horns open Friday evening in the first game against James Madison, followed by Oklahoma State playing Stanford. The Saturday night games are Michigan against Maine, and then Arizona State playing Alabama in the last first-round game.

The games will all be played in the evening for television purposes, to give ESPN the biggest possible viewing audience. However, due to some already scheduled programs like USFL football, some of the games will not be broadcast live this year, so fans back at home will have to tune it to a radio broadcast or wait until late at night to see the ESPN replays. The fans here in Omaha like the games being scheduled at night. One UT fan said that a typical day consists of "A round of golf in the morning, going to the Ak-Sar-Ben racetrack in the afternoon to bet on the horses, baseball at night, then a late dinner and drinking until 2 AM. Then we get up the next morning and do it again!"

ESPN has announced that they will be using 10 cameras this year, double what they started with 4 years ago. They are bringing a staff of 60 to Omaha, compared to 30 when they first started covering the CWS. They even have a monitor set up in the box seats just to the left of home plate, there to be used by the NCAA officials if there is a rules dispute. It is not to be used to change a call on the field – no instant replay – but the rules committee members can use it to settle an issue if there is a game protest by one of the teams playing – and the issue will be settled immediately.

Every team has one or more stars that can win games in clutch situations. Alabama has Dave Magadan, who leads the country in hitting with a .523 average. The Alabama coach said, "Pitchers have tried every conceivable way you can imagine to get him out, including throwing behind him. He has trouble hitting that pitch." Oklahoma State has Pete Incaviglia, who has been hitting towering home runs for OSU all year, even though he is just a freshman. Michigan has Barry Larkin and Chris Sabo. Arizona State starts Oddibe McDowell and Barry Bonds, the son of former major leaguer Bobby Bonds. And Texas has their pitching staff, probably the best in the country.

June 1st

The team flew to Omaha Thursday morning early, because coach Gustafson had to be at the opening press conference Thursday afternoon. The team took a bus (provided for the team by the CWS) to their hotel and checked in, and then went to lunch while the coaches went to the press conference. Texas is staying at a Holiday Inn for the second year in a row, one of the new "Holidomes," moving out from the Red Lion downtown hotel they used in past years (this is UT's 22nd trip to the College World Series). This place has an indoor heated swimming pool, a putt-putt course, ping-pong tables, and video games – a nice touch and place to unwind after games. The pool is supposed to close at 10:00 each night, but since Texas will be playing late games Al Lunsteadt, UT's Business Manager that accompanied the team to Omaha, has negotiated with the hotel and got them to keep the pool open late for the team. This place is a lot more fun than the downtown hotel where the team used to stay, and allows for a lot of time with family, fans, players from other teams, and don't forget girlfriends!

The press conference was a bundle of laughs, as usual. Alabama's coach, Barry Shollenberger, went first, and didn't talk very long. He said, "I left all my one-liners at home." Arizona State's Jim Brock and Oklahoma State's Gary Ward picked on Cliff Gustafson. Brock said, "It's good to have Cliff back. In fact, it's good to have Cliff on the road anywhere. We went down there to play them this year. That's quite a place to play. You get your pitcher ready to go for a 7:30 ballgame. Then they hit you with a 45-minute medley of I love Texas songs. But Cliff is the most honest coach we have in the game. When we met at home plate before the game, he didn't hesitate a bit when he introduced the umps as his brother-in-law and his first cousin."

Oklahoma State's Gary Ward, bringing OSU to Omaha for the 3rd straight year, said, "I've been trying to figure out the difficulties we've had here the last couple of years, and I've come to the conclusion it's been Texas. I got to thinking about every little detail. I decided it wasn't coaching or talent. It's this press conference. Each year Gustafson comes in with a pair of shiny boots and a nice-looking belt buckle and intimidates everyone else." He then lifted up his pants leg, showing off his new boots – "Anaconda!" he added. He then stepped out from behind the podium to show off his huge belt buckle. "Silver, with my name inscribed in gold script. That takes care of Texas." Gus, sitting next to the podium, just put a foot up on the table and showed off his boots. "You got your initials on your boots?" Ward just shook his head and sat down.

Brad Bobcock, the James Madison coach, was hilarious. He started off saying, "This is a first-class thing. We put two people in a room here when normally, on road trips, we put eight in a room – with only one bed. We've got guys taking ground balls because there is so much space in our rooms. We never really talked about getting to Omaha. In fact, I didn't even know where Omaha was except you go north through Virginia to Washington, D.C., and take a left." Talking about Texas, he said, "Someone asked me if I thought we could stay on the same field with them. I said, Sure! Unless they ask us to get off…"

James Madison lost in their conference tournament, and Bobcock had already sent everyone home when they got the NCAA's last wildcard invite to the Regional in North Carolina, and he had to regather his team. "Our guys were working summer jobs already. We had one guy working at the casinos in Atlantic City. He was on a roll, and he didn't want to come back."

One thing the coaches were unanimous on is that they hate the idea of the major league draft occurring during the World Series. They all felt the draft was a big distraction that none of their star players needed, and that players not drafted could be adversely affected, too. The first rounds of the draft are scheduled for Monday, with the process continuing through Wednesday. Maine coach John Winkin said, "That's got to be changed. The players' minds are on the draft, and not the national championship." Michigan coach Bud Middaugh said, "This is the ultimate, and I hate to see anything share the importance of the College World Series."

They polled the coaches as to who they thought would win this week, with them not being allowed to pick their own team. Ward said Stanford. Gus and Bud Middaugh, the Michigan coach, both picked Oklahoma State. Everyone else said Texas. Brock commented that Ward had picked on almost every coach on the dais. He closed with, looking at Ward, "Is this going to be the year that the nice guy wins it?"

Late Thursday afternoon Texas took the team bus out to Creighton University and worked out on their ballfield. They took both batting and fielding practice, just like a normal warmup for a game, mostly just to get loose after the plane ride. Gus seemed to be pretty loose, too, considering what was about to start. Maybe it was just an act to keep the team from getting too tight. He did tell the press, "When I quit getting jittery at Omaha, I will quit coaching."

Our outfield seems to have settled down a little with Johnny Sutton playing. He is great at yelling "Mine!" when he is going after a ball, but when playing left he also knows to defer to the centerfielder when that guy is going after a fly ball. Gus has tried 32 combinations of outfielders this year, including 8 different right fielders, 8 in left, and 6 in center. Part of that is due to Mark Reynolds signing with the pros at mid-term, and Mike Simon having knee surgery 3 weeks ago. Bud Ray, who the coaches thought might be a regular starter, is only hitting .176. After Johnny won the MVP award at the Regional, the team has started referring to him as "MVP Johnny Sutton" every time they see him. He is already getting tired of hearing, "Hello MVP Johnny Sutton. How are you today?"

The press and ESPN wanted some pregame interviews, so UT provided several players. Doug Hodo commented that instead of Aggie jokes, the Texas team tells right field jokes. Alan Brown, who misplayed a ball against Arkansas in the conference tournament, said, "We need three right fielders. One who can jump over the other two as they are falling down." Deron Loy, normally a catcher but sometimes inserted into right, said, "I asked the ground crew if they can plant a tree in right field, so we can hide behind it." The usual left fielder, David Denny, strained his elbow in the Regional, and Texas thought he was done for the year – but he has been cleared to start swinging a bat. Johnny Sutton, new to the outfield, did show some confidence. He said, "I feel like I've been a 3-year starter in the outfield. I bet I've taken 8,000 fly balls there in practice, if not more."

Clint Thomas, who will be scouting all the other games in the series, has quite the responsibility – picking up on hitting and pitching trends, how teams set up their infield and outfield against certain players, which teams like to run, or prefer to play for the long ball (like Oklahoma State).

Because some of the games will be replayed late at night on EXPN, Gus will probably relax curfew a little if Texas keeps winning, especially when UT will have the following day off later in the week. Another incentive to stay in the winner's bracket!

Thursday evening the Longhorns went to their "Sponsor's Dinner" at Mr. C's Steakhouse, one of Gus's favorite places to eat here in Omaha. Each team is assigned a sponsoring organization from here in Omaha to help facilitate the team's needs, and to help keep the team entertained on off days. The UT sponsor is one of the local Kiwana's Clubs. Gus was introducing the players to the sponsor group, going down the list, naming players by number, but when he got to #13, he couldn't remember who that was, and asked, "Who's #13?" Bud Ray raised his hand, forgotten again!

Friday, June 2nd

Baseball will come at the end of an exceedingly long day. The team's day started at 11:45 with the traditional Chamber of Commerce lunch for all the teams and coaches. Today's main speaker was supposed to be Dick Howser, the Manager of the Kansas City Royals, but his flight got fogged in during his transfer in Chicago, and he couldn't get to Omaha in time for lunch.

Replacing Howser as keynote speaker was Irv Brown, an ESPN analyst and color announcer for the games this week. He gave a fairly good speech, considering he was a last-minute stand-in. He was the baseball coach at the University of Colorado before going to work for ESPN, so he does know the game. He told the players that the coaches were not just trying to drill everyone in athletic skills, but that they were "trying to prepare you for the bloody noses in life." The Chamber of Commerce people talked about how ticket sales were up over previous years, with both reserved seats and general admission ticket books selling well above expectations.

They announced the American Baseball Coaches Association All-American team at the lunch, and Calvin Schiraldi was named a first team All-American. Houston's Rayner Noble was the only other Southwest Conference first-teamer. There were multiple players on other teams that are here that were also named, led by Dave Magadan, the nation's leading hitter at Alabama.

The Chamber of Commerce people also introduced the new College World Series mascot, the Baseball Maniac. He looks a little like the mascot at the University of Miami, like a clown with a baseball-shaped head. He is played by John Routh, who was the mascot at the University of South Carolina (Cocky) before graduating and moving south to Miami. He had apparently impressed the CWS staff when he was here with the South Carolina team. The Texas players really don't care, and it helps that Miami did not make the field this year – but the 'Horns would have voted for Bevo, since UT has been here more than any other team!

After lunch all the teams moved over to Rosenblatt, and at 3:00 they introduced everyone on every team, with all the teams on the field at the same time. A pretty colorful sight! Then the teams not playing cleared out, and Texas and James Madison started their pregame warmups.

Texas vs. James Madison

Everybody was a little tight. The UT coaches and players know very little about James Madison, except that they beat some good teams in their Regional to get here. So, Texas was a little tentative starting the game. It was 0-0 for the first 2 innings, and UT looked pretty bad all the way through the 4th. The JMU starting pitcher, Justin Gammon, struck out 6 in the first 4 innings, including 5 of the Texas hitters looking at called 3rd strikes. José Tolentino looked like he had never seen live pitching before. Jeff Hearron ran through Gus's stop sign, signaled from the third base coach's box, after Steve Labay singled in the 4th, and Jeff was thrown out at third base by about 10 feet. In the bottom of the 2nd (James Madison was the home team this afternoon) the JMU left fielder hit a dribbler between the pitcher's mound and first base, and both Calvin Schiraldi and Tolentino acted like it was someone else's problem.

The good news is that the infield single was one of only five hits Calvin gave up all afternoon, and Texas ended up winning the game 12-0, with JMU acting like they were more nervous than the 'Horns were. The 3 pitchers James Madison used in the game gave up 16 hits, walked 9 batters, balked in 2 runs, gave up another on a wild pitch, and UT capitalized on the 2 JMU errors. Mike Trent was the Texas star at the plate, tying a World Series record by scoring 4 times – and he almost had the record by himself. He thought he scored a second time in the 8th when Bryan Burrows hit a shot to center, but Burrows' ball bounced over the fence for a ground-rule double, and Trent had to go back to third base. Mike said after the game that "It's kind of like a climax to the end of my career. Maybe one of these days my son will get to read that in the record book." He talked about how he had been through an up-and-down season, and how he would "hit for two weeks and then not hit for two weeks – and when you don't hit at Texas, you're on the bench because we have so many great players."

Every starter had at least 1 hit except for José Tolentino. Jeff Hearron and Steve Labay were both 3 for 6 in the game, Bill

Bates was 2 for 4 and stole a base, Trent was 3 for 4, and Burrows was 2 for 3. Mike Brumley and Deron Loy, the UT designated hitter, both had 3 RBIs in the game. It took Texas a while to get going, but when the dam burst...

UT started their scoring in the 3rd. Trent beat out a bunt single for the first Texas hit of the game. Dennis Knight, the JMU third baseman, was playing back and Mike dropped the bunt halfway to third. By the time Knight got to the ball Trent was crossing first base. Burrows hit a fly down the right field line that probably should have been caught, but it dropped in front of the right fielder. Trent had been forced to wait and see if the ball was going to be caught, so he was only able to make it to second. Bill Bates singled to left, going with an outside pitch, loading the bases. Then Gannon slipped off the mound during his delivery, falling down, and the pitch was called a balk, scoring Mike Trent with the first run of the day.

The game was 1-0 until the 5th, when Texas picked up another run. Trent beat out another bunt single to start the inning. This one Mike pushed past the pitcher as he fell off the mound after his delivery. Burrows then drew a walk, putting 2 on. Bates sacrificed, moving both runners up a base. Mike Brumley followed with a sharp single to center, scoring Trent for the 2nd time in the game.

UT got a little insurance in the 6th. With 1 out, Steve Labay bounced one over the mound for another infield single. After Johnny Sutton popped out for the 2nd out in the inning, Mike Trent coaxed a walk from Gammon, putting 2 on base. Bryan Burrows singled to left, driving in Labay. Gannon walked Bates and Brumley, allowing Trent to walk home from third. At that point Texas was up 4-0 and starting to breathe a little easier.

Gannon was pulled after the RBI walk to Brumley and was replaced by Randy Foster. Foster lasted until the 8th.

The 8th was when everything fell apart for James Madison. Johnny Sutton started things off with a walk, followed by Mike Trent's 3rd bunt single of the day. Bryan Burrows walked to load the bases. Bates singled to left, again, scoring Sutton. Mike Brumley hit a ground ball to the JMU third baseman, Dennis Knight, and he booted the ball trying to short hop it. Trent scored on the play. Deron Loy doubled into the right field corner, clearing the bases, scoring Burrows, Bates and Brumley. Loy, now on third, faked going home and caused Randy Foster to balk, allowing Deron to score. Jeff Hearron walked. Steve Labay beat out an infield single. Having batted around, Johnny Sutton came up for the second time in the inning and hit one of his patented line drives right over second base into centerfield, scoring Hearron. Mike Trent hit into a fielder's choice that forced Sutton at second. Burrows hit his ground-rule double over the wall in right, and Labay scored from third.

It was a great team win, but the Longhorns also have to look at the level of competition. James Madison now goes into the loser's bracket, and has to play at 5:10 on Sunday against the loser of tonight's late game between Stanford and Oklahoma State. Texas gets the winner of that game on Monday. But at least UT gets Saturday and Sunday off (I'm sure Gus will have the team out practicing!). Texas didn't use any relivers tonight, and they got the opening round jitters out of their system.

Now the 'Horns get to sit back and watch Stanford and Oklahoma State. While the Texas players can't say they have a rooting interest, most of them really want to play the Cowboys again, because they can't stand Gary Ward and his antics. He doesn't believe in good sportsmanship – he won't even allow his team to shake hands with the opposition after a game. His excuse is that "Teams need a 10-minute cooling off period after a game - if you try and shake hands during that time that is when most fights occur." That is a BS excuse! And, after the team heard about Ward dissing Coach Gus at the opening press conference – that stuff was in the local paper this morning – they have even more incentive to want to play Oklahoma State again – and beat them again.

One interesting thing tonight was that Randy Christal was the umpire at second base for the Texas – James Madison game – the first time UT has seen him since early in the year, when he quit umping the games in Austin after his dust up with Roger Clemens and Jeff Hearron. Jon Bible, another ump from Austin, is also here, but didn't do the Texas game this evening. There are only 6 umpires here, so Texas will probably see them both later in the series. Umps for the series were chosen in early April before anyone knew what teams would make the field in Omaha. Both umpires have said they will not be behind home plate for a UT game, as that might cause too much controversy. Bible said, talking about the two umps from Austin having worked in games all around the country, "I know 5 of the 8 teams here, and Randy knows 6. I think we've got the respect of every coach we know." Randy said that "Nowhere is the pressure worse on umpires than at UT, Arizona State, Florida State and Oklahoma State. If an umpire can stand the heat there, you can stand it anywhere."

The stands were full, which the team was not really expecting for a game starting just when a lot of people were getting off work, and the fans were great. They cheer good plays by both teams. They tend to root for the underdog, but that is understandable. They don't boo mistakes, with one exception. When the ball boy behind home plate comes out to try and grab a foul ball coming off the net, and misses it, he gets the business. They also cheer when the kid makes a nice catch. The youngster with that job, Eugene "Chopper" Rosales, is 13. He just finished 8th grade, and is in his 3rd year as a ball boy. He catches more than he misses!

Clint Thomas said he counted 10 ESPN cameras recording the game tonight. That is about double what the 'Horns saw here just a couple of years ago. That network is putting a good deal of effort into making this into a showcase event, and the coaches all say they appreciate the money and time ESPN is putting into college baseball. Hopefully the exposure will help the sport to grow all around the country. These teams are not the pros, but they do put an excellent product on the field, and some fans say the college players' passion for the game makes the college game more exciting than the pro game. The Dodgers playing the Yankees in the Major League World Series is also exciting, but the College World Series can be just as great. ESPN is blacking out the local area, trying to make sure that fans In Omaha and across the river in Iowa actually attend the games, but the network will be showing the game replays during the late night and early morning hours. Some of the Texas players say they will be getting up at 3 AM to watch the broadcast of their game from the comfort of their hotel room!

Jeff Hearron struck again. On the plane ride to Omaha, Bill Little handed out questionnaires from ESPN, wanting background info on each player so that the network could say something about the player when he came to bat. Hearron, assisted by Deron Gustafson, put down that his favorite things were "riding bulls and roping cows." He said he was never happier than when he was "busting broncs." And ESPN bought into it hook, line, and sinker. When Hearron came to the plate, the announcers were falling all over themselves to talk about how Hearron was the "Californian turned Texas cowboy," and how he liked nothing better than riding and roping. The Texas players are not sure that Jeff has ever been on a horse! The guys watching the replays back at the hotel were rolling on the floor, and Jeff was getting high-fives from everybody for pulling one over on ESPN.

The team left after their game to get a late dinner, but Clint Thomas stayed to watch the Oklahoma State – Stanford game. He did get a couple of hotdogs between games. Listening to Clint talk about what he learned after he scouts a game is quite educational. He looks at trends (what pitch is being thrown in what situation), what pitches hitters seem to be able to handle and which ones give them the most trouble – type of pitch, location, speed, everything. He looks at where defenses are playing against certain players, the leads runners are taking, even how good the catchers are at framing the ball. One big thing is the size of the ump's strike zone. Sometime later this week Texas might see this same guy behind home plate for one of their games, and Clint wants to be prepared.

Stanford vs. Oklahoma State

While the Texas – James Madison game was almost ordained to be a cakewalk, considering who was playing, this game had #2 Stanford facing #3 Oklahoma State – two good teams in what was probably the marquis opening game of the Series. Stanford coach Mark Marquess was pitching Brian Myers (10-4) against the 5 OSU sluggers that have contributed 75 home runs to the team's 86 total this year. Stanford was the Pac-10 champ, and 14 of the last 16 CWS champions have come from the west coast – the two exceptions were UT in '75 and Miami this past year.

Oklahoma State was matching their ace, 2nd-team All American Dennis Livingston (15-2) up against Myers. OSU is 47-14 on the year, and they have hit at least one home run in 44 of their 61 games so far this year. Yes, their ballpark is smaller than the Disch, but their power numbers are still pretty impressive. Clint commented before the game that he would probably see a 1-0 pitching gem, since everyone was expecting a shootout.

And as it turned out, he was pretty close. Oklahoma State won 3-1, hitting 2 home runs while Stanford just got 1. Both starting pitchers pitched fairly good games, with Myers only giving up 6 hits in his 6 2/3 innings, and Livingston allowing the same 6 hits, but over 8 innings. The Texas team got their wish, and they get to face Oklahoma State Monday night. On Sunday Stanford will play James Madison in the loser's bracket.

Stanford actually struck first, in the top of the 2nd, with the Pac-10 Southern Division's Player of the Year Eric Hardgrave putting a ball over the centerfield fence right over the 410 sign for a 1-0 lead. But in the 5th, with 2 outs, OSU shortstop Gary Green singled into center, and leadoff hitter Tim Knapp put one off the ESPN television camera platform in right field. The ball actually bounced back onto the field, and Knapp stopped at second until he saw the umpire circling his finger, signifying a home run. It was only Knapp's second homer of the year – He said after the game that normally he is content just to get on base and let one of the sluggers coming up behind him in the lineup to put one over the fence and let him stroll home. And then in the 7th Pete Incaviglia hit his 22nd of the year – extending his Big

Eight record – a monster shot to left that Clint Thomas said that he thought was going to clear the stands.

Livingston got in trouble in the 6th, 7th, and 8th, but was able to get out of the jams each time to keep Stanford from getting back into the game. In the 6th, he loaded the bases on 3 walks, but got Stanford shortstop John Verducci to ground out to end the threat. In the 7th, catcher Lyle Smith led off with a single, and Livingston put 2 on with a walk – but struck out the next 2 batters and got Eric Hardgrave to ground out to end the inning. The 8th was probably Stanford's best chance at another run. With third baseman Vince Sakowski on first and 2 outs in the innings, Verducci drove one past the third baseman and down the left field line. Left fielder Scott Wade retrieved ball in the corner and threw to the relay man, shortstop Gary Green. Green fired a one-hop strike to catcher Robbie Wine, who was acting like there was no play to be made. Wine's decoy act worked, and he was able to tag out the sliding Sakowski to stop Stanford's last scoring chance. Green said after the game that he was surprised Sakowski tried to score. Marquess said he thought it was the right move, because it took two perfect throws to nail the guy at home. In the 9th, Gary Kanwisher relived Livingston and struck out the side, allowing 1 walk. This was an interesting move by Gary Ward, as this was Kanwisher's first relief appearance of the season – he had been a weekend starter for most of the year.

OSU's Gary Green was 2 for 3 in the game. Tim Knapp was 2 for 4 with his homer, and Pete Incaviglia was 2 for 3, including his moon shot. Stanford's Hardgrove was 2 for 4, including his solo shot, and Verducci was 2 for 3, including his double in the 8th.

Jon Bible and Randy Chrystal both umped in this game. Oklahoma State players did not shake hands with the Stanford players after the game – both teams met (separately) in the outfield outside of each of their dugouts for the coaches to talk to their team after the game was over. One thing Clint said he noticed in this game was how funny the PA guy was. Besides just announcing who is coming to bat, he cracks jokes. In the 1st inning, he told the crowd that it was time for them to get acquainted with the people sitting around them. In the bottom of the 2nd, he announced, "Two cars are parked in the zoo lot across the street. They must be moved, or they will be towed." About 20 seconds later he added, "The NCAA record from the ballpark to the zoo is 7 minutes, 2.3 seconds." The crowd broke up!

Now it is back to the hotel for the team. Tomorrow, Saturday evening, Michigan plays Maine, followed by Arizona State and Alabama. That second game might be a good one! And, hopefully, no rain this week to mess up the schedule. Omaha is known for thunderstorms this time of year. In the past Texas has seen games here go on until the wee hours, and they don't want to be a part of that!

Saturday, June 4th
Michigan vs. Maine

Maine was the last team to make the field here in Omaha, winning their 3rd straight NE Regional title this past Tuesday (after a LOT of rain in New England this past weekend). It helped them a little to be in the bracket starting on Saturday, as it gave their pitchers another day of rest. Maine has been hot. They are 22-3 since their spring break trip to Florida back in March – but, again, you have to look at the level of competition they have been playing. Beating Harvard to go to the CWS is not the same as Alabama beating Miami. Michigan will be a big favorite in tonight's first game.

And the Wolverines did beat Maine – but just barely as it turned out. Michigan was able to hold on for a 6-5 win in a game that was pretty close most of the game. Maine showed the same fighting spirit that got them to the semifinals of last year's CWS. Maine picked up the first run of the game in the bottom of the 2nd on a home run by the Black Bear's first baseman, Kevin Bernier. But Michigan came right back in the top of the 3rd when right fielder Mike Watters drove in Barry Larkin after Larkin had doubled with 2 outs.

The game stayed 1-1 until the 5th, when Chris Sabo hit a 3-run homer over the wall in right off of Maine's top pitcher, Billy Swift. Maine came back in the bottom of the 5th with a home run of their own, by left fielder Brad Cotton – but Maine didn't have anyone on base in front of Cotton, so that only brought Maine within striking distance at 4-2.

Michigan got a couple of insurance runs in the top of the 7th when Barry Larkin hit his 2nd double of the game, driving in center fielder Dale Sklar. Their 2nd run in the 7th scored on a nice hit-and-run play with Sabo getting his 4th RBI of the game, and Larkin scoring for the 2nd time. It was 6-2 at that point, and Michigan pitcher Rich Stoll, a guy that Texas saw couple of years ago, seemed to be rolling.

But Stoll tired a little in the 8th, giving up 3 runs on back-to-back doubles by second baseman Jeff Paul and Cotton, followed by a sharp single by right fielder Tom Vanidestine that scored Paul. Suddenly it was 6-4, and Maine had the tying runs on base. Reliever Tim Karazin gave up a single to pinch hitter Peter Bushway, scoring Cotton, and Karazin was replaced by Dave Koph, Michigan's 3rd pitcher of the inning. He was able to retire

Maine's shortstop Fred Staples to end the 8th, and then shut Maine down in order in the 9th to get the save. It was Koph's 3rd relief appearance of the year.

Maine's pitcher Billy Swift, who pitched a complete game but took the loss to fall to 9-3 on the year, Michigan pitcher Rich Stoll, and Michigan third baseman Chris Sabo all played together last summer on the U.S. College All-Star Team that played in a couple of international tournaments. Maine coach John Winkin said Sabo should have been an All-American this year. He added, "He was an All-American today."

The first three hitters in the Michigan lineup looked awesome at the plate, going a collective 7 for 13 on the night. Barry Larkin was 2 for 5, Mike Watters was 2 for 4, and Sabo was 3 for 4. If Texas gets the Wolverines later in the tournament UT is going to have to pitch very carefully to those guys – they can all beat you with one swing. Maine's Brad Cotton was 2 for 3, and Tom Vanidestine was 3 for 4, but they didn't get enough help at the right time to beat Michigan.

The win puts Michigan into a Tuesday night game against the winner of the Arizona State – Alabama game, and Maine gets the loser of tonight's second game in an elimination game late tomorrow (Sunday) night, following the James Madison – Stanford game.

Alabama vs. Arizona State

There was a standing-room only crowd of over 13,000 here for game 2, with most of them here to see Alabama's Dave Magadan – and he didn't disappoint. In fact, it was a great game, with Alabama beating Arizona State 6-5 in 11 innings. It wasn't a well-played game, with the two teams combining for 6 errors – more opening day jitters?

Magadan was 5 for 5, hitting every type of pitch and location you can throw. After tonight's game he is hitting .535 for the year. His catcher, Greg Freel, calls him "Megahit." After his 5th straight hit the fans gave him a standing ovation, something Clint said he had never seen in Omaha. Arizona State tried 4 different pitchers, and nothing worked on the Alabama first baseman. If the pitcher throws it inside Magadan is going to pull it. If the guy on the mound throws it outside Dave is going to go opposite field. And if the hurler makes a mistake and puts one down the middle, forget it! Umpire Hank Roundtree was behind home plate for this game, and he has a pretty tight strike zone – so the Wildcat pitchers couldn't get away with stuff a couple of inches outside like you can with some umpires. Tonight, Magadan hit 5 singles off of 2 fastballs, 2 curveballs, and a changeup. The Texas team had talked on the plane ride up about how no one could legitimately hit over .500 if facing decent pitching, and maybe Magadan was doing it against scrubs in the SEC. But he showed everyone something tonight – the guy is fantastic!

The game went back and forth all night. Alabama struck first in the bottom of the 1st. Leadoff hitter third baseman Bret Elbin started things off with a single and went to second on a balk by Arizona State's starting pitcher Kendall Carter. DH Ted McClendon walked, and Magadan, batting 3rd, singled to score Elbin and put McClendon on third. Rob Skates hit into a 6-4-3 double play, but McClendon scored on the play. Allan Stallings got a 2-out single, stole second, and scored on Frank Velleggia's single to right. Kendall was yanked at that point, relieved by Jefferson. It was 3-0 Alabama before a lot of people got to their seats.

Alabama's starter Dean Hayes kept Arizona State off the board for the first 4 innings, got the first 2 outs in the 5th, and then things fell apart. First baseman Tim McNaughton, batting 9th, singled. Center fielder Oddibe McDowell also singled, and then left fielder Barry Bonds got the Wildcat's 3rd straight hit to score McNaughton. Right Fielder Steve Moses hit a Texas League double to score McDowell, with Bonds stopping at third. Catcher Dan Wakamatsu drew a walk, loading the bases. Third baseman Bert Martinez singled for Arizona State's last hit of the inning, but the runners were going with 2 outs and both Bonds and Moses scored to give the Wildcats a 4-3 lead. Tim Meacham relieved Hayes at that point, and he ended up pitching the rest of the game for Alabama.

The Crimson Tide came right back in the bottom of the fifth to retake the lead. Bret Elbin led things off with a walk, and Jack Turek, the replacement DH for McClendon, singled to put 2 on. Magadan shot one over second for his 3rd hit of the night, scoring Elbin. Both runners moved up on a wild pitch, and then Allen Stallings got his 3rd hit of the game, scoring Turek. Alabama was back up 5-4.

In the top of the 8th Arizona State tied it up one more time. Dan Wakamatsu got on when second baseman Fermin Lake made a bad throw that went into the dugout, allowing Wakamatsu to take second. Bert Martinez hit a dribbler that turned into an infield single, putting Wakamatsu on third. Shortstop Romy Cucjen hit into a 4-3 out, but Wakamatsu scored on the play. Then came one of the strangest plays of the game. With 2 outs and Bert Martinez on second, Greg Steen hit an easy ground ball back to the pitcher, Tim Meacham. But instead of flipping the ball to first for the 3rd out of the inning, Meacham (who must have lost count of the outs) decided he needed to try and get Martinez going to third. Meacham's throw beat Martinez to the base, putting him in a rundown. Third baseman Bret Elbin ran Martinez back towards second, and then threw the ball to shortstop Craig Shipley – but Shipley bobbled the ball, and Martinez made it back to second safely. The good news for Alabama is that Meacham then got Tim McNaughton to fly out to end the inning, with no harm done by Meacham's brain fart.

The game remained tied until the bottom of the 11th. In that inning, reliever José' Rodiles, who had come on in the 9th, threw the ball past first for a 2-base error, allowing Allan Stallings to reach second. Frank Velleggia was given an intentional walk, setting up a force at third or a possible double play. Fermin Lake flied out, with the runners not being able to advance. Former Austin Crockett High School player Dee Smithey singled, which should have loaded the bases – but Stallings made too wide a turn around third, and was thrown out by a nice relay throw from shortstop Romy Cucjen. Then, with runners on first and second and 2 outs, Alabama shortstop Craig Shipley hit the ball off the end of the bat right at Arizona State's second baseman Greg Steen. Steen bobbled the ball just for a second, allowing Shipley to beat the throw to first and Velleggia to score. That was the ball game on what was called an infield single, but could have been scored as another error. The final score was 6-5, Alabama.

Now Alabama gets a couple of days off, playing Michigan in the Tuesday night game. Arizona State has to turn right around and play tomorrow, Sunday, in the late game, facing Maine. While Magadan and Shipley (with the game winner) were the guys getting interviewed after the game, Allen Stallings also had a good game. He went 3 for 5, scored once, and had an RBI. Arizona State's stars also did well, with Oddibe McDowell and Bert Martinez both going 2 for 5, and right fielder Steve

Moses batting 2 for 4. Both teams remind the Texas coaches of Mississippi State at the plate – aggressive, not taking many pitches, and hitting it all over the ballpark. There is a reason they made it to Omaha!

Sunday, June 5th

Elimination day. Two teams will be going home this evening, but UT will not be one of them. Winner's bracket, baby! The only way to go! The first game will be James Madison against Stanford, followed by Maine playing Arizona State. The two smaller school programs are probably the ones that will be 0-2 and BBQ, but stranger things have happened in Omaha. Bill Bethea said that even if he wasn't part of the Texas program, he wouldn't go to Vegas and bet on the games – too many variables! Clint Thomas was at Rosenblatt for both games, as there is a chance Texas may see one of these teams later in the tournament. The coaches want to be prepared for any contingency. As Coach Gus always told his teams, we may not be the best team, but we will be the best prepared team. That goes for scouting potential opponents, too!

James Madison vs. Stanford

James Madison's team is known as the "Dukes." And they played like gentlemen in their game this evening against Stanford. Calvin Schiraldi limited them to 5 hits in the opening game against JMU, and tonight they only got 4 hits off of two Stanford pitchers, Steve Cottrell and Kevin Kunkel. Stanford won 3-1. At least James Madison was able to score in this game! It was cool tonight – 59 degrees at game time – and maybe that had something to do with this being a low scoring affair.

James Madison actually scored first in the game, when in the 2nd catcher Steve Cullers singled, went to third on a single by third baseman Jeff Urban, and scored on a sacrifice fly from first baseman (and #9 hitter) Tom Estepp. The run was unearned after an error by the Stanford shortstop.

Stanford came back in the 4th to take the lead 2-1. First baseman Mike Aldrete led off the inning with a sharp single to left, followed by a walk to DH Eric Hardgrave. Third baseman Vince Sakowski moved the runners up with a sacrifice bunt. Right fielder Greg Lorenzetti grounded to short, but Aldrete beat the throw home to score Stanford's first run. Left fielder Mike Dotterer then singled to bring home Hardgrave.

The Cardinal got an insurance run in the 5th. Catcher Lyle Smith walked, went to third on a double by second baseman Pete Stanicek, and then scored when center fielder Mark Davis hit a sacrifice fly to left.

Stanford was sloppy, with 3 errors in the game. But their pitchers were superb. Steve Cottrell went 7 innings, and at one point Clint Thomas noted that Cottrell had thrown 57 straight fastballs. Cottrell is a 2-sport star at Stanford, also serving as the backup quarterback on the football team. He might be starting some places, but Stanford has John Elway at QB, so Cottrell is trying to make his mark on the mound. Kevin Kunkel came in and relieved Cottrell in the 7th and held JMU hitless for the last 3 innings of the game, facing only 9 batters. Stanford only had 5 hits themselves – they are not hitting well so far in this tournament – but James Madison pitcher Dennis Knight issued 7 walks to go along with those 5 hits, so Stanford was taking a lot of pitches.

Stanford now gets a couple of days off while the winner's bracket games are played. They get the loser of the Tuesday Michigan – Alabama game in the first game Wednesday evening. James Madison is going home, but they did make the College World Series, and that is something their team can take home with pride. They ran into a couple of college powerhouse teams, and they have nothing to be ashamed of – and they showed a lot of fight the way they played against Stanford after their first game against Texas.

Maine vs. Arizona State

The Sun Devils continued the Pac-10 conference dominance tonight with a 7-0 win over Maine. Freshman right hander Pat Henry pitched a 1-hitter for Arizona State, and he probably should have had a no-hitter. In the 3rd, with 1 out, Maine third baseman Bill Reynolds hit a ball to the right of ASU first baseman Tim McNaughton. McNaughton dove for the ball, but it went under his glove, and official scorer Lou Spry called it a hit. ASU coach Jim Brock thought it should have been scored an error. He said on a close play like that, the scorer should check with the home plate umpire (Jon Bible was behind home for this game) to get his opinion. After the game, when Bible was asked what he thought, all he would say is that he "would like to talk to Spry about it." From the stands, Clint said he thought it should have been called an error – but it was close. McNaughton said the ball was right in front of him, and he froze for a second, and then booted it. He thought it should have been an error, too. But what the official scorer says is what counts, and in the scorebook it goes down as a 1-hitter.

Until that alleged single, Henry had retired the Maine batters in order. After a walk to shortstop Fred Staples, a double play ball got Henry out of the 3rd. He retired the side in order in the 4th, but walked 2 batters in the 5th. Those were the last 2 Black Bear base runners until the 8th, when Staples drew another walk. He was forced on a fielder's choice ground ball by DH Doug Whitten, and then Henry struck out Maine's leading hitter, left fielder Brad Colton. Colton swung twice, and then took a called strike 3 to end the game. It was Colton's 2nd strikeout, and Maine coach John Winken commented that, "When you throw the ball past Colton, you're pretty impressive." Winken, who will coach the USA team this summer, added, "I'm telling you right now, if any of the juniors on the USA team get drafted, he's (Henry) going to play for me."

Arizona State didn't waste any time jumping on Maine's starting pitcher, right hander Stu Lacognata. In the bottom of the 1st, Right fielder Steve Moses drew a walk, followed by singles from catcher Don Wakamatsu and Henry, who was also the starting designated hitter. Wakamatsu's hit drove in Moses, and Henry's single drove in Wakamatsu. Henry later scored when Maine's third baseman Reynolds booted a grounder from ASU shortstop Romy Cucjen, giving Arizona State an early 3-0 lead. ASU also picked on the Maine catcher, with 3 stolen bases in the inning.

The Sun Devils picked up 2 more runs in the 2nd. McNaughton opened the inning with a double down the right field line, just inside the first base bag. Barry Bonds then launched one over the right field fence to give ASU an early 5-0 lead. In the 4th, McDowell tripled, and Bonds hit a sacrifice fly to bring him home, making it 6-0. In the 5th, Wakamatsu homered deep to left, against the wind, to make the final score 7-0. All the runs were off of Lacognata, who pitched through the 5th. He was relieved by John Kowalski, who did pitch 3 innings of scoreless relief – but it was too little, too late.

Maine is going back to Orono – wherever that is – but they have been here before and may be back in future years. Arizona State gets a couple of days rest, and next plays in the late game on Wednesday against the loser of the Texas – OSU game tomorrow, Monday – which means UT hopes they will be playing Oklahoma State!

Monday, 6/06

A big day for UT. Game day. Draft day. And after 2 days of practice and intrasquad games, the Longhorns are ready to take on Oklahoma State tonight. But first comes the start of the Major League draft. The first picks will come right after noon, and by early afternoon Roger Clemens and Calvin Schiraldi should know which team now has the rights to those guys. Mike Brumley may go later in the first round, but since his batting average slipped this year (.283) his draft stock has dropped a little.

Texas has several other guys who will probably be drafted in later rounds over the next couple of days – Mike Capel, Kirk Killingsworth, Jeff Hearron, José Tolentino, and Bryan Burrows should all have a chance to play pro ball as soon as the 'Horns finish here in Omaha. Texas will be losing a lot of talented players, but UT doesn't rebuild – they reload. UT will be good next year, too!

Texas did have one issue here last night, as Killingsworth had his knee pop out again while stepping off a curb at the restaurant where the team had dinner. That has happened to him several times this year – he has torn cartilage – but he has tried to keep his injury under wraps. The Longhorn's head trainer, Eddie Day, and student manager John Turman were able to pop Kirk's knee back into place, and Killer says he is ready to go if needed. A couple of times this year it happened while Killer was on the mound, and he was able to get it popped back into place and keep pitching – showing again just how competitive UT players can be!

The coaches here at the World Series have been unanimous in their complaint about the draft occurring during the competition, as it can be a distraction. As Bud Middaugh put it, "Who drafted me? How did that agent get my room number to call me so quickly? Or conversely, why haven't I gotten the call that I was drafted? I was told I would probably go in round X – but since that didn't happen, when will it happen? Now I'm frustrated and depressed over something where I have no control. You can see how the draft could affect a kid's thinking and emotions going into a game, when they need to be 100% focused on what is going on between the foul lines."

By mid-afternoon, the team stars all knew where they were headed as pros. Roger Clemens was the 19th player drafted, going to the Red Sox. He commented that he had always been a fan of the NY Yankees, but that now he would probably "have to throw away my Yankee hat." Calvin Schiraldi went to the New York Mets as the 27th player drafted, in the compensation part of the first round. After Roger found out that Calvin had been drafted, he said, "Maybe we'll see each other in the World Series. In 1999." Mike Brumley wasn't drafted until early in the 2nd round, going as the #33 pick to the Red Sox, too. Mike and Roger may get to play some together as they move up the organization's minor league team hierarchy. Calvin talked about how Spike

Owen had felt draft pressure last year, but then how Spike had played well after the draft. "Maybe that will happen to us." The rest of the Texas draft-eligible players will have to wait to hear their names called over the next couple of days.

Now the Longhorns have to head to the ballpark, to face a bitter rival. OSU is pretty much the antithesis of how the Texas team plays, with both teams taking on the personality of their head coaches. UT tries to be cool at all times, winning with pitching and defense – and, as far as anyone can remember, Gus has never been thrown out of a ballgame by an umpire – whereas the Cowboys are loud, brash, and want to bludgeon other teams with a dozen runs per game. They are always trash talking, just like their head coach, Gary Ward. Gary is great at teaching hitting, and his teams usually average about one run per inning.

Texas will have their hands full. Oklahoma State is a hot team, having won 24 of their last 25 games. Gus said that OSU reminds him a lot of the Miami team that won the CWS last year, with a good balance of hitting and pitching. However, last year Texas did beat Oklahoma State here in Omaha, with Roger Clemens throwing a 5-hitter in a 9-1 win. Roger will be on the mound for UT again tonight, and the 'Horns hope they get a repeat of his performance from a year ago! Roger was being polite when he said about the two teams, "There's no love lost between the two." OSU's latest hitting star, Pete Incaviglia, put it more bluntly, saying, "Nobody likes Texas. It's going to be a war."

Oklahoma State is starting Eric Schmidt, who has a record of 7-6 on the year. However, he has pitched well lately, and has moved ahead of their usual Saturday starter, Gary Kanwisher, in the rotation. Schmidt made the All Big-Eight team as a relief pitcher and has lowered his Earned Run Average to a respectable 3.02. And while Texas had 16 hits in their Friday night win, about half of them were infield singles and bunts, so Gus is worried about hitting. The team spent a lot of time in practice over the last couple of days trying to get everyone in the groove at the plate.

Oklahoma State vs. Texas

Someday, when it counts, Oklahoma State will beat Texas. But not tonight! For the 3rd straight year, UT put OSU into the loser's bracket in Omaha. The 'Horns beat the Cowboys 6-5, and this time it took 11 innings. OSU Coach Gary Ward had to be livid. Before the game, he told Jamie Doughty, "Well, I guess we'll see if you made the right decision" (as to which school to attend). Tactful as usual. But in the bottom of the 11th, Doughty doubled to right center, scoring Mike Trent from second base, and Texas is staying in the winner's bracket here at Omaha. Jamie did show Ward that the right decision was to go to Texas!

Roger Clemens pitched a great game, until he got tired in the 9th, but Texas did not play well behind him. UT had 4 errors in the game, including 3 consecutive miscues in the 3rd, giving OSU a couple of gift runs. The Longhorns had to come back in this one – they were losing 4-1 going into the bottom of the 7th – and that made the win even sweeter.

Roger started off looking like the Roger that won 9 straight in the middle of the season. He struck out the side in the 1st. OSU's center fielder Tim Knapp swung on a 1-2 pitch, left fielder Scott Wade swung and missed on a big curve at 1-2, and right fielder Glenn Edwards swung and missed on a 1-2 pitch. A 16-pitch inning for Roger, which bodes well for a possible long outing tonight.

In the bottom of the 1st, Texas didn't look that great, either. UT actually had 2 hits in the inning – Bates singled under the shortstop's glove, and then Brumley, batting left-handed, singled into the hole to put 2 on with no outs. But then things fell apart. Doug Hodo squared to bunt, pulled the bat back, and Robbie Wine, OSU's All-American catcher, threw behind Bates at second. Bates headed for third and was called out even though it looked like he beat the throw. Hodo then hit into a 5-4-3 double play to end the inning. No score after a promising start! And Schmidt, even after giving up 2 hits, got out of it with a 10-pitch inning.

Roger was throwing bullets again in the 2nd. Robbie Wine struck out on 3 pitches – 2 called strikes and a swing. First baseman Joe Gorman got 4 pitches – a ball, a called strike, a swing, and a K looking. Incaviglia came swaggering to the plate and took a couple of pitches outside. He swung and missed at the 2-0 pitch, took a slider on the outside corner for a 2-2 count, and then took a pitch right now the middle for strike 3. 6 strikeouts in a row to start the game for Roger! And 28 pitches through 2 innings.

Texas drew first blood in the bottom of the 2nd. José Tolentino, leading off, got his first hit of the series when he bounced a 2-2 pitch right over second base. Jeff Hearron followed with another single, this one again past OSU shortstop Gary Green. With 2 on, Steve Labay, playing right field tonight, laid down a great bunt between the pitcher and first base. It would have been a tough play for Joe Gorman, the OSU first baseman, so he peeled off and let Schmidt field the ball. Labay was out, 1-4, but the sacrifice moved both runners into scoring position. Left fielder Johnny Sutton hit a grounder to second on a 2-1 pitch and was thrown out – but Tolentino scored on the play. UT led 1-0, and nearly had some more. The Longhorn centerfielder, Mike Trent, hit a shot to deep center, but the OSU center fielder, Tim Knapp, made a great running catch over his head to end the threat.

The top of the 3rd was when Texas decided they didn't need to play defense. Oklahoma State's #7 hitter, Gary Green, grounded to Bryan Burrows at third – but Burrows hurried his throw to first, and the ball almost went into the dugout, sailing about 5 feet inside of first base. José didn't have a chance to even grab the throw. OSU third baseman Chris Beck laid down a sacrifice bunt between first and the mound, but when Roger threw to Tolentino José lost the ball in the sun, and it went past him into foul territory. Oklahoma State had runners on second and third with no outs, when there should have already been 2 gone. Then Randy Whisler, the OSU second baseman and #9 hitter, grounded to Brumley at short with what looked like a perfect double play ball – but the ball went right between Brumley's legs, allowing Green to score from third and Beck to take third. Tim Knapp flied out to Sutton in left field, but not deep enough to score Beck. With one out, Scott Wade hit a fly to Steve Labay in right center that was deep enough to allow Beck to tag and score. Oklahoma State took the lead, 2-1, with two unearned runs. Glen Edwards singled to left for OSU's first hit of the game, putting 2 on with 2 outs. But Roger struck out Robbie Wine for the 2nd time in the game to end the damage with just 2 runs scored. It was 2-1 OSU after 2 ½ innings, with both teams feeling like they should have scored more.

Texas went quietly in the 3rd, with Burrows grounding to first, Bates popping up to the shortstop in foul territory behind third, and Brumley grounding one right over first base for another easy play by Gorman at first. In the top of the 4th, OSU also went 1-2-3. Gorman lined to Labay in right, Incaviglia grounded to short, but Brumley's throw to first was high, and Tolentino had to bring the ball down and tag Incaviglia right before he got to the bag. There was a pretty good collision between the two, and a few words were exchanged. Gary Green then popped up to Bates in short right center to end the inning. Texas did get a runner on in the bottom of the 4th, when Hodo reached on an error by the Oklahoma State second baseman, Randy Whisler. The ball took a bad hop when it hit the lip between the infield dirt and the outfield grass and scooted past Whisler. However, Schmidt bore down, and got Tolentino to fly to the track in left, and then struck out Jeff Hearron and Steve Labay – with Steve taking a called 3rd strike. The score was still 2-1 OSU after 4 complete.

OSU scored 2 more runs in the 5th and 6th, with Glen Edwards and Gary Green both getting run-scoring singles off of Roger. So, Oklahoma State was leading 4-1 going into the bottom of the 7th. That's when things started to get interesting. The inning started off inauspiciously enough, with José Tolentino popping out to third just in foul territory by the bag. But then Jeff Hearron and Steve Labay both hit first pitch singles to center, putting 2 on with 1 out. Johnny Sutton worked the count to 3-2, squatting as he has been doing about every other pitch, and then hit one of his patented singles right over second base to score Hearron. Mike Trent came to the plate, and hit a 2-2 pitch deep to right, in the corner. He thought he had just hit his first homer of the year. He went into a trot, as did Labay and Sutton. The ball ended up just off the top of the wall, dropping straight down and hitting the right fielder and bouncing away. It should have been at least a triple for Trent, and possibly an inside-the-park home run – but he had to hustle to get back to second when OSU got the ball back to the infield. At one point Sutton and Trent were running almost in tandem between second and third.

Sutton had to stay at third after Trent's hit, but then scored when Alan Brown, pinch hitting for Bryan Burrows, hit a soft fly to center that was just deep enough to allow Sutton to tag and beat the throw home. Alan's RBI came in his first at-bat of the series, and it was good enough to get UT into a tie game. Bill Bates then tried to bunt for a base hit but was thrown out by Beck from third to end the inning. Texas should have taken the lead, but the game was 4-4 after 7 innings.

In the top of the 8th, Jamie Doughty came in to play third, after Alan Brown had pinch hit for Burrows. Robbie Wine led off, and struck out for the third time against Roger, who now had 10 total Ks for the game. Joe Gorman grounded out to Bill Bates for out 2 on a 2-1 pitch. Incaviglia managed to get the count to 3-2, but then swung and missed for Clemen's 11th strikeout of the game. Roger was pumped, and said something to Incaviglia as Clemens was coming off the mound. When he got back to the dugout, Cliff had to remind him that pissing off the other team's best homerun hitter might not be the best idea...

Texas picked up a run in the bottom of the 8th to take their first lead in the game since the 2nd inning. Mike Brumley led off and took a 3-1 pitch high for the first walk of the ball game by either pitcher. Tom Holiday, the OSU pitching coach, went to the mound, but left Schmidt in the game. Doug Hodo followed Brumley with a nice sacrifice bunt on the first pitch, but Hodo was thrown out at first on a nice play by OSU catcher Robbie Wine. Brumley was now on second, and UT needed to find a way to get him home.

At this point Holiday came back out, and Schmidt was relieved by Gary Kanwisher. José Tolentino, the first batter to face Kanwisher, hit a shot behind second base on a 1-2 pitch that probably should have been a base hit, but Whisler was playing him perfectly, and easily threw José out at first. Brumley went to third on the play, but now the 'Horns had two outs in the inning. Jeff Hearron, who has been hot at the plate, took the first pitch low for a 1-0 count. The next pitch was way outside and in the dirt, and Wine couldn't handle it. It didn't bounce away very far, but Brumley, with his great speed, was able to safely slide home before Kanwisher could make the tag. Labay then struck out to end the inning. Texas had a 5-4 lead, and only needed 3 more outs for the win!

Like previously mentioned, Gus always said the hardest outs to get in a game are numbers 25, 26, and 27 – the last 3 outs in the game. And this time UT didn't get it done. Roger looked great to start the inning. Steve O'Donnell, pinch hitting for Green, hit a shot up the middle that Roger deflected over towards second. Bill Bates, who had been moving toward second on the hit, had to reverse course back towards first base, but he got there in time to get the ball and throw out O'Donnell. Bill sat down for a moment and took off his glove – the guys in the dugout thought he might have hurt his back with the sudden change of course – but he got up and moved back into position for the next pitch.

Chris Beck struck out on 3 pitches, and suddenly Texas just needed one more out to move into the Thursday winner's bracket game. That was Roger's 12th strikeout of the night, his season high. But apparently, he was getting a little tired. Kevin Jagielo, pinch hitting for Whisler, worked the count to 3-2, fouled off a pitch, and then singled to left. He was replaced on first by pinch runner Kevin Fowler. That put Oklahoma State back at the top of the batting order. Tim Knapp again worked the count to 3-2, fouled off a pitch, and singled to right. That put 2 on with 2 outs, and brought Gus to the mound. He pulled Roger, putting Kirk

Killingsworth on the bump to try and save the game. The Killer was by far the best choice at that point. He was 11-3 on the year, had a 2.63 ERA, and has saved 7 games this season. If you only need one out, he was the guy to put out there. But Scott Wade singled to left on a 1-0 pitch, scoring Fowler to tie the game. Johnny Sutton's throw was a little up the line, allowing Knapp to take third. With runners at the corners, Killingsworth got Glenn Edwards to foul off a 2-1 pitch, and then Edwards swung and missed to get UT out of the OSU half of the 9th. But OSU had managed to tie the game at 5-5.

In the bottom of the 9th, OSU had to make some defensive changes after subbing in a pinch hitter and pinch runner in the top of the inning. They ended up with an almost completely new infield. Fowler went to third, Steve O'Donnell, who had pinch hit, went to shortstop, and Beck moved from third to second. Kanwisher was still on the mound for Oklahoma State.

Texas had Johnny Sutton, 1 for 2 in the game with 2 RBIs, leading off. He did his usual squat before coming to the plate, and he has been stepping out and squatting between almost every pitch. He took the 1st pitch for a ball, and the 2nd for a strike, giving him a 1-1 count. He fouled off a pitch into the right field stands, and then hit a hard liner right at O'Donnell at short. Steve short hopped the ball and threw Sutton out at first by a couple of steps.

Mike Trent followed Sutton in the lineup. Mike had a double and an RBI earlier, when he through he had put the ball over the fence. He took the 1st pitch for a strike and the next was high for a ball, giving him a 1-1 count. He fouled the next pitch off the end of the bat for a 1-2 count, and then swung and missed on a nice slider from Kanwisher for out number 2.

Jamie Doughty was the last Texas hope in the 9th, having come into the game in the 8th as a defensive replacement for Bryan Burrows after Alan Brown had pinch hit for Burrows in the bottom of the 7th. Kanwisher started Doughty off with a fastball on the outside corner for a strike, and then a curve stayed high for a ball, giving Jamie a 1-1 count. He fouled the next pitch off, took the next pitch high for a 2-2 count, and then slammed his bat down after taking a called strike 3 on the outside corner.

Free baseball. Extra innings. Texas had a slight advantage, being the home team, but the 'Horns had not played very well the entire game, and OSU had the momentum after tying the game in the 9th. OSU has their 4-5-6 batters coming to the plate, with Robbie Wine leading off, followed by Joe Gorman and then the ever-dangerous Pete Incaviglia. But UT had the Killer on the mound, and that evened up the odds considerably.

Wine was 0 for 4 on the night and had struck out 3 times in the game. He took Killingsworth's first pitch outside for a ball, then hit the ball to the wall in left. Johnny Sutton had a play, but misjudged the ball when he grazed the wall as he tried to make the catch, and the ball bounced off his glove. Wine ended up on second. He probably should have made third, but he was just trotting between first and second. He was assuming that the ball was going to be caught. The hit was ruled a double, but probably should have been another UT error.

Gorman lined Killingsworth's 1st pitch just foul past first. Six more inches fair and OSU would have easily had the lead. He was 1 for 4 for the night, with a hit in the 6th. It was obvious he was trying to hit the ball to the right side to move Wine up a base. The next pitch was inside for a 1-1 count. The next pitch might have caught the inside corner, but the ump called it a ball.

Gorman hit the next pitch on the ground to Bates at second for an easy first out, but Wine did move to third on the play.

That brought Incaviglia to the plate. Pete was 0 for 4 for the night, but all he needed here was a long sacrifice fly to give OSU the lead. Infield came in to cut off the run at the plate. Gus had Wade Phillips warming in the bullpen, just in case. And with the first pitch Killer came inside and hit Incaviglia on the elbow. That put runners on the corners with 1 out but did set up the double play.

That brought Steve O'Donnell back up. Steve had pinch hit in the 9th and had stayed in the game to play shortstop. He had been thrown out in the top of the 9th with a great play by Bill Bates. Gus could have gone to double play depth in the middle of the infield, but decided to keep the entire infield in for O'Donnell. Killingsworth's first pitch was taken for a ball, and then the Killer hit the inside corner for a strike. A foul tip put the count at 1-2. O'Donnell fouled off another pitch, protecting the plate. And then Killer's fastball, which always had good movement, jumped outside just as the left-handed hitting O'Donnell swung for the strikeout. Texas was 1 out away from getting out of the jam!

Cliff, wearing his usual glossy UT jacket, and with his hands in his pockets, strolled out to the mound to check on Killingsworth – who did have a bad knee. But Coach Gus left Killer in to face Chris Beck, now playing second for OSU. Beck was still looking for his first hit of the series, 0 for 6 for the week at this point. He had struck out on 3 pitches against Clemens in the 9th. He took Killingsworth's first pitch for a ball, and then took a low strike for a 1-1 count. The next pitch was grounded to Bates, moving to his left half-way to first. It was a slow roller, usually an easy play, but Bates' hard sidearm throw 10 feet from first base had the fans in the stands gasping! José was able to grab it, and Texas had somehow managed to escape without giving up any runs in the inning. Now, they just needed one score to win it!

And UT had the top of the order coming up in the bottom of the 10th – Bates, Brumley, and Hodo. Kanwisher was still on the mound for OSU. But no joy in the Texas dugout. Tolentino and Hearron did get on, but with the bases loaded Steve Labay struck out on a called low strike to end the inning, and the two teams were on to the 11th, still tied 5-5. Steve jumped about 10 feet into the air after the called strike 3 and could have been thrown out of the game – he thought he had just walked in the winning run.

OSU had Kevin Fowler leading off. He had come on as a pinch runner in the 9th and ended up scoring the tying run. He had stayed in the game to play third. Fowler lined the first pitch off of Killingsworth's calf, with the ball bouncing towards third. Doughty made a great bare-handed play on the ricochet, falling as he threw, to get Fowler at first by 2 steps. Gus went to the mound again to check on Killingsworth, but Kirk said he was OK, and Cliff left him in the game.

That took Oklahoma State back to the top of the order one more time. Tim Knapp was 2 for 4 for the game, with 2 singles and a sacrifice fly. Another left-hander to face the righty Killingsworth. The first pitch to Knapp was a high slider that dropped into the zone for a called strike. A foul out of play put Killer up 0-2. And then Kirk blew the ball by Knapp for a swinging strike 3, and a quick second out in the inning.

That brought up left fielder Scott Wade. Scott was 1 for 4 for the night, but he did have 2 RBIs. He swung and missed on Killer's first pitch and took the next pitch high for a 1-1 count. The next pitch was in the dirt, giving Wade a good hitter's count at 2-1. Kirk's next pitch was hit to Jamie Doughty about 10 feet behind third. Jamie's throw was a little up the line toward home plate and hit Wade in the back. He ended up on second on the throwing error. Tolentino was in another hard collision at first on the play.

Next up was Glenn Edwards. He was 2 for 5 for the game, but had struck out against Killingsworth to end the top of the 9th with the game tied. A base hit would give OSU the lead. Edwards fouled the first pitch back over the OSU dugout. The next pitch was high for a 1-1 count. Kirk's next pitch resulted in a soft liner to Mike Trent in centerfield, and the game headed to the bottom of the 11th.

Texas had the bottom third of the order coming to the plate – Johnny Sutton, Mike Trent, and Jamie Doughty. Not exactly Murderer's Row, but each a player capable of getting on. And Texas knew they had been playing with fire, putting OSU runners in scoring position in both the 10th and the 11th. Kanwisher was still on the bump for OSU. Sutton was 1 for 3 and did his usual squat as he approached the plate.

Kanwisher's first pitch was a strike right down the middle. The next was high for a 1-1 count. The next was a little lower, but still high. The next hit the outside corner, making it 2-2. In the dugout, everyone had turned their hats backwards – rally cap time! Sutton fouled off a pitch and took the next pitch outside for a full count. The next pitch was in the same location as the one where Steve Labay was called out in the 10th. Sutton also thought he had drawn a walk, but the ump, Hank Roundtree, felt otherwise. 1 out, and 7 Ks for Kanwisher in his short outing.

That brought up Mike Trent, who was 1 for 4 for the night with a double – the one that should have been a triple. Kanwisher's first pitch bounced and caught the home plate ump in what looked like his hip, with no padding to slow it down – and Hank had to take a minute to gather himself. Kanwisher's next pitch was high, putting Trent at 2-0, but then Mike took one on the inside half of the plate to run the count to 2-1. The next pitch was way inside, and it looked like Kanwisher might be losing it a little. His last pitch to Trent was about where Roundtree had been calling strikes, but this time Mike got the call, and Texas had their first baserunner of the inning on a walk.

That brought Jamie Doughty to the plate. Kanwisher's first pitch was right on the black on the outside corner for strike 1. Jamie swung and missed on the next pitch – a good breaking ball – but the ball bounced right behind home plate, bounced up and hit Robbie Wine in the mask, and by the time Robbie found the ball – it had rolled just behind him - Trent, with his good speed, had taken off and just beat the throw to second base. Trent had gotten a late break, and Wine had a great arm, but Trent made a nice slide and now UT now had the winning run at second. But Jamie now faced an 0-2 count. And then Jamie came through! He lined the next pitch all the way to the wall in right center, just to the right of the Marlboro Man sign! Mike Trent scored easily, diving face first into home, and then he just laid there on top of home plate. Bill Bates was the first one to reach Mike, and picked him up off the plate. Texas had done it! And Jamie had shown Gary Ward that Doughty did pick the right team! Most of the post-game-hugs were for Jamie Doughty. Bill Bates said he thought José Tolentino was going to crush Jamie!

The team celebrated, and everyone got to play in the pool back at the Holiday Inn when they got back to the hotel. But the Longhorns knew they had more work to do. Texas won this same game last year, too – but then lost the next two to be sent home with no championship. But this team has a quiet confidence, and a determination to see things through to that final out dogpile. Gus also seems a little more relaxed. He has even smiled a couple of times since Texas got out of the Regional. And him being less uptight has rubbed off on the team, and helped UT to relax and just play ball, too.

Now the Longhorns get a couple of days off, and they get to watch Michigan and Alabama duke it out tomorrow, Tuesday, for the right to play Texas on Thursday. Wednesday will be the loser's bracket games between Stanford and the Alabama – Michigan loser, and then Arizona State playing Oklahoma State.

Tuesday, June 7th

Texas had two more players drafted by pro teams today while they wait to see who they will play on Thursday. Jeff Hearron went to the Toronto Blue Jays in round 4, and Kirk Killingsworth, the winning pitcher last night, was picked by the Texas Rangers in the 7th round. The draft goes on for two more days, and everyone expects several more UT players to hear their names called.

UT also found out that one of their recruits, Jackie Davidson from Everman, Texas, is going to sign with the Chicago Cubs today. He was the 6th overall pick in the draft and will get a sizeable signing bonus. Dallas Green, the Cubs' General Manager, called Coach Gus to tell him they were signing Davidson. Green and Gustafson have been friends for a long time, but it was still nice for Green to give Gus the advance warning. Coach Gus had expected Davidson to sign after he was drafted that high, but it is always a disappointment when you can't get star players on campus.

Alabama – Michigan

Dave Magadan might be human after all. He actually made an out, flying out to left field in the 6th inning of the Alabama – Michigan game. Of course, by that time, he already had gotten 3 more hits, making it 8 straight to start the College World Series. And those hits had helped Alabama to a 6-0 lead after just 4 innings. Michigan starter Dave Koph gave up 3 straight hits to start the game, including a leadoff home run from Alabama's third baseman Brett Elbin. Alabama led 2-0 after the 1st, scored another run in the 3rd and then 3 more in the 4th (all unearned) to give them their 6 total. But then Michigan started coming back, holding Alabama scoreless after the 4th, and scoring 3 in the bottom of the 4th, and 1 each in the 6th and 7th to make it a 6-5 game. In the 6th, Rich Blair singled, and Barry Larkin tripled to bring Blair home. In the 7th, Chris Sabo doubled, and scored on Jacobson's single.

Magadan was the hitting star for Alabama, again, going 3 for 4 for the game with 2 RBIs. Jeff Jacobson, the Michigan second baseman, led their team at the plate with a 3 for 4 night, but only 1 RBI.

Tim Meacham, who had come in for Alabama in the 6th to relieve starter Rick Browne (from Arlington), gave up 2 singles in the bottom of the 9th to give Michigan a chance – but he was pulled for Trey Brauchle, who got the final out for the save. Brauchle played high school ball in San Antonio – both Michigan and Alabama like to recruit in Texas! So, now Texas knows they will be playing Alabama on Thursday night, and Michigan falls to the loser's bracket, having to play Stanford tomorrow.

Wednesday, June 8th

The Texas team has scheduled their annual fajita cookout at Elmwood Park this afternoon. Sonny Falcón, the "Fajita King" from Kyle, is a big UT baseball fan, and has had reserved seats close to the Wild Bunch for years. Those of you not familiar with Sonny – shame on you! Every Texan should know about Juan Antonio "Sunny" Falcón, the man who invented the fajita! Every year he supplies the team with frozen fajitas to take to Omaha for a Texas-style meal. The parents that are driving up to Nebraska bring the ice chests with the fajitas, along with tortillas since no one is sure they could get those in Omaha. The rest of the materials are bought locally, so that they will be fresh.

The parents set up portable grills in the park, and also use what grills that park already has available at the gazebo – probably a half-dozen grills in all. The Wild Bunch guys are the cooks, assisted by some parents. The drill is simple. A player gets a plate, starts at a grill where tortillas are being toasted, moves on to get meat, and then on to add veggies, cheese, and condiments. Most players start with two tortillas and are back in line within a couple of minutes after finishing their first offerings.

There weren't enough picnic tables for the whole team and the parents and other relatives, girlfriends, and fans to sit and eat, so almost everybody was eating standing up. José Tolentino's gorgeous big sister was there, and she looked like she was about 17. Other player's cute sisters were there, too, including Calvin Schiraldi's and Mike Brumley's, and there was a flock of unattached players gathered around the ladies like moths attracted to a flame. It was a relaxing afternoon, and it helped knowing that the team didn't have a game later tonight! Gus was going to make everyone go practice later, as usual, but that wasn't a big deal.

The team found out while they were eating at the park that Oakland had picked José Tolentino in the 7th round of the draft, and the Chicago Cubs drafted Mike Capel in the 17th. Two more players headed to the pros! That makes 7 UT players drafted so far – Clemens, Schiraldi, Brumley, Hearron, Killingsworth, Tolentino, and Capel. José was happy he had gotten his U.S. Citizenship papers, to ensure that he was eligible for the draft!

After the picnic lunch, almost everybody followed the team bus out to practice, and having a crowd there made practice even more enjoyable, almost like a game atmosphere. UT fans come to Omaha in droves every year – The Texas team has been here so many times the fans have shirts saying, "The University of Texas at Omaha." People were cheering good plays, solid hits, and clapping and singing like the team was playing in Austin!

The team left for dinner, and Clint Thomas went to Rosenblatt to watch the elimination games. Tonight, Oklahoma State has to quickly regain their composure after losing that extra inning game to Texas and play Arizona State in the opening game at 5:10, and then Michigan will be facing Stanford in the nightcap at 8:10. The losers will have two losses and be heading home. Texas will face one of the winners on Friday, depending on who wins tonight. Last year, Texas lost the Thursday winner's bracket game to Miami, and then the Friday game to Wichita State to end their season. The Longhorns plan to change that scenario this year!

Bryan Burrows, the Texas third baseman, has a little extra incentive to win a ring. His dad, Eddie, has two of them, having been on the UT championship teams that won the CWS in 1949 and 1950. Bryan says he wants at least one, to keep his dad from having all the bragging rights! Bryan did get a little good news tonight. He was drafted by the Pittsburgh Pirates in the 33rd round of the major league draft. He is the 8th Longhorn to be drafted this year. Gus says he doesn't know what the record is for UT in one draft, but this year's team has to be close to it!

Joe Schiraldi, Calvin's dad, is a die-hard Texas A&M Aggie. He refuses to do a "Hook 'Em" hand sign, even as he roots for UT to win this year. Joe told Scott Wilson, from the Wild Bunch, that if UT wins the championship that Joe will finally give in and stick his horns up – but only once!

And starting tonight, ESPN is bringing in the varsity broadcasting team. Joe Boyle and John Sanders have been doing the play-by-play up to this point in the series, with Irv Brown and University of Arizona coach Jerry Kindell doing the color. Tonight, ESPN will have Jim Simpson announcing the Michigan – Stanford game, and he will be here for the rest of the series.

Arizona State vs. Oklahoma State

When Kendall Carter, the Arizona State pitcher, pitched on Saturday against Alabama, he only lasted 2/3 of an inning, giving up 4 hits and 3 runs in the 1st inning of that game. Tonight, he held Oklahoma State to 5 hits, and made it into the 9th before tiring. He was relieved by Jim "JJ" Jefferson, who gave up a grand slam home run to Pete Incaviglia – but it wasn't enough for OSU. Jefferson struck out Oklahoma State's Steve O'Donnell after the Incaviglia home run, to preserve a 6-5 Arizona State win.

Carter was asked about the difference in the two games after this game was over, and he said there really wasn't any difference – "That tonight the ground balls just went to somebody." That would have been a nice humble statement, but then he proceeded to start talking trash about Texas. "I think I'm as good as Clemens and those other Texas guys. They play Texas Christian and teams like that and play at home all the time. Anybody can get a shutout against teams like that. We played Houston in a Regional last year, and they were terrible. They (UT) play a lot of weak teams. They wouldn't be as great in our league." He has a short memory – UT beat ASU twice back in March, including a 6-0 shutout by Clemens. But Arizona State did send Oklahoma State home tonight, so there is a bright side to this game and having to listen to this guy after the game.

Arizona State scored first, in the top of the 1st, with 3 straight hits off of OSU's starting pitcher and All-American Dennis Livingston. ASU catcher Don Wakamatsu got the RBI. But then, with the bases loaded, shortstop Romy Cucjen hit into an inning ending double play to get OSU out of the jam. Oklahoma State tied the score in the bottom of the 1st, when OSU's right fielder Glenn Edwards put one off the top of the screen behind the centerfield fence – about 430 feet in the air. It might have gone 450 or 460 if the screen had not been there. But Carter settled down and didn't give up another run until the 9th.

In the 3rd, Arizona State scored 2 when third baseman Bert Martinez doubled, bringing home a couple of guys that had drawn walks off of Livingston. In the 4th, Arizona State's second baseman Gregg Steen made a nifty, heads-up play. Oklahoma State's Gregg Edwards was running on the pitch, but catcher Robbie Wine hit an easy popup to Steen. But Steen went down like he was going to field a ground ball, and Edwards kept running toward second. By the time Edwards realized the ball was in the air, even with the umps already calling it an out under the infield fly rule, it was too late for Edwards to retreat, and Steen easily doubled him off of first. Smart play by Steen!

The 2 runs ASU got in the 3rd ended the scoring until the 6th, when Barry Bonds homered – his 5th in the last 6 games. Unfortunately, Oklahoma State's left fielder Scott Wade banged hard into the wall going back for Bond's hit, and ended up having to leave the game later with a cracked rib. That homer gave ASU a 4-1 lead, and they scored 2 more runs in the 7th and 8th. In the 7th, Martinez came through again, this time off of reliever Mike Henneman, with an RBI single. In the 8th, Bonds doubled, and came home on a single by ASU designated hitter Doug Henry.

That set the stage for the fireworks in the bottom of the 9th. OSU's Tim Knapp doubled off of Carter, and then Kevin Jagielo walked. Jim Brock then pulled Carter for Jim "JJ" Jefferson. Jefferson struck out the first two guys he faced – Glenn Edwards and Robbie Wine – but then Joe Gorman singled to load the bases. Pete Incaviglia then hit his grand slam home run, making it a 1-run game at 6-5. But Jefferson came right back and struck out Steve O'Donnell to end the game and OSU's season.

Arizona State's Martinez was the hitting star for the Sun Devils, going 3 for 5 for the night, including a double. Bonds was 2 for 3, including his home run. For OSU, Knapp and Edwards were both 2 for 4. Edwards homered, and Incaviglia had his grand slam. Carter was the winning pitcher for Arizona State, and Jefferson got the save, even with his shaky 9th. Livingston was the losing pitcher for OSU, as ASU got the lead early and never gave it up, even as the game got close.

Incaviglia was jumping for joy in between first and second after his homer, but he said after the game that he had realized by the time he was rounding third that his team was still down a run with 2 outs in the 9th. He said he felt that OSU had a better team than they did 2 years ago, when they finished 2nd, and that they had played flat against Arizona State after losing the heart breaker to Texas. Oklahoma State again refused to shake hands with the Arizona State players after the game, with the OSU team gathering in the outfield, until booing from the stands forced them to come back into the infield and shake. Gary Ward said again that he thought shaking hands "was a bad tradition," and that the crowd pressure forced his team to do it. Most of the UT players are glad OSU is gone!

Michigan vs. Stanford

The team now knows Texas will be playing Michigan Friday night, after they beat Stanford 11-4 in the late game this evening. That score looks like the game was a rout, but it was a 4-4 game going into the 9th, when Stanford ran out of pitching. The game times haven't been set for Friday. If UT beats Alabama, they get the late game Friday night. If Texas loses tomorrow, they will have to turn around and play the first game Friday evening, and Alabama will get Arizona State in the nightcap.

Stanford scored first in this one, with a homer by first baseman Mike Aldrete in the bottom of the 1st. They added another run in the 2nd when third baseman Vince Sakowski reached on Michigan shortstop Barry Larkin's error, followed by a walk to left fielder Mike Dotterer. They attempted a double steal, but Sakowski was thrown out at third. Stanford shortstop John Verducci then doubled, scoring Dotterer and giving Stanford a 2-0 lead off of the Michigan starter, Rich Stoll.

Michigan cut the lead to 2-1 in the top of the 3rd, when the Wolverine's catcher Rich Bair homered off of the Stanford starter, Brian Myers. In the top of the 5th, Myers hit leadoff batter Blair with a pitch, and he was sacrificed to second by center fielder Dale Sklar. Barry Larkin singled, with Blair stopping at third. Stanford coach Mark Marquess then pulled Myers, bringing in reliver Jeff Ballard. Michigan's right fielder, Mike Watters, doubled on Ballard's first pitch, scoring both Blair and Larkin, giving Michigan a 3-2 lead.

In the top of the 7th, Michigan struck again. Barry Larkin led off with a walk, tagged and went to second on Chris Sabo's long fly ball to the left field corner, and then Larkin scored when first baseman Ken Hayward singled. That gave the Wolverines a 4-2 lead. But in the bottom of the 7th, Stanford came right back to tie the game. Right fielder Mike DeBonen led off with a single, followed by a walk to John Verducci. Catcher Lyle Smith then moved them up a base with a nice sacrifice bunt. Stoll, still pitching, then got second baseman Pete Stanicek to pop up for the second out of the inning. But then center fielder Mark Davis hit a sharp single to right center, scoring both DeBonen and Verducci, tying the game at 4-4. Davis stole second, and first baseman Mike Aldrete was given an intentional walk. But then Stoll got out of the jam when designated hitter Eric Hardgrave hit an easy fly to Michigan's Dale Sklar in centerfield.

Neither team scored in the 8th, and then Michigan came to bat in the top of the 9th. John Radtke had come in to pitch for Stanford in the 8th, and he gave up a leadoff single to Barry Larkin. Chris Sabo then doubled, scoring Larkin, and giving Michigan a 5-4 lead. Ken Hayward and Jeff Jacobson both singled, with Jacobson's hit driving in Sabo, making it a 6-4 game. Left fielder Dan Sygar was given an intentional walk, bringing up Michigan's designated hitter, Casey Close. Close had not come into the game until the 6th – Michigan coach Bud Middaugh said after the game that he had been keeping Casey out in the bullpen in case Close was needed as a pitcher to help hold a lead late in the game. Close didn't need to pitch to help win the game. He put the ball into the left field stands for a grand slam home run, giving the Wolverines a 10-4 lead. Catcher Rick Bair then tripled, and he scored on Dale Sklar's triple to end the scoring at 11-4. Kunkel came in to pitch and got the final 2 outs in the top of the 9th, but by that time the cow was out of the barn.

Rich Stoll is now 13-2 on the year, and undefeated since he had a cast removed before the Big Ten tournament. He had broken a bone in his hand fielding a ball a couple of months ago. He scattered 7 Stanford hits tonight. If Michigan makes it to the final game on Sunday, Texas might see him again! Michigan had 16 hits in this game, and their hitting stars were numerous. Barry Larkin was 2 for 5 and scored 3 times. Mike Watters was 2 for 6 with a double and 2 RBIs. Chris Sabo was 2 for 4 with a double. Rich Bair was 3 for 4 with a triple. And Close had his grand slam.

Stanford coach Mark Marquess commented after the loss that this year's team wasn't as talented as last year's bunch, but that they had accomplished quite a bit just getting to Omaha. He said that unfortunately, they did not play well after they got here. In tonight's game, Mark Davis was 2 for 5, with 2 RBIs. Shortstop John Verducci was 2 for 2 with a couple of walks. But Stanford did not take advantage of early opportunities against Michigan's Stoll, and now the California team is headed back home.

Late Wednesday night the Texas team watched the rebroadcast of the game on ESPN. The broadcast was pretty bad. Jim Simpson was totally unprepared, and Jerry Kindle had to keep correcting Simpson's errors. Simpson misidentified players, base coaches (wrong team), and even claimed a batter walked, forcing in the tying run, when the count was 1-2. Does the guy even know baseball? Jerry Kindle was great, and very patient. Someone commented that they might have walked out on Simpson after his horrible performance behind the microphone. If this is the "star" that ESPN brought in for the rest of the series, the players are almost wishing they would go back to the crew they were using the beginning of the week. The team feels sorry for fans watching on television – a bad announcer can ruin a broadcast.

Thursday, June 9th

Texas has been here before. Last year the probably better Texas team was undefeated going into the Thursday game, too – and lost a close one to Miami. The 'Horns know what's at stake. Win this one, and they are in the finals on Sunday for sure, no matter whether or not they beat Michigan on Friday. The way the rules work, if there are 3 teams left with one loss after the Friday games, the last undefeated team (the Thursday winner, which hopefully will be Texas!) gets the bye into the final Sunday game. And if UT can beat both Alabama and Michigan, then whoever wins the Friday game between Alabama and Arizona State would have to beat the 'Horns twice to win the championship. Texas is a confident team, and they expect to win 3 straight and go back to Austin as champions, undefeated in the World Series this year. But all the remaining 4 teams are good, and Texas still has to prove it on the field!

Gus is pulling another of his cerebral moves tonight, starting Steve Labay. Steve is Texas' best left-hander, and 3 of the first 4 Alabama hitters hit from the left side of the plate. Gus was remembering what Labay did to Mississippi State's left-handed dominated lineup in the Regional, and said before tonight's game that he thought Steve had a better chance of shutting down Alabama's vaunted hitting attack than a rested Calvin Schiraldi.

Alabama, led by Dave Magadan's .539 average for the year, is hitting .339 as a team. They may be a newcomer to the national scene – their coach, Dr. Barry Shollenberger, commented about how their field didn't even have lights until 1981, and that they average about 200 fans per game – but they have recruited well nationally and internationally. Shortstop Craig Shipley is from Sidney, Australia. Only 6 of their 22 players call the state of Alabama home. 3 of their players are from Texas. Shollenberger has not announced his starter for tonight, saying it will be one of 2 right hand pitchers, either Dean Hayes (11-2, 5.02 ERA) or Alan Dunn (3-0, 6.47 ERA). The Alabama coach commented that while their pitchers may not have the gaudy ERAs of the Texas staff, the Alabama team more than makes up for it with their hitting. The old saw about good pitching beating good hitting will get a good test tonight!

Texas is starting their usual lineup, except that with Labay pitching they need a different right fielder – and Gus is going with another hunch and putting Deron Loy in right. UT has Bill Bates leading off as usual, followed by Mike Brumley and then Doug Hodo as tonight's designated hitter. José Tolentino is batting cleanup, with Jeff Hearron batting 5th and Loy 6th. Johnny Sutton is batting 7th and holding down left field. Mike Trent is in center, batting 8th, and in the 9 hole is Bryan Burrows, playing third base.

Alabama is the home team tonight, and the top half of their lineup is pretty tough. Brett Elbin leads off and plays third. Ted McClendon is their DH and is batting .376. You can't pitch too carefully to him, because behind him is Dave Magadan and his

.539 average. The cleanup hitter is Rob Skates, their left fielder. Batting 5th is Allen Stallings, playing centerfield. Frank Velleggia, their catcher, bats 6th. The bottom 3rd of their order is down in the order for a reason – Fermin Lake, the short second baseman, bats 7th, Dee Smithey bats 8th and plays right, and the last guy is the order is the Australian shortstop, Craig Shipley – but he is hitting .323, not too shabby for a #9 hitter! Labay has his work cut out for him!

Alabama is on a 15-game winning streak and is now 45-9 on the year. Texas has played a lot more games, with a 63-14 record. That 63 wins is already a school record and sounds impressive – until you realize that Alabama's winning percentage, .833, is better than Texas' percentage of .818. This game is no pushover for either team!

Texas vs. Alabama

Game time, finally. Wind is blowing out a little towards left at about 10 mph. Not horrible, but it will help fly balls hit in that direction a little. In warmups, Sutton and Trent were having to back up a little more than what their original judgment told them on flies hit in their direction. It is about 86 degrees and humid, with rain clouds in the vicinity. The teams need to get this game in tonight so that they don't crowd the schedule for the rest of the week! The humidity may help keep balls in the ballpark – the ball flies better when it is cool and crisp, and tonight is just the opposite of that! But both teams are from the south, and used to playing in these types of conditions, so that should not be a problem for either team. Rosenblatt is a concentric ballpark. The dimensions are 343 down the lines, 370 in the alleys, and 420 to centerfield. A pretty good-sized park, but with the metal bats used in college balls do seem to jump out of here with regularity!

Dale Williams is the home plate umpire, and he is known for having a generous strike zone. It will be interesting to see how that plays into each team's pitching strategy. Randy Cristal is umping at third, and hopefully he will not have any close plays to judge tonight! If he does, either way he rules is going to be criticized by one team or the other, with the team not getting the call claiming that he was prejudiced against them.

Top of the 1st

The Alabama coaches decided to start Dean Hayes. He is 11-2 on the year, but has a 5.05 ERA. Texas would love to get that number of runs off of him this game!

The UT leadoff hitter, Bill Bates, came to the plate with his closed stance, no longer looking like the freshman he is – the guy looked confident at the plate. Bill took the 1st pitch high, and the 2nd outside. The 3rd was over the plate, but about 6 feet high – Hayes was overthrowing everything. He stopped at this point to retie a shoe, but the pitchers in the Texas dugout could tell when adrenaline had gotten to a guy. A loose shoelace was not the problem! Hayes got the automatic strike at 3-0, with Bates taking all the way, but then lost Bill with a walk on another high pitch. A nice way to start the game!

Mike Brumley came up batting left-handed – he is a switch hitter. He took the first pitch outside and squared to bunt on the second. He took that pitch for a strike, running the count to 1-1. He is hitting .380 in the post season, so Hayes has to be careful where he puts the pitch. When Hayes went into his windup for the next pitch, Bates took off for second. Hayes threw to first, and Alabama probably should have had Bill picked off on the steal attempt. But Magadan glanced at Bates, and then when he looked back at Hayes, he lost the ball in the sun. It ended up rolling all the way to the infield tarp out in right field, and Bates ended up on third! But the umps ruled that the ball had gotten lodged under the tarp, and made Bates go back to second base. Gus wasn't happy with the call, but he almost never argues a call, and he didn't in this case. The guys in the dugout could hear the coach muttering under his breath out in the third base coaching box! Brumley, now with a runner on second, squared again to bunt on his 1-1 pitch – but popped it up to Magadan at first base for the 1st out of the inning.

Doug Hodo, another freshman, dug in and took the first two pitches for a 2-0 count. He swung and missed on a low slider, making it 2-1, but on the next pitch lined a shot off of Hayes' foot on the mound. By the time the ball was recovered, Texas had runners on the corners with just one out!

José Tolentino came to the plate not hitting well in the series. He took the first pitch low, took the second for a strike, and then hit a liner to Stallings in center. The fly ball was deep enough to allow Bates to tag and score, giving UT a 1-0 lead in the game. It was José's 72nd RBI of the year, tying Keith Moreland's UT record.

With Hodo still on first, Jeff Hearron came up to bat. He swung and missed the first pitch, and then grounded out to Shipley at short for a 6-4 fielder's choice out. The top half of the inning was over, but Texas had an early lead!

Bottom of the 1st

Brett Elbin, the Alabama third baseman, is a great leadoff hitter. He knows the strike zone well and will wait for his pitch. He showed that against Labay. Steve's first pitch was outside, Elbin then took a strike giving him a 1-1 count, and then 2 more pitches just outside to run the count to 3-1. Steve's 5th pitch was low, and Alabama also had their leadoff batter on with a walk.

Ted McClendon also took the first pitch outside for a ball, and Jeff Hearron went to the mound to try and settle down Labay. Steve did throw a strike on the 2nd pitch – but McClendon looped it over Bates head at second for a single, putting two on with no outs. Not a good start for Labay, especially with Dave Magadan coming to the plate.

Magadan is a tall drink of water, with a very open, unusual left-handed stance. But it works for him! Labay's first pitch nicked the outside corner for a strike, with Magadan taking. The next pitch was just a little more outside, putting the count at 1-1. Dave then fouled off 3 straight pitches, one back to the screen, one down the right field line, and one to left. It is easy to see that he will hit the ball where it is pitched! But then Labay threw a great slider, low, and Magadan grounded into a 6-4-3 double play! Elbin went to third on the grounder, but at least UT now only needed one more out in the inning.

That brought Rob Skates to the plate, the left-handed hitting cleanup hitter and left fielder. Labay's 1st pitch was in the dirt and bounced toward first base – but Hearron was able to corral it quickly and hold Elbin on third. The next pitch was inside for a 2-0 count. Skates took a strike on the outside corner, making it 2-1. He fouled off the next pitch, and then swung and missed on the low slider from Labay! Steve was out of the inning, with a runner left on third.

Top of the 2nd

Texas had Deron Loy leading off. He is playing right tonight, since Labay is pitching. Deron is batting .321 for the year, so he made sense as a replacement for Labay in the outfield. He took Hayes' first pitch high, but then took a strike on the outside corner for a 1-1 count. He hit a long foul to left, took the next pitch low for a 2-2 count, and then took a pitch just outside to get the count full. But then he swung and missed on a low slider, and Alabama had their 1st out in the 2nd.

Johnny Sutton followed Loy to the plate. After his now expected squat to get loose, he swung at the first pitch and hit a 2-bouncer to short for the second out in the inning.

Mike Trent came up, batting .500 this week in the series. He took the first pitch for a called strike, and then hit a 4-3 grounder to Lake off the end of the bat to end the UT half of the inning. An easy 1-2-3 inning for Hayes – maybe he is settling down a little.

Bottom of the 2nd

Allen Stallings, the Alabama centerfielder, led off this inning. He bats right and is hitting .298 for the year – but he is 6 for 8 in the CWS. He took the first pitch for a ball, swung and missed for a 1-1 count, and then hit a sharp single between third and short to get the leadoff batter on base for the Crimson Tide for the second inning in a row.

Frank Vellegia, the Alabama catcher, was next up. He is 2 for 9 this week. Labay's first pitch was fouled back to the screen, and then Frank hit another foul down the right field line. Labay's next pitch was just outside, running the count to 1-2. But Steve then nicked the outside corner with a nice changeup to get the strikeout looking. One out, and Stallings was still on first.

Fermin Lake, the vertically challenged second baseman, came up, also batting right. He swung and missed on a fastball from Labay. Steve threw to first to hold Stallings, and then threw a changeup to Lake that fooled him badly. He made a one-handed swing that ended up as a fly ball to Loy in right for the second out of the inning.

Dee Smithey, the right fielder, was next up. He bats right, and is only hitting .257 on the year. Labay's first pitch was low, and Stallings stole second, getting a good jump off of Labay. Steve's 1-0 pitch was grounded to Brumley at short, and the throw got Smithey easily. Another runner left on base, but Texas still had the lead, 1-0, after 2 complete.

Top of the 3rd

Bryan Burrows led off the 3rd. He is hitting .294 for the year, but batting 9th in this lineup. He took Hayes' first pitch on the outside corner for a called strike, took a pitch low for a 1-1 count, swung and missed to run the count to 1-2, and then swung again on a nice slider that broke 6 inches outside for the first out in the 3rd.

That brought UT back to the top of the order, and Bill Bates. He took a strike looking, fouled off a pitch, and then took one high for a 1-2 count. He fouled off another good pitch, protecting the plate, and then hit a low pitch off the wall in right center for a triple!

Brumley took Hayes' first pitch outside for a 1-0 count, and then singled past short, scoring Bates. The 'Horns had a 2-0 lead!

Hodo watched as Hayes made a couple of throws to first, trying to hold Brumley close – Mike has 30 stolen bases on the year. Doug hit Hayes' first pitch foul down the first base line, and then watched 2 more throws to first. Hayes next pitch was low, and Brumley was going on the pitch. Valeria dropped the ball at home plate, and Mike had stolen base #31. Hayes' next pitch was outside, running the count to 2-1, but then Doug grounded to Lake at second for the 4-3 out, with Brumley going to third on the play.

Tolentino came up already having 1 RBI in the game and wanting another – but he popped up on the first pitch to Lake at second base, and Alabama was out of the inning. Texas had also left a runner on third, but Bates did score earlier in the inning, so UT had that 2-0 lead!

Bottom of the 3rd

It looks like the storms are getting closer. It is pretty dark out over the right field fence, and the wind has really picked up, now blowing hard towards left. Shipley, the Alabama #9 hitter, led off and hit the first pitch hard to right. But Loy tracked down the liner with a nice running catch, and UT had the 1st out in the inning.

Elbin came back up, took Labay's first pitch for a strike right down the middle, took a called strike 2 on a nice changeup from Steve, and then flied out to Mike Trent in center for out #2.

McClendon fouled off the first pitch to left, and fouled the next one to right for an 0-2 count. He then hit a grounder to

Burrows, who tried to short hop the ball and misplayed it for an error.

That brought Dave Magadan back to the plate. Steve had pitched him mostly in on the hands during Magadan's first trip to the plate, which seemed to be Clint Thomas' strategy on how best to pitch to the left-hander. Magadan fouled off the first pitch, took a pitch outside and low for a 1-1 count, took the next pitch inside to make it 2-1, and then hit an easy grounder to Tolentino at first to end the inning. Texas had held Alabama scoreless through 3 complete, but the Crimson Tide had gotten people on base every inning – Steve was pitching well against the left handers, including Magadan, but the Alabama right-handed batters were giving Labay a little trouble.

Top of the 4th

Jeff Hearron led off the 4th and flew out to right on a 1-1 count. Deron Loy followed, and also flew out to right after taking a strike. 2 quick outs for Hayes!

Johnny Sutton followed Loy to the plate. Johnny, after his usual squat to loosen his legs, took the first pitch on the outside corner for an 0-1 count. A braking ball also caught the corner, dropping him into an 0-2 hole. But then he singled right over a jumping Lake at second base. Somebody taller than 5-3 would probably have caught Sutton's ball.

Mike Trent strolled to the plate. Hayes threw to first, holding Sutton close. Trent swung and missed a changeup. Another throw to first. Mike took a pitch outside for a 1-1 count. Hayes threw to first again. Mike took another pitch outside for a 2-1 count, but then hit an easy ground ball to Magadan at first base to end the UT half of the inning.

Bottom of the 4ᵗʰ

Rob Skates led off this half of the 4ᵗʰ. It has started to rain a little, but not too bad so far. Skates hit a foul tip off of Hearron's leg just above his knee, and Hearron shook it off as usual. Skates fouled the next pitch out of play, took one high over his head for a 1-2 count, and then hit a foul tip that Hearron hung onto for the 1ˢᵗ out of the inning.

Stallings swung and missed on Labay's first pitch, took one low and then one outside for a 2-1 count, and then hit a grounder to Brumley at short. His throw to Tolentino was low, but José got down on his knees, foot still on the bag, and managed to hang onto the throw.

Vellegia took the first pitch low, and then flew out to Sutton in left for a 1-2-3 inning for Labay, his first of the game.

Top of the 5ᵗʰ

Another easy inning for Hayes. Burrows hit a high fly to short right field on the first pitch. Bates took 2 quick strikes, the first on the outside corner and the second on the black on the inside edge of the plate. He took a pitch high for a 1-2 count, fouled off 3 consecutive pitches, and then popped up to Elbin at third in foul territory.

Brumley took the first 2 pitches for balls, swung and missed on a slider for a 2-1 count, took a pitch outside to make it 3-1, and then flew out to deep right center, with Stallings making a catch out on the track. 3 quick outs for Hayes, but Texas still had a 2-0 lead halfway through the game.

Bottom of the 5th

Fermin Lake started things off quickly, with a first pitch single to left off of Labay. Dee Smithey, who is from Austin, fouled off the first pitch. Labay threw to first to hold Lake, but then put a pitch where Smithey could get it. The ball was a liner to right field, and Loy misplayed it at the fence to add an error on the play. Lake scored, Smithey was given a double, and went to third on Loy's error. Coach Gustafson was seeing Labay start to get the ball up, so Gus got Schiraldi to start warming in the bullpen.

Shipley, the #9 hitter, singled to center on his first pitch from Labay. Smithey scored from third, tying the game at 2-2.

Elbin follows with another single to right. Loy slipped, and the ball rolled almost to the fence. Shipley went to third, and Elbin to second on Loy's 2nd error of the inning.

Ted McClendon, the DH, came up and took Labay's first pitch low. He swung and missed the second for a 1-1 count. The ball got away from Hearron and bounced 5 or 6 feet down the third base line – but Jeff was able to corral it and hold the runners. The next pitch was low, making it 2-1, but then McClendon grounded back to Labay on the mound. He looked the runner back to third and got the 1-3 out at first for the first out of the inning.

With runners on second and third, Gus wasn't going to take any chances with Magadan at the plate, so he was given an intentional walk, loading the bases. Rob Skates came up, took a strike looking, and then hit a sacrifice fly to Sutton in left, allowing Shipley to score. Alabama had their first lead of the game at 3-2. Sutton's throw from the outfield went to Burrows at third, so Alabama had runners on first and second with two outs.

Gus had seen enough, so he pulled Steve, putting Calvin Schiraldi on the mound. Calvin came in with his 13-2 record, 1.74 ERA, and 134 innings pitched this year, second only on the team to Clemens. Allen Stallings came to the plate after Calvin's warmup tosses. The first pitch was a fastball on the outside corner, with Stallings taking. The second pitch was in the same spot. With an 0-2 count, Stallings swung and missed on the 3rd pitch. Three pitches by Schiraldi to get UT out of the inning, with two more left on base by Alabama – but they did now have the lead.

Top of the 6th

Labay had been inserted as DH, replacing Hodo, so UT had Steve leading off the 6th. He took the first pitch for a strike on a nice changeup from Hayes. He fouled off the second pitch to put him in a hole. The next pitch was high, but Steve didn't go for it, running the count to 1-2. But then he took the next one on the inside corner for a strikeout looking.

Tolentino fouled off the first pitch, took one low for a 1-1 count, took the next one outside to make it 2-1, fouled off a pitch, and then flew out to right. 2 more quick outs for Hayes.

Hearron came up, with it starting to rain harder. He took a strike looking, and then the umps called for the tarp. The teams ended up with about a 20-minute rain delay. Hayes sat in the Alabama dugout with a jacket on, to keep his arm warm, but you never know how a delay like this will affect a pitcher.

After Alabama retook the field, with Hearron back at the plate, he swung and missed on Hayes' second pitch to run his count to 0-2. The wind had completely died down, with the flags in the outfield hanging limp on the flagpoles – completely different from what the game conditions had been before the rainstorm. Jeff took a couple of pitches inside to get to 2-2, and then singled down the line in right. Texas' first hit after 6 straight outs!

Loy followed Jeff to the plate. Deron swung and missed the first pitch from Hayes on a nice cut fastball. The next pitch was inside, the next high, and the next inside to run the count to 3-1. The next pitch was low for 4 straight balls from Hayes, and UT had 2 guys on base after the walk.

Sutton, up 3rd after the storm, took the first pitch for a strike. It looked to be outside, but he didn't argue the call. The next pitch was low, and then Johnny swung and missed a low slider for a 1-2 count. But then he singled to right field, going with the pitch! Hearron scored, tying the game at 3-3, and Loy went all the way to third, running with two outs.

Mike Trent took a fastball down the middle for an 0-1 count, and then took one in the dirt (but the ball was recovered quickly by Vellegia) to make it 1-1. Then Sutton took off from first on a delayed steal. Vellegia went ahead and threw to second, but the ball was dropped – and that allowed Loy to score from third! Sutton was eventually tagged out in a rundown, but he had done his job, getting Loy home – and Texas had retaken the lead, 4-3.

Bottom of the 6th

Gus sent Bud Ray in to play right field, replacing Deron Loy. Frank Vellegia, the Alabama catcher, led off their half of the 6th. He swung and missed Schiraldi's first offering, and then grounded out back to Calvin for the 1st out in the inning.

Lake took a fastball on the outside corner for an early strike, and took the next pitch outside for a 1-1 count. The next two pitches were both called high, running the count to 3-1. Calvin nicked the outside corner to get to a full count. Lake fouled off a pitch, and then hit a low liner to Bates at second for out #2.

Smithey looked at a low strike, and then hit an easy fly to Sutton in left to end the 6th. Calvin had gotten the first 4 batters he faced!

Top of the 7th

Mike Trent led off and took the first pitch for a strike. He tried to bunt for a base hit, but fouled off the pitch for an 0-2 count. Hayes wasted a pitch high, but then Mike flew out to Skates in shallow left field for out 1.

Burrows came up, took the first pitch inside for a ball, and the second looked like it was over the plate but called inside, too. Hayes threw a good curve for a strike, making it a 2-1 count, but then Bryan doubled over the shortstop! The centerfielder, Stallings, had been playing Burrows toward right field, and by the time he got back to the ball Bryan was standing on second. Not bad for the #9 Texas hitter!

Bates grounded out to Magadan at first on his first pitch. Burrows went to third on the play. With Brumley up, the first pitch from Hayes got by Vellegia, and Burrows broke for home. But Vellegia was able to corral the ball pretty quickly, and the throw to Hayes covering home was in time to get Burrows. Bryan got a late break on the play, not noticing at first that the ball had gotten away from the catcher. It was a close play, but the call was correct, and he was the third out of the inning. The good news is that Texas still had the lead, 4-3, with 9 outs to go.

Bottom of the 7th

Craig Shipley led off for Alabama, this time batting left-handed against Schiraldi. He was 1 for 2 for the evening up to this point. He took 3 straight pitches low, took the automatic strike to run the count to 3-1, and then swung and missed two pitches for the first out of the inning.

Elbin came back up, also 1 for 2 tonight. He took a strike looking, took one under his chin for a 1-1 count, and then took one low to make it 2-1. And the rain came back. The second rain delay of the evening, this one about 40 minutes.

After the shower passed, Elbin fouled off a pitch to make it 2-2, and then swung and missed. Two strikeouts this inning for Schiraldi, and 6 straight outs since coming into the game! McClendon hit a one bounce ground ball to Burrows at third, and Alabama's 7th was over.

Top of the 8th

Troy Brauchle has come in to pitch for Alabama, relieving Hayes. Brauchle is 5-3 on the year, but looks like their top reliever with 12 saves. He has a nice ERA at 2.51.

Brumley led off for UT. He was 1 for 3 for the game. He fouled the first pitch out of play, and bunted foul on the second. He took a waste pitch high, fouled off another pitch, and then grounded to Lake at second. Lake's throw to Magadan bounced in the dirt, but Dave made a nice scoop to get the out.

Labay fouled off the first pitch, took one on the outside corner for strike 2, took one low for a 1-2 count, and then watched a slider nip the inside corner for strike 3. Two quick outs for Brauchle.

Tolentino took a strike looking, hit a long foul down the left field line, fouled another down the right field line, and then flew out to Skates in left. It looked like the ball might drop in, but it held up enough for Skates to get to it to end the top half of the inning.

Bottom of the 8th

Dave Magadan came up as the leadoff hitter, just where Texas wanted him – up with no one on base. He took Schiraldi's first pitch high, and the second outside. The third was a fastball low and away, but Magadan guessed right and drove it over the left field wall. Tie game at 4-4!

Skates took the first pitch at his feet for a 1-0 count, fouled one off to make it 1-1, and then hit a liner down the line in left for a double. Both batters had gone opposite field on Schiraldi on what looked like good pitches – but that is what good hitters can do!

Stallings fouled off the first 2 pitches to get in a hole. Calvin's next pitch was high, but Stallings swung and missed for the 1st out of the inning.

Vellegia came up, swung and missed on Schiraldi's first 2 pitches, and then Calvin tried another high fastball – but unlike Stallings, Vellegia let it go for a ball. He took the next pitch inside for a 2-2 count, but then swung and missed on another fastball for out #2.

Lake came up, 1 for 3 on the night. He took Calvin's first pitch on the outside corner for strike 1, and then took one a little more outside for a 1-1 count. He swung for the fences on a nice curve, actually falling to his knees, but missed for strike 2. He took a pitch high for a 2-2 count, but then swung and missed again to end the 8th. But Magadan's home run had tied the game, and Alabama had the advantage, being the home team.

Top of the 9th

Hearron took a strike down the middle from Brauchle to start the inning. The next pitch was outside, and the third was even more outside – but called a strike. Jeff swung at the next pitch and missed for out 1.

Bud Ray came to bat for the first time since replacing Loy in right field. He is only batting .176 for the year. He took the first pitch on the outside corner for strike 1, and took the second for strike 2. The third pitch was outside for a 1-2 count, took a pitch high to make it 2-2, but then he swung for another strikeout.

Sutton took the first pitch on the outside corner for a strike, bunted a pitch foul for an 0-2 count, took a close pitch outside for a ball (ump had been calling that a strike), but the next pitch got the corner for strike 3. Brauchle was looking tough, and now Texas was into a sudden death situation – tied going into the bottom of the 9th.

Bottom of the 9th

The inning started off easy enough. Smithey, 1 for 3 for the game, took a strike looking, and then flew out to Ray in right field for the 1st out.

Shipley, also 1 for 3, swung on an outside pitch for an 0-1 count, fouled off a pitch to make it 0-2, took a couple of balls, and then swung and missed on a nice slider for the 2nd out of the inning. Calvin already had 6 strikeouts in his short outing and appeared to be cruising through the lineup.

But with two outs Elbin hit Schiraldi's first pitch off the wall in right center for a stand-up double, and Alabama suddenly had the winning run in scoring position.

McClendon came up, batting .376 on the year, and fresh off of being the MVP of the Southern Regional. He took the first 2 pitches low, a pitch outside for a 3-0 count, and then one high for a walk. Alabama had 2 on with 2 outs, and Dave Magadan strolling to the plate.

Gus strolled out to the mound, hands in his pockets as usual, just to make sure Calvin was OK and understood how he wanted to throw to Magadan. Calvin took a deep breath, and hit the inside corner for strike 1. The next pitch was high for a 1-1 count, but then Magadan swung and missed on a nice changeup to get in a hole at 1-2. He had tried to check his swing, but couldn't hold up enough. The next pitch was high to make it 2-2, but then Schiraldi blew it past a swinging Magadan for strike 3! Extra innings!

Top of the 10th

Texas' second extra inning game in a row. UT came out on top against Oklahoma State, so they had shown they can handle that pressure – and the Longhorns had survived Alabama's attempted rally in the 9th. Mike Trent led off and took a strike looking for an 0-1 count. He took a pitch inside to make it 1-1, and then grounded to the right of Lake at second. The ball skidded on the wet dirt and made it through for a single!

Bryan Burrows tried to sacrifice Trent to second. He fouled off his first bunt attempt, and then popped the second bunt foul back behind the catcher. He then grounded to Shipley at short, who threw out Trent coming to second for the fielder's choice out. Burrows barely beat the relay throw back to first.

Bill Bates, 1 for 3 for the game with a triple back in the 3rd inning, swung and missed the first pitch from Brauchle. The pitcher threw to first, and then missed outside giving Bates a 1-1 count. On the next pitch Bates doubled into the left field corner, scoring Burrows! Skates, the Alabama left fielder, had been playing Bates to pull the ball, and when the ball got in the corner it rattled around enough to allow Burrows to come all the way around from first for the run.

Brumley swung and missed on the first two pitches from Brauchle, and then took a waste pitch high for a 1-2 count. But then he hit a liner down the line in right, scoring Bates from second. The relay throw to second was close, and it looked like Brumley beat it – but the ump called him out. Mike stuck a finger in the ump's face, and was lucky he wasn't thrown out of the game. The ump may have known he had blown the call. But Texas led, 6-4.

Labay, 0 for 2 for the night, took the first pitch outside, took a strike looking for a 1-1 count, and then hit a weak grounder between third and the pitcher. Brauchle made a nice play and threw out Labay to end the UT half of the inning. Three more outs!

Bottom of the 10th

Alabama has the middle of their lineup coming to bat, their 4-5-6 hitters. But they are facing probably the top pitcher in the country this year, and Calvin already has 8 strikeouts since relieving Labay in the 5th.

Skates led off, having gone 1 for 3 in the game. He swung and missed on Calvin's first fastball, took a pitch outside to make it 1-1, swung again for a 1-2 count, and let one go by outside to make it 2-2. He fouled off a pitch, just protecting the plate, but then swung again on a high heat fastball for the 1ˢᵗ out of the inning.

Stallings took the first pitch outside, took a strike looking for a 1-1 count, missed on another fastball to make it 1-2, and then swung and missed on a pitch identical to what Calvin threw to Skates. Calvin had struck out Stallings 3 times in the game, as part of his 10 Ks. One more out!

Vellegia came up, 0 for 4 in the game. He swung and missed on Calvin's first pitch, but then took a couple of pitches high to run the count to 2-1. It looked like Schiraldi was getting a little too excited, so Hearron went out the mound to settle him down a little. Calvin took another deep breath and threw a strike down the middle to make it 2-2. Vellegia fouled a pitch off the screen, and then swung and missed. Ball game, and Texas was in the finals!

The 6-4 UT win means the 'Horns will be playing Sunday for sure, whether or not they beat Michigan on Friday. If Texas beats Michigan, then whichever team wins in the early game between Alabama and Arizona State will have to beat UT twice, and the finals will start on Saturday. If Michigan wins tomorrow, then Michigan and the other game winner will play on Saturday, with the winner of that game facing Texas in a winner-take-all game on Sunday. The Longhorns are assured of going to the Sunday game as the last undefeated team in the tournament, whether or not they win tomorrow night.

Bill Bates was the MVP of this game, with his two extra base hits. Johnny Sutton was 2 for 4 in the game, and Mike Brumley

2 for 5. Calvin Schiraldi was the winning pitcher, for his second win of the tournament. He had 11 strikeouts in just over 5 total innings, including striking out the side in the bottom of the 10th. Magadan got to Schiraldi in the 8th to tie the game with his home run, but Calvin got Magadan back with a strike out in the 9th, when a hit would have won the game for Alabama. Extra innings, rain delays, whatever – this UT team just continues to battle and comes through when it counts! Calvin said after the game that he had never thrown harder in his life. And everyone on the team felt that this was sweet vindication for what happened to him last year against Wichita State.

Friday, June 10th

The Holidome is starting to feel almost empty. There are only four teams left playing in this College World Series, and the eliminated teams' fans, families, and players have all left to head back home. Either Alabama or Arizona State will be heading home tomorrow after their game tonight, and if Texas beats Michigan tonight the Wolverines will be heading back to Ann Arbor, too. Now there is more room in the pool, and the other hotel recreation areas are a lot less crowded. The Texas team knows they will be here until at least Sunday, but they want to win it all Saturday night, and go home after a blowout Saturday night party!

The first game tonight is Alabama against Arizona State. Both are good teams. Alabama may be a bit down after losing to UT in extra innings last night. Oklahoma State came out a little flat in their next game after Texas beat them on Tuesday, and that is one of the main reasons Arizona State is still here instead of OSU. Arizona State is considered to be one of the "blue bloods" of college baseball, consistently having good teams and making it to Omaha on a regular basis, including 5 national championships. Alabama, on the other hand, is considered to be an upstart newcomer. Only time will tell whether or not Alabama can be good in the years to come. But this year there is no question – they are a good team, and Dave Magadan is the best player in baseball this year. Arizona State has their share of stars, too, so tonight's first game should be a good one! Alabama did beat Arizona State earlier in the tournament, but "past performance is not a predictor of future results" as those in the stock market keep telling us.

In the Texas-Michigan game, Gus is starting Mike Capel. Mike has almost been the "forgotten man" this tournament. He has gotten up and warmed up a couple of times in the bullpen, but has yet to throw a pitch in a game this week. He thought he might get the starting role against Alabama last night, but when Gus started Steve Labay Mike thought that it might be because Gus thought Mike was still waiting to hear from the Major League draft. But Mike had already gotten the telegram saying he had been drafted by the Chicago Cubs, so he didn't have that distraction. Gus said after the game against Alabama he had started Labay because of all the left-handed hitters early in the Alabama lineup, and that made sense – but Capel was disappointed at being passed over. At least he will get his chance tonight! Mike has won 13 in a row since losing his first game of the year, and there were times this year when he had the best stuff of all of the Texas pitchers. The team knows they can count on him to give them a good game tonight!

Alabama vs. Arizona State

The announcers said before the game that they were predicting a high scoring game on both sides, with somebody winning an 8-7 game with late inning heroics. Instead, two Alabama pitchers, Alan Dunn and Tim Meacham, combined to shut out Arizona State with a 1-hit pitching gem. Alabama ended up winning 6-0. The Sun Devils didn't even get that hit until the 7th inning, and by that time the game was out of hand.

With both Stanford and Arizona State eliminated, the Six-Pac has failed to win the CWS championship for the second straight year – and that hasn't happened for over 20 years! Alabama may be a flash in the pan, but this year they have proven to be a very good team.

Dunn started for Alabama and was crazy wild. He walked 8 batters in 4 1/3 innings, but ASU got too aggressive with men on base and couldn't get the hit they needed to get people home. Dunn also struck out 7 – including striking out the side in the first inning, with Arizona State leaving the bases loaded. That set the tone for the game. Alabama's coach Barry Shollenberger said Dunn "was just wild enough to be effective." Jim Brock said, "We never could get in a rhythm against him."

In the 5th, Schollenberger relieved Dunn with Meacham. Meacham gave up Arizona State's single hit, a pinch-hit single by Lew Kent in the 7th. Meacham, Alabama's top reliever, ended up striking out 4 more Crimson Tide batters, and only walking 1 in his 4 plus innings pitched. Meacham ended up with the win.

Alabama scored 5 in the 6th inning to put the game away. Doug Henry, the Arizona State starter, had held Alabama scoreless through 5 innings, and it looked like the fans were going to get a pitching duel. But in the sixth, with one out,

Brett Elbin singled, and went to second on a groundout by Ted McClendon. Henry then gave Magadan an intentional walk (no need to give him a shot with a runner in scoring position), but the move backfired when Rob Skates, after getting behind in the count at 1-2, hit a bad-hop single past the Arizona State first baseman, Tim McNaughton. That scored Elbin with the first run of the game. Henry got Allan Stallings down 0-2, but then Stallings hit a low line drive just past the reaching Romy Cucjen at shortstop, and Magadan scored. Jim Brock had seen enough, and relieved Henry with Jim Jefferson. But Alabama catcher Frank Vellegia, who had looked bad at the plate on Thursday night, put Jefferson's first pitch over the right center fence for a 3-run homer – and you could hear the fat lady starting to sing. Alabama picked up their sixth run in the 7th inning, when after a 2-base error by McNaughton that put Elbin into scoring position, McClendon singled for the RBI.

Henry had shut out Maine on Sunday with a 1-hitter, and hadn't given up a run in over 22 innings until the Alabama 6th. Brock said after the game that he had probably made a mistake when he had Henry walk Magadan, as that seemed to get Henry out of his rhythm. Whatever the reason, Arizona State was going home, and Alabama had lived to play another day. At this point they didn't know if they would be facing Michigan or Texas on Saturday, but they knew they were still in the hunt!

Michigan vs. Texas

Game 13 of this College World Series. It is beginning to feel like the Longhorns have been in Omaha forever, but that is not a bad thing – a lot better than going home early! The big question tonight is whether or not they can keep their focus, since UT already knows they are guaranteed to be in the final game on Sunday, even if they lose tonight. Jerry Kindle, the Arizona coach and one of tonight's ESPN announcers, thinks that Michigan has the edge tonight because they know they have to win to stay in the tournament.

And Michigan is good – they are still here for a reason. Their young stars, Barry Larkin and Chris Sabo, lead the team – but they have a lot of other firepower, too. Rich Bair is a great catcher with a nice arm, and he is hitting .388 on the year. Ken Hayward, the Michigan first baseman, reminds the coaches of José Tolentino – and Hayward is hitting .355, which is a great average for a guy in the cleanup spot. Their #2 hitter, Mike Watters, is considered the team's "spark plug" – and he has 34 walks on the year. But the stars are Larkin and Sabo. Larkin has a 13-game hitting streak and is 5 for 14 in the CWS. Sabo leads the team in home runs and stolen bases – an unusual combination unless you are a great athlete. Michigan will be starting Scott Kamieniecki, who is a bit of a surprise. Texas thought they would be facing Dave Kopf, who is 9-1 on the year. Kamieniecki is 5-0, has pitched 52 innings this year, and has an ERA of 2.39. He has apparently been pitching well the latter part of the year. It is 71 degrees at game time, with rain in the area – they had a little rain in the first game tonight, but both teams are hoping to get this one in without any delays. The wind is blowing out toward left center at 14 mph. That will help the ball carry!

Top of the 1st

Texas had an advantage this game in that they got to be the home team, so Michigan came to the plate to start the game. Terry Hunter was coaching first for Michigan, with head coach

Bud Middaugh in the third base box. Joe Driscoll is the home plate ump tonight, with Dale Williams at first, Jon Bible umping at second, and Dick Runchey at third.

Barry Larkin, the Wolverine's shortstop, led off. Mike Capel started Larkin with a strike down the middle, missed outside and then low for a 2-1 count, and then got a fly ball to Labay in right field for the 1st out of the game.

Mike Watters, the right fielder, came in batting 4 for 14 in the CWS. He took Capel's first pitch low, and then watched as Mike nipped the inside corner for a 1-1 count. The next pitch was a little too far inside – Mike was testing Joe Driscoll, the home plate ump, to see how much leeway the ump would give him – but then Capel came back on the outside corner for a 2-2 count. The next pitch was a nice slider right down the middle, and it fooled Watters completely. 2 quick outs for Capel!

Chris Sabo hits 3rd in the Michigan lineup. He is 6/13, batting .462 in the CWS. He is hitting .376 for the year, with 16 home runs. A dangerous hitter! He took Mike's first pitch for a called strike, and then another on the outside corner for an 0-2 count. Capel threw a pitch in the dirt, and then Sabo fouled off a pitch. But with a 1-2 count, Sabo swung and missed on a low slider – and Capel was out of the 1st with a 1-2-3 inning.

Bottom of the 1st

Kamieniecki started Bill Bates off with a low strike, and then a pitch high for a 1-1 count. Bates has turned into a great leadoff hitter. He is hitting .298 for the year, and has gotten a lot more selective on the pitch he wants to hit. The next pitch was a foul down the left field line, and looked to be out of play in the stands– but the wind carried it back onto the field (still in foul territory), and over left fielder Fred Erdmann's head. Hard to judge the ball in this wind! Bates hit another foul down the line in left, took a pitch inside for a 2-2 count, and then flied out to Erdmann. It looks like Michigan had Bates scouted well – they were playing him to hit to left the entire at bat.

Mike Brumley came up, batting left-handed tonight against the right-handed Kamieniecki. Mike is at .289 for the year, and leading the team with 31 stolen bases. He took a strike, and then hit an easy grounder to Hayward at first base for an unassisted out.

Doug Hodo, the leading Texas freshman hitter at .354 for the year, is not having a great CWS – he is only batting .167 this week. He swung and missed Kamieniecki's first offering, and then hit a soft foul to left field. Erdman dove but couldn't make the catch – he is not having a great inning! But then Hodo took a breaking ball right down the middle for strike 3, and both teams had gone down quickly in the 1st.

Top of the 2nd

Ken Hayward led off for Michigan. He is batting .355 for the year and has a 4-game hitting streak going. But he hit Capel's first pitch right at Burrows at third, and Bryan made the throw to Tolentino at first for the 1st out of the inning.

Jeff Jacobson, the Wolverine's second baseman, also has a gaudy average at .361. He took Capel's first pitch low, fouled off a ball for a 1-1 count, took a pitch inside to make it 2-1, and then took a slider on the outside corner to even the count at 2-2. Capel's next pitch was low, Jacobson fouled off a pitch, and then Mike missed low to make Jacobson the first baserunner of the game with a walk.

Fred Erdmann followed Jacobson to the plate, batting 6th. He is another good hitter at .341 for the year. Capel threw to first to hold Jacobson, and then Erdman fouled off the first pitch to the plate. The next pitch was a pitchout, but Jacobson was not running. Another throw to first was a little high, or it might have gotten Jacobson. Capel again threw to first – apparently, they were worried about the attempted steal. Capel went home, and Erdman swung and missed – but Jacobson was running. And Jeff Hearron gunned him down at second! It looked like an attempted hit-and-run, but Erdmann didn't hold up his part of the play. Erdmann took the next pitch high for a 3-2 count, fouled off a pitch, and then grounded out to Bates to end the inning.

Bottom of the 2nd

José Tolentino led off and hit a liner in the hole. He probably would have beaten the throw, but he twisted his ankle and stumbled at home plate trying to get in motion. A bit unlucky, but at least he made good contact!

Jeff Hearron came up, leading the team at 6 for 13 in the CWS. He fouled off the first pitch from Kamieniecki, took a pitch high, and then managed to check his swing to get the count to 2-1. Kamieniecki did throw a strike on the next pitch – but Jeff hit it to left for the first hit of the game by either team.

Steve Labay, playing right tonight after pitching and serving as DH last night, followed Hearron. Steve is batting .290 on the year. Texas doesn't have the fancy batting average numbers that they see on the Michigan team, but UT is hoping that the old adage about good pitching beating good hitting still holds true! Steve took the first pitch high, and then hit a pitch just foul down the right field line. The next pitch was high to bring the count to 2-1, and Middaugh came out for a quick mound visit – the announcers said they didn't know if he saw something in Kamieniecki's delivery he didn't like, or if the coach was just out there to tell his pitcher to take his time and make his pitch. Labay swung and missed a slider, and Rich Bair, the Michigan catcher, threw to first and caught Hearron too far off base for a pickoff. Maybe that is what Middaugh was telling his battery? Whatever, UT now had two outs and no one on base. Labay took the next two pitches high and outside and drew a walk.

Johnny Sutton, playing left, did his usual squat before settling in at the plate. He is 4/13 this week, and has had some key hits during the series. He took Kamieneicki's first pitch inside, took another pitch that caught the inside corner to make it 1-1, took a pitch high, and then grounded to Sabo who threw out Labay at second for the fielder's choice. No score through 2 full innings.

Top of the 3rd

Capel has retired the first six batters he faced – off to a great start!

Chuck Froning, the Michigan DH, led off the 3rd. He is batting .297 for the year, but is 0 for 8 in the CWS. He took the first pitch inside, and then grounded back to Capel for out #1.

Rich Bair, the catcher, came up as the #8 batter in the lineup. He is hitting .388 for the year – another good hitter. He took the first pitch from Mike on the outside corner, and then fouled off a pitch to go to 0-2. He hit a grounder to Bryan Burrows at third, but a bad hop caused the ball to bounce off Burrows' chest – that's why you are taught from Little League on to always get in front of the ball! Bryan grabbed the loose ball and fired to first, getting the slow-footed Bair by a step. Tolentino made a nice stretch to help get the out.

The #9 hitter was Dale Sklar, the center fielder. Sklar is only hitting .286 for the year, but has been hot this week, going 6 for 11 for a .545 average at the World Series. On the first pitch he hit a soft fly to Bates in shallow right field, and Capel had no-hit Michigan for the first 3 innings!

Bottom of the 3rd

Mike Trent, the UT center fielder led off their half of the 3rd. He is hitting .297 for the year, but is 5 for 12 this week. He took a strike looking, and then a pitch outside for a 1-1 count. He squared to bunt and hit a ball that bounced back up and hit his hand while he was still in the box for a foul ball and a 1-2 count. He hit another foul to left, hit a foul tip that Bair dropped, but then swung and missed a good fastball for the 1st out of the inning.

Burrows hit his first pitch to Sklar in center for out #2. Bill Bates came back up for the 2nd time in the game. He took the first pitch outside, but Kamieniecki hit the outside corner to even the count at 1-1. Another pitch in the same location put Bates in a hole, and he then hit a 2-hop grounder to Hayward at first base for the unassisted out. No score after 3 innings, and it looks like the two teams might get the game in before 10:00!

Top of the 4th

Barry Larkin came back up for the second time. He took a pitch on the outside corner, but then Mike threw a pitch in the dirt to even the count. Larkin then hit a sinking line drive to shallow center, but Mike Trent made a great sliding catch with a "snow cone" in his glove to get the out. Trent picked the ball just before it hit the grass, and replays showed that the umps got the call right when they called Larkin out.

Mike Watters took a pitch on the outside corner for an 0-1 count, and then grounded to Bates for the second out of the inning. Chris Sabo, with his 16 home runs and team-leading 77 hits, took the first pitch inside, fouled one off at the plate for a 1-1 count, but then grounded out to Bates at second to end the Michigan 4th.

Bottom of the 4th

Mike Brumley led off and hit the first pitch for a clean single right up the middle. A good start to the inning!

Doug Hodo took his first pitch high, and then Kamieniecki threw to first 2 times to hold Brumley close. Doug squared to bunt on the next offering, but took the pitch for a strike to run the count to 1-1. Another throw to first, and then another that almost got Brumley – he was leaning a little too much toward second. Kamieniecki stepped off the mound to settle himself, and then threw to first one more time. Hodo swung and missed the next pitch for a 1-2 count, fouled off a pitch and then took a nice breaking ball for strike 3 and the 1st out of the inning.

José Tolentino is in a pretty bad slump – he is only 1 for 14 in the CWS. Kamieniecki went to first one more time, with Hayward doing a good job digging out the low throw. José took the first pitch high for a 1-0 count, and then Kamieniecki went back to first – and this time he got Brumley! Mike was picked off for the 2nd out of the inning. The next pitch almost hit José for a 2-0 count, and then he took a strike to make it 2-1. José then singled to right – the second Texas hit of the inning.

Jeff Hearron followed José to the plate. Jeff had singled back in the second, and with a runner on Kamieniecki was pitching Hearron carefully. The first pitch was inside, as was the second. The third was low, and the 4th inside for a 4-pitch walk. 2 on with 2 outs!

Steve Labay waited at the plate while Mike Middaugh leisurely strolled out to the mound to talk to Kamienieki. In college ball, you get three free trips to the mound before you have to pull the pitcher, and this was Middaugh's second mound visit in just 4 innings. But then on Kamieniecki's first pitch to Labay, Steve popped up to Jacobson at second back behind the mound, and UT had left 2 on base in the inning. Still no score after 4 complete!

Top of the 5th

Ken Hayward led off, took a strike looking, and then fouled off a pitch for an 0-2 count. He took a waste pitch high, fouled a ball off his foot, and then fouled a pitch down the left field line. But then he doubled to the left field corner for Michigan's first hit of the game!

Jeff Jacobson, who walked his first time up, hit Capel's first pitch right back up the middle for a single. Mike Trent's throw went home, but Hayward scored, and Jacobson went to second on the throw. Michigan had drawn first blood, and led 1-0.

Fred Erdmann squared to bunt and popped up to Hearron in foul territory down the third base line for the 1st out of the inning.

Chuck Froning, the designated hitter, was hitting left-handed against Capel. He took Mike's first pitch in the dirt, and Hearron went out to the mound to talk to Capel. Mike's next pitch was fouled back to the screen, and the next was low for a 2-1 count. Froning hit a liner to Sutton in left, who tried to double Jacobson off of second after snagging the liner. It was close, but Jacobson made it back to second safely.

Rich Bair hit Capel's first pitch just to the left of second base, and off the glove of a diving Mike Brumley. The ball rolled into short centerfield. With 2 outs, Jacobson was running on the play, and scored ahead of the short-hopped throw to Hearron. A good relay throw from Brumley might have gotten Jacobson, but it didn't happen, and Michigan was up 2-0. And all this from the bottom half of the Michigan batting order!

Dale Sklar, batting 9th, hit a foul out of play, fouled a second pitch, and then hit a grounder to Brumley at short. Mike threw Sklar out, but the throw was low, and Tolentino had to take it on his knees. But he got the out, and UT was finally out of the inning. Half-way through the game, and the 'Horns were behind, even with Capel pitching well. Texas just hadn't been able to get the timely hit with men on base.

Bottom of the 5th

The Wild Bunch still hoists their cups to the heavens and toasts Frank Erwin in the bottom of the 5th – Frank was known to imbibe a little – and maybe this half inning was his way of letting the Longhorns know he could hear the toasts.

It started off inauspiciously. Johnny Sutton took the first pitch low, and then took one on the outside corner for a 1-1 count. He then hit a one-hop screamer to first that Hayward snagged and stepped on the bag for a quick 1st out in the inning.

Mike Trent took the first pitch in the dirt, took one on the inside corner to even the count, took a pitch low, and then one outside to run the count to 3-1. The next pitch was over the plate but low, and Trent had drawn a one-out walk.

Bryan Burrows took Kamieniecki's first pitch high for 5 straight balls, and the Michigan catcher Bair immediately went out to the mound to try and settle down his pitcher. But the next pitch was high, too, and the count was 2-0. Michigan has their bullpen warming, and Middaugh came to the mound for his last free trip before he had to pull Kamieniecki. But the next two pitches were outside the zone, and Texas had two straight walks!

Bill Bates came up with 2 on and 1 out. Bill is only 5-7, weighs about 155, is playing with a strained thumb, but like they say about feisty fighters, he hits above his weight class! He took Kamieniecki's first pitch outside for a 1-0 count, and then took the pitcher's first strike in a long while to even the count. Bates called time and stepped out, swinging the bat a couple of times. He then hit the next pitch between first and second to load the bases! Mike Trent, running from second, had to hold up because he thought Bates' shot might be caught, so he was only able to get to third.

Mike Brumley came up, and the umpire called time. Brumley looked up, and Joe Driscoll was pointing to Gus in the third base box. Coach Gus was motioning for Brumley to join him, and Brumley hustled down the line. Gus was known for making players take a lot of pitches. Some guys even got frustrated and ignored the take sign, getting in trouble when they swung after being told not to do so. Last night, against Alabama, Gus had told Steve Labay to take a pitch, and it ended up being strike three. So Brumley was surprised when Gus told him, "If you get a pitch you can handle on the first pitch, go ahead and swing." With the bases loaded, not making the batter take at least one strike was highly unusual for Gus! Brumley marched back to the plate, and with the surprising green light from the coach deposited Kamieniecki's first pitch over the wall in right, out by the Budweiser sign, for a grand slam home run! The pitch was low, but Mike looked like a golfer hitting a long high wedge into the green. He hit a hanging curve about as square as you can do so! Mike Watters, the Michigan right fielder, had tracked the ball all the way to the wall – and then slammed his glove into the fence in frustration. Brumley was mobbed at home plate after he touched home, and Middaugh came out to pull Kamieniecki – but the damage had been done, and Texas was leading, 4-2. Brumley had hit a grand slam back on April 2nd, against TCU, so the team knew he was capable of doing that – but Brumley wasn't known as a home run hitter, and this one came as a big surprise to everyone – except Mike, and maybe Coach Gustafson!

The new Michigan pitcher coming in for relief was Casey Close, 5-1 on the year with 50 innings pitched and a 3.58 ERA. He is right-handed and has a good strikeout to walk ratio. Doug Hodo came up, now with the bases empty, and took the first pitch from Close low. Hodo swung on a slider for a 1-1 count, and then took one low to make it 2-1. Doug, tall and thin for a freshman at 6-1 and 195, fouled off the next pitch to even the count. He took the next two pitches for balls and drew the 3rd walk of the inning.

Tolentino fouled off his first pitch, back to the net, and Close threw to first to hold Hodo. The next pitch was outside, and then another foul got the count to 1-2. Another throw to first was followed by an inside pitch for a 2-2 count, but then José grounded back to Close for a 1-6-3 double play. Michigan was out of the inning, but the big blow by Brumley had given UT the lead!

Top of the 6th

The 'Horns were now up 4-2, but had to hold that lead, and Mike had not pitched that well in the 5th. Gus had Wade Phillips starting to throw in the bullpen, just in case. And Michigan had the heart of their lineup coming to bat, with Larkin, Watters, and Sabo due up this inning. Killer is doing the pitch charting in the dugout, and while Capel hasn't thrown that many pitches, if he starts getting the ball up, Gus will not hesitate to get someone else in there.

Larkin took the first pitch from Capel high, and then fouled a pitch back to the screen for a 1-1 count. Barry fouled a pitch down the right field line, took a pitch just outside to even the count at 2-2, and then took a pitch inside to run the count full. But then he swung and missed on a nasty slider from Capel, and Texas had the first out in the 6th.

Watters, 0 for 2 on the night, took the first three pitches high, low, and outside for a 3-0 count. Capel got the automatic strike with Watters taking all the way, but then threw another pitch high to put Watters on first with a free pass.

Chris Sabo took Capel's first pitch low, and then a strike down the middle for a 1-1 count. He then flew to Mike Trent in centerfield for out #2.

Ken Hayward, batting left, followed Sabo to the plate. The Longhorns are playing him the other way pretty strongly – Clint doesn't think Hayward can pull the ball against Capel. Hayward took the first pitch inside, and the second outside, for a 2-0 count. He hit a foul to left for a 2-1 count, fouled a ball down the first base line to even the count at 2-2, and then took a pitch inside to run the count full. Capel threw to first to hold Watters, and then Michigan tried a hit-and-run with Watters going – but Hayward fouled off the pitch. Capel then again threw to first, but put the ball way over Tolentino's head – it looked like Capel was shot putting the ball – and by the time the ball was retrieved Watters was on third base. Hayward fouled off another pitch, but then grounded out to Brumley to end the inning, leaving a runner stranded on third. 9 more outs for the win!

Bottom of the 6th

Jeff Hearron led off the Texas 6th. He fouled the first pitch off the screen, and then took a pitch inside for a 1-1 count. He barely managed to check his swing on an outside pitch, and then fouled off another to even the count at 2-2. And then lined a single to center. Jeff is 8 for 15 in the CWS and flirting with Jeff Magadan status!

Steve Labay has been struggling at the plate. He squared to bunt on the first pitch and took it high. Same result with pitch 2. He took a strike, watched a throw to first, and then fouled off a pitch on a hit and run attempt. With 2 strikes, he swung and missed on a high breaking pitch for the 1st out in the inning.

Johnny Sutton followed, 0 for 2 on the day. He took the first pitch inside, watched Close throw to first, and then Sutton took the next 2 pitches high for a 3-0 count. At that point Middaugh pulled Close. The new pitcher was Tim Karazim. 46 innings pitched, with 7 saves. He, too, throws mostly breaking stuff. His first pitch to Sutton was a curve that nicked the plate for a 3-1 count. The next pitch was low, but called a strike, running the count full. Sutton was taking all the way on that pitch. He fouled off a pitch, and then took another strike for out 2. Hearron was going on the pitch – probably a hit-and-run call that Sutton missed – and Jeff made it safely to second when Larkin dropped the ball. It was Jeff's first stolen base of the year! He would have been out by 3 feet if the shortstop had been able to handle the throw, but a stolen base is a stolen base...

Mike Trent came up, 0 for 1 for the day with a walk. He took the 1st pitch inside, the 2nd low, the 3rd high, and then Karazim called time to retie his shoe. But his next pitch was low, and Trent had his second walk of the game.

Bryan Burrows followed, 0 for 1, but he also had worked a walk. He and Trent scored on Brumley's grand slam back in the 5th. But this time Bryan hit into an easy 6-4 fielder's choice out, with Larkin to Jacobson forcing Trent at second base.

Top of the 7th

Jacobson led off for Michigan. He is 1 for 1 for the game, with a single, a walk, and an RBI. He took the first pitch for a strike and took the second outside for a 1-1 count. The next pitch was low, and then he fouled off a pitch at the plate to even the count at 2-2. And then Capel threw him a great slider, and Jacobson swung and missed for the first out in the 7th.

Erdmann followed, 0 for 2 on the day. He took a strike looking, fouled off a pitch, and then hit a ground ball to Bates for out 2. Gus still has Phillips warming in the bullpen, but it looks like Capel has settled back down after the 5th.

Chuck Froning, the DH, was also 0 for 2 for the evening. He took a strike looking, a pitch low, and then another on the inside corner for a 1-2 count. Capel threw one way outside that went all the way to the screen – it looked like the ball just slipped out of his hand as he was making the pitch. But then Froning hit a soft grounder to Tolentino at first, and he stepped on the bag to end the Michigan 7th.

Bottom of the 7th

Bill Bates led off. He was 1 for 2 with a walk, and also scored on Brumley's home run. He took four straight pitches outside the zone for another walk.

Mike Brumley, 2 for 3 on the day with the big hit in the 5th, squared to bunt but pulled the bat back and took the first pitch for a strike. Karazim threw to first a couple of times, and then Brumley fouled off the next pitch for an 0-2 count. Michigan had a couple of guys warming in their bullpen, too. Three more throws to first followed. But then Brumley struck out. Bates was running on the play, and Larkin again dropped the throw, allowing Bates to reach with a stolen base.

Hodo, 0 for 2 with a walk, swung and missed on a first pitch breaking ball, and then hit a grounder to Hayward at first base for out 2. Bates went to third on the play.

Tolentino came to the plate, but had to wait as Middaugh decided to again change pitchers. The new guy on the mound was Dave Kopf, who the UT coaches thought might have been the starter tonight. He is 9-1 on the year, has a 3.38 ERA, and has 2 saves with 72 innings pitched. José took the first pitch outside, but then popped up to Jacobson at second to end the inning.

Top of the 8th

Capel was getting close to 100 pitches. He had gotten 9 ground ball outs in the game, and he was still keeping the ball down – critical against a good hitting club like Michigan. The question for Gus was whether or not to leave him in, or bring in Phillips or another reliever to finish the game. Texas needed six more outs, and Gus's decision at the moment was that Capel was staying on the mound. But, just in case, Wade and Kirk Killingsworth started warming in the bullpen. Michigan has the bottom two in the order due up this inning, and then back to Barry Larkin.

Rich Bair, the catcher, led off. He is 6-2, 185, and can hit it a long way if he connects. He was 1 for 2 in the game. He took Capel's first pitch on the outside corner for a strike, and then singled past Burrows at third for Bair's second hit of the game.

Dale Sklar, 0 for 2 tonight, took Capel's first pitch outside for a ball. But then hit into a 4-6-3 double play! Bates took the grounder just inside the baseline, flipped the ball back to Brumley, and he threw it to Tolentino, over a sliding Bair, to barely get Sklar at first. Two quick outs! Middaugh came out, arguing catcher interference, but home plate umpire Joe Driscoll said no, and the outs stood!

Larkin came to the plate, and took a strike looking, followed by a pitch that looked like it was off the plate outside, but Hearron did a beautiful framing job, and the ump said strike 2. The next pitch was outside, for a 1-2 count, and then Larkin bounced one back to Capel, who easily threw Larkin out at first. Capel was through the 8th, and Texas still had a 2-run lead!

Bottom of the 8ᵗʰ

Jeff Hearron led off, 2 for 2 in the game with a walk thrown in for good measure. He fouled off the first pitch, and then swung and missed for an 0-2 count. He then hit a ground ball to Larkin at short, and Michigan had the first out of the inning.

Steve Labay took Koph's first pitch high, took a strike looking for a 1-1 count, watched a pitch sail back to the screen, and then one inside for a 3-1 count. He then grounded to Larkin, just like Hearron – but the ball took a bad hop, and only great reflexes by Larkin helped him snag the ball as it came up on him. He managed to corral it and throw Labay out for the second out of the inning.

Johnny Sutton took the first pitch about six inches outside, but Driscoll called it a strike. The next pitch was low, and then Sutton swung at a good slider and missed for a 1-2 count. He stepped out and did his usual squat to loosen his legs, and then took a pitch outside. Koph had started off the mound, thinking he had struck out Sutton. But then Koph did get him, with Sutton swinging and missing on another low slider. On to the 9ᵗʰ.

Top of the 9ᵗʰ

Gus left Capel in the game. He was at 108 pitches, but still being effective – so why make the change? Michigan had the heart of their lineup coming to bat, with their 2-3-4 hitters due up this inning. Mike Watters, the right fielder, led off. He fouled off the first pitch, and then popped up to Bates in shallow right for the first out.

Chris Sabo, 0 for 3 in the game, took a pitch on the outside corner for strike 1. The next pitch was a little more outside, and the count evened. He fouled off a pitch, and then hit a dribbler past Capel. But Bates was playing him up the middle and was able to get to the ball and throw out Sabo. Having Bill Bates (and the other defensive players) know where to play each batter is where the pregame scouting comes into play, and shows how valuable Clint Thomas' contributions are to this team's success.

Hayward came up, the last hope for Michigan. He was 1 for 3 for the game, with a double in the 5th and a run scored. He bats left against Capel, and Texas was playing him toward right. He took Capel's 1st pitch outside, and the 2nd inside. The 3rd was low for a 3-0 count, and Hearron went out to the mound to try and settle down Capel. Mike threw two strikes, with Hayward taking on both pitches, but then with a full count put a pitch high to put Hayward on first.

Middaugh put a pinch runner in for Hayward, and Jacobson came to the plate. He took Capel's first pitch outside, and then popped up to Bates! Ball game, and the Longhorns were still undefeated this week. Now, Alabama would have to beat UT twice or Texas would be CWS champions! Lots of hugs for Mike Capel, and he even got a handshake and grin from Coach Gustafson – a rare thing for Gus!

The team watched the Irv Brown interview of Capel after the game – Mike had been named game MVP – and Brown teased Mike about the lob throw to first that went over Tolentino's head. Mike said, "I have no move at all!" But he had pitched a 4-hit complete game, and thanks to Mike Brumley's grand slam the 'Horns will be playing for the championship Saturday night.

Texas only had six hits in the game, against the 3 Michigan pitchers. But the one big one by Brumley won the game. UT overcame 2 more errors – the team has not been playing great defense this week – but the 'Horns got the outs when they needed them. Capel is now 13-1 on the year, and has won 13 straight since his opening week loss. He doesn't get the attention that Schiraldi and Clemens get, but this year Capel has been just as outstanding on the mound, and he is a big reason the Texas team is where they are – playing for the trophy in Omaha!

Saturday, June 11th

The Finals. UT has been here before, and blown the last game. Last year, Texas didn't even make the finals, even though they were probably the best team in the country in '82. Baseball is a game of breaks, and sometimes the breaks just don't go your way – but Texas thinks this is their year! UT just has to just win one of two games, and hopefully they can close out this tournament tonight and not have to play on Sunday. As much as the team and fans like Omaha and the Holidome, they all feel they have been here long enough!

It was a long day, sitting around, before it was time to head to Rosenblatt. The team had a late lunch, and then bussed to the ballpark to start batting practice. But before they got on the bus, Gus sat everyone down, and gave a speech no one had ever heard him give before. As much as he has chewed on this team in the past, today he was almost just the opposite. He told his players that he was very proud of this team, that they were not just overachievers, but that they well deserved to be where they were – in the finals. And he closed by saying, "You guys are going to be National Champions. I don't know if it will be tonight or tomorrow night – I'm pretty sure it will be tonight – but you guys are destined to win it all." That speech relaxed a lot of the pregame tension everyone was feeling, and got everyone into the mood to go kick some Alabama behind!

Texas is now 65-14 on the year, and the team has set a UT record for wins in a season. Alabama is 46-10. Texas now has a slight advantage in winning percentage, .823 to .821, and they have the psychological advantage, having beaten the Crimson Tide just a couple of nights ago. The Longhorns are pitching a well-rested Roger Clemens, 12-5 on the year, with 1 save and a 3.04 ERA. He has pretty much recovered from his inflamed elbow issues and should be in peak form. Roger has pitched 157 innings this year, leading the team, and has only walked 22 and struck out 142 while on the mound.

Alabama is countering with Rick Browne. Browne is a tall, lanky left-handed pitcher (and left-handers seem to give UT the most trouble). He has a high leg kick, and sometimes an almost side-armed delivery. Batters say his pitches look like they are coming from somewhere around first base! His record for the year is 11-1, with one save, and a 3.71 ERA. He has pitched 78 innings this year, walked 40 and struck out 56 in those innings. He is a junior college transfer and pitched in the Junior College World Series last year – so he is comfortable with a big game atmosphere.

The wind is blowing out towards left center, right now at about 14 mph. Looks like no rain delays tonight! It is about 75 degrees, with 64% humidity – about normal this close to the river in Omaha on a summer evening.

Umpires for tonight's game are some of the best in college baseball. Joe Driscoll behind home plate, Hank Rountree at first, Randy Christal at second, and Jon Bible at third.

There was a lot of burnt orange in the crowd, but the pre-game announcement applause seemed to favor Alabama. The average fan roots for the underdog, so the Texas team can understand the cheers – and that just makes them more determined to show everybody why UT is the best team!

Texas is the visiting team tonight and will start what has been their usual lineup against left-handers, at least the usual lineup since the Regional. The UT second baseman, Bill Bates, with his still taped up thumb, leads off. Mike Brumley is at shortstop and batting second, followed by Kirk Killingsworth as the designated hitter. First baseman José Tolentino bats cleanup, with catcher Jeff Hearron hitting 5th and Steve Labay, back in left field, batting 6th. Johnny Sutton hits 7th and is playing left, followed by centerfielder Mike Trent in the 8 hole and third baseman Bryan Burrows batting 9th. As usual, Gus will be in the third base coaching box, and Bill "Sweets" Bethea is coaching first.

Alabama is countering that order with a defense that has Bret Elbin at third, Craig Shipley, the Australian, at shortstop, Fermin Lake, the (maybe) 5-foot-2 tall kid at second, and Dave Magadan at first. The outfield has Rob Skates in left, Allan Stallings in center, and Dee Smithey in right. Catching is Frank Velleggia, who had a big home run last night against Arizona State to put Alabama in the finals.

And finally, it was time for some baseball. 27 outs to the National Championship!

Top of the 1st

Bill Bates led off the game. He is hitting .298 for the year, with 1 home run and 34 RBIs. In the College World Series, he is 6 for 16, with a triple, a double, and 4 singles. He had 3 hits against Alabama on Thursday. He took the 1st pitch inside, the 2nd a little low, and the 3rd was another breaking ball called a strike. He swung at a pitch just off the dirt to even the count at 2-2, and then swung at a slider for the 1st out of the game.

Mike Brumley is having a great series. He is 7 for 17, hitting .412, with a double, the grand slam home run that beat Michigan last night, and 5 singles. He has 9 RBIs this week! He is only hitting .292 for the year but is pretty hot right now. He took the first pitch high, and then singled up the middle past a diving Fermin Lake for Brumley's 8th hit of the series.

Killingsworth, the do-everything Texas pitcher, outfielder, and DH, is only hitting .225 on the year. But Gus wanted another right-handed bat in the lineup against Browne, and Kirk is used to big-game situations. He took Browne's first pitch outside, watched one just catch the black on the outside corner of the plate for a 1-1 count, took the next pitch high and then one outside to run the count to 3-1. The Alabama manager took a rosin bag out to Browne, but I'm not sure his early control issues are due to a sweaty hand! His next pitch was again outside, and Texas had 2 on with 1 out.

José Tolentino came up, only 2/17 in the tournament, in a terrible slump. He leads the team in hitting in most categories for the year, batting .346 with 12 home runs and 72 RBIs – but right now he is struggling. He took a first pitch breaking ball on the outside corner for a strike, another similarly located to run the count to 0-2, and then swung and missed on a big curve for the second out of the inning.

Jeff Hearron followed José to the plate. Jeff is 8 for 16 in the CWS, all singles and has added 3 walks this week. He is having an outstanding series. He took Browne's first pitch for a strike, took one low for a 1-1 count, and then grounded out to Shipley on a 6-4 fielder's choice play to Lake at second for the third out of the inning. Texas had threatened, but wasn't able to do any damage against Browne.

Bottom of the 1st

Dick Wiggins was coaching first for the Crimson Tide, with Roger Smith coaching third for the team in cream-colored uniforms with a red "Alabama" across the front of their jerseys. Alabama had Bret Elbin leading off. Elbin is a switch-hitter, batting 5 for 19 in the CWS, including being 3 for 4 against UT in the Thursday game. Elbin is hitting .344 on the year. Roger Clemen's first pitch was high, and then Elbin took one on the inside corner to even the count. Clemen's next pitch was almost too good, and Elbin flew out to Johnny Sutton on the track in left for the first out in the bottom of the 1st.

DH Ted McClendon was batting 2nd. He is 5/13, .385, in the CWS, and is hitting .376 for the year. The Texas coaches say this batting order reminds them a lot of Mississippi State's – everybody can hit the ball! McClendon fouled off Roger's opening pitch, took one on the outside corner for an 0-2 count, and then hit a one-hopper to Bates at second for the 2nd out of the inning.

That brought up Dave Magadan, just where you want him – with no one on base ahead of him. He is 9 for 16 in the CWS, hitting .563. The critics that said he had feasted on bad SEC pitching had all been shut up by this point – Magadan had proven he could hit the best pitchers in the country. He fouled off Roger's first 3 pitches, took a pitch high and inside for a 1-2 count, fouled another pitch back out of play, and then swung and missed on a low slider from Clemens. It was only Magadan's 11th strikeout of the year. The two teams had a 0-0 ballgame after 1 inning, and both pitchers looked to be throwing great stuff.

Top of the 2nd

Steve Labay, the Longhorn's right fielder tonight, led off the 2nd. Steve is batting .286 for the year and is 4 for 16 in the CWS. He took the first pitch low – looked like a strike from the bench – and the second pitch was low and inside. He took a strike looking, took a low pitch for a 3-1 count, and then Browne hit the outside corner to run the count full. Steve then got fooled, with a strike right down the middle for the 1st out of the inning, and Browne's 3rd strikeout.

Johnny Sutton followed Labay to the plate. Johnny is 4 for 17 in the CWS, but hitting .377 in his abbreviated season. Browne hit the outside corner twice to put Johnny in a hole, 0-2, wasted a pitch high and outside, and then Johnny grounded out to Fermin Lake at second for the 2nd out of the inning.

Mike Trent, the UT center fielder, is batting 8th. He is at .297 for the year, and is having a good CWS, hitting 5 for 13 for a .385 average here in Omaha. He started his at bat by attempting to bunt but hit the ball foul. He took a ball low and outside to even the count, but then grounded out to Dave Magadan at first to end the 'Horn's half of the inning. It looked like Browne was settling down and throwing more strikes as he got into his rhythm.

Bottom of the 2nd

Rob Skates led off the second for Alabama. He was 1 for 4 against UT on Thursday and is 4 for 18 for the CWS. He is hitting .349 for the year, so he can be dangerous. He swung and missed a high fast ball from Roger to open the at bat. He fouled a ball just outside third for an 0-2 count, took a pitch outside to make it 1-2, and then swung and missed on another high fastball for the first out in the Alabama 2nd.

Allen Stallings, the Crimson Tide center fielder, is having a good CWS. He is 7 for 19 this week, for a .368 average. He took Roger's first pitch low, and then swung and missed a slider to even the count at 1-1. Roger hit the outside corner to put Stallings behind at 1-2, and then hit a foul tip that Hearron dropped. Stallings fouled off a couple more pitches, and Jeff went to the mound to discuss with Roger how to pitch to this guy. Stallings checked his swing – barely – on the next pitch to even the count at 2-2, took a pitch inside to work the count full, and then singled to right. A good at bat, and the first hit for Alabama tonight.

Frank Velleggia, the catcher, was up next. He was 0 for 4 against UT on Thursday, but hit a 3-run homerun last night that helped Alabama beat Arizona State. He took a strike looking from Roger, watched a throw to first, and then Roger hit the same spot as the first pitch on the outside corner for an 0-2 count. Velleggia took a pitch high, watched as Roger threw to first again to hold Stallings, and then swung and missed, swinging way late on a Clemens' fastball. 2 outs in the inning!

Fermin Lake, the 5-2 second baseman (looks more like 4-9) does like to swing from his heels, and can put the ball out of the park. He is only 3 for 17 in the CWS, but when he gets behind the ball, it can go a long way. He hit Roger's first pitch pretty hard, but a retreating Johnny Sutton tracked it down near the warning track in left for the 3rd out of the inning. No score after two complete!

Top of the 3rd

The Texas #9 hitter, Bryan Burrows, led off the 3rd. He is 3 for 11 in the CWS, but does have 2 doubles in those 3 hits. He is hitting .295 for the year. He took Brown's 1st pitch outside, and the 2nd was low and outside for a 2-0 count. Bryan took a strike looking, nearly got hit by a pitch way inside, and then took a high pitch for ball four and a walk.

That brought Bill Bates back to the plate. Bill has hit safely in every CWS game so far this week. He took a pitch on the outside corner for strike 1, squared to bunt but pulled the bat back and took strike 2, and then swung and missed on a pitch way outside for the first out of the inning.

Mike Brumley, with the only UT hit tonight, is batting right tonight against the lefty Browne. He took the first pitch low, but the second from Browne caught the black on the outside corner to even the count. Brumley took a pitch high, and then one outside, to run the count to 3-1. He fouled off the next pitch to make it 3-2, but then popped up to Shipley at short for the 2nd out of the inning.

Killingsworth took a strike on the outside corner for 0-1, took a pitch inside to even the count, and then took another pitch on the outside corner to fall behind 1-2. Gus finally let him swing with 2 strikes, but Kirk swung and missed on a good curve ball, and Alabama was out of the inning. Browne had 6 strikeouts in only 3 innings of work – the kid was dealing!

Bottom of the 3rd

Dee Smithey, the Alabama right fielder, led off. He is only 3/17 in the CWS, and is batting .261 for the year. He bunted Roger's first pitch foul, and the second was outside and went all the way back to the screen for a 1-1 count. Smithey then hit a slow roller to Brumley at short and beat Mike's throw to first base for an infield single.

Craig Shipley, the shortstop, bats 9th for Alabama in tonight's lineup. He is only 3/16 this week but is hitting .290 for the year. After a couple of Roger throws to first to help hold Smithey, Shipley bunted to Burrows at third, trying to move Smithey up into scoring position. Burrows got to the ball in time to throw Smithey out at second for the 4-3 fielder's choice out, and the first out of the inning. There was no throw to first, so Shipley was on with 1 out.

That brought Bret Elbin back up for the second time in the game. He took a strike on the inside corner for an 0-1 count, but then Roger bounced a wild pitch curve just behind home plate that Hearron couldn't handle, and the ball went all the way back to the screen. Jeff had tried to catch the ball instead of just blocking it, and the short hop got past him. Shipley made it to second easily. Elbin took the next pitch outside for a 2-1 count. The next pitch was inside, and Jeff was up and throwing, trying to catch Shipley off second. But Bates was late in covering the bag, and the ball went all the way into centerfield. Shipley was on third, with just 1 out in the inning. Bates pounded his chest, telling Jeff it was his fault – but the damage was done. With a 3-1 count, Elbin popped up to Bates in shallow right, but he was running away from home plate. He turned and threw home, and the ball and Shipley arrived at home at the same time. Shipley was able to kick the ball loose, and Alabama had the first run of the game. Clemens threw the ball to Burrows at third, appealing that Shipley had left early, but Randy Cristal ruled Shipley safe.

Ted McClendon, the DH, was next to bat. He took a strike looking, swung and missed for an 0-2 count on a good fastball, but then singled to center. His hit was off the handle of the aluminum bat, way inside, and would have broken a regular wooden bat – but it still went for a hit.

That brought back up the dangerous Dave Magadan. He swung and missed on Roger's first offering, and then fouled a pitch to left for a quick 0-2 count. Roger threw to first a couple of times to hold McClendon, and then Magadan foul tipped a ball that Hearron was able to hang onto, and UT had the third out in the bottom of the 3rd – finally! But Alabama had scratched home a run on some throwing miscues, and they led in the game, 1-0.

Top of the 4th

José Tolentino came back up, 0 for 1 tonight. He leads UT with 98 hits for the year, but has looked pretty bad at the plate most of this week. José took the first pitch from Browne low and in the dirt, but then popped up again to Fermin Lake at second for the first out of the 4th.

Jeff Hearron took Browne's first pitch low, and then one inside for an 0-2 count. He took a good curve to make it 2-1, tried to hold back on a checked swing to even the count at 2-2, and then took a strike on the outside corner looking for the second out of the inning.

Steve Labay swung and missed on the first pitch, fouled off a pitch to make it 0-2, and then took a pitch inside for a 1-2 count.

But then he grounded out to Shipley at short, and Browne had another quick inning.

Bottom of the 4th

Rob Skates took a curve for an 0-1 count, and then hit an easy grounder to Bates for the 1st out of the inning.

Stallings, 1 for 1 with a single in the second, tried to square and bunt himself on, but ended up taking the pitch for a strike. Roger's next pitch was outside, then Allen hit a foul out of play down the right side to make it 1-2. And then Roger painted the outside corner, and Texas had 2 quick outs in the 4th.

Velleggia took the first pitch inside, and then fouled off a pitch to even it at 1-1. Roger hit the outside corner for a 1-2 count, and then Velleggia popped up to Burrows in foul territory outside of third base to end the 4th. But Alabama still led, 1-0.

Top of the 5th

Johnny Sutton led off the 5th. He took the first pitch from Browne outside for a 1-0 count, but then hit a one-hop grounder to Magadan at first for an easy out.

Mike Trent, 0 for 1 in the game, was hit by the first pitch from Browne – a breaking ball that didn't break. UT had their first baserunner in a while, stopping a string of 7 outs in a row from Browne.

Bryan Burrows fouled a pitch back to the screen, and then popped up to Lake at second for the second out of the inning.

Bates, crowding the plate, took a pitch outside from Browne. Browne threw to first, with Trent running. Shipley took his eye off the throw from Magadan, and Trent made it safely to second – a good play would have had him. The ball skipped into centerfield, but was retrieved quickly enough that Trent couldn't go to third. Bates squared but pulled the bat back and took a strike to make it a 1-1 count. He then hit an easy fly to Skates in left field, and Alabama ended the UT threat. Browne had held Texas to 1 hit through 5 innings.

Bottom of the 5th

Alabama had the bottom part of the lineup coming up this inning, but everybody on this team can hit, so Roger couldn't relax. Fermin Lake led off, squared, and missed a bunt attempt. Then Roger dropped a splitfinger in over the plate for an 0-2 count. A high pitch got Lake to 1-2, but then Roger threw another great breaking ball right down the middle to get Lake looking for the 1st out of the inning.

Dee Smithey (from Austin) already had a single in this game. He fouled the first pitch back to the screen, and then fouled another off into the stands. He hit a 3rd foul down the right field line, but then Roger left a pitch hanging up in the strike zone and Smithey homered to left center, out by the scoreboard. Alabama had a 2-0 lead, and Texas looked to be in some trouble.

Craig Shipley followed Smithey to the plate but grounded to Bates on Roger's first pitch for the second out of the inning. Shipley can fly, and Bates barely got him at first.

The Crimson Tide was back at the top of the order and Bret Elbin, 0 for 1 in the game. He did get the first RBI in the game with his sacrifice fly to short right back in the 3rd inning. He took Roger's first pitch high, and the second outside for an 2-0 count. Hearron went to the mound to make sure Roger was settling down after the home run. On the next pitch Elbin hit a liner to Labay in right, and Texas was finally out of the inning – but Alabama had doubled their lead to 2-0.

Top of the 6th

Mike Brumley led off and hit Browne's first pitch to Elbin at third for an easy 5-3 out.

Kirk Killingsworth took a pitch outside, and then a pitch low for a 2-0 count. He then hit a line drive single past Lake at second. This was only Texas' 2nd hit in the game.

José Tolentino was up next, and he hit Browne's first pitch past third for only his 3rd hit of the week. A great time to break out of a slump!

Jeff Hearron came up, hitting .500 for the week before tonight, but 0 for 2 so far tonight. Alabama just sent a couple of guys, including Troy Brauchle, down to the bullpen to start warming. And Browne's first pitch hit Jeff in the leg, loading the bases with just one out!

Steve Labay was up next, 0 for 2 for the game. He took the first pitch from Browne inside for a ball. He squared to bunt for a safety squeeze, but pulled the bat back and took the pitch as a strike. Browne's next pitch was outside, running the count to 2-1, and then Labay checked his swing on an outside pitch to get to 3-1. Gus gave Labay the take sign, and Browne's next pitch was just low, giving Labay the walk, giving Texas their first run of the game. It was 2-1 Alabama, and UT still had the bases loaded.

Johnny Sutton came up, took the first pitch low, and then took a strike for a 1-1 count. He then grounded to Shipley at short, who got the 6-4 fielder's choice out at second – but Sutton beat the relay throw to first, Tolentino scored, and the 'Horns had tied the game! Shipley had trouble getting the ball to Lake at second, or Alabama might have gotten the double play. Velleggia was backing up first on the plate, and no one covered home – if Hearron or Coach Gus had noticed that home plate was wide open, Jeff could possibly have scored from third – but everyone was watching the play at first, and Jeff didn't attempt to score.

Mike Trent took Browne's first pitch low, and the second outside for a 2-0 count. Browne hit the outside corner to get a strike, and then Trent fouled off a pitch to even the count at 2-2. Mike then popped up to Velleggia behind home plate to get Alabama out of the inning, but Texas had come back to tie the game!

Bottom of the 6th

Ted McClendon, the DH, led off for Alabama. He was 1 for 2 tonight. He fouled off Roger's first pitch, took one high to make it 1-1, fouled off another pitch, and then grounded back to Roger for an easy out at first.

Dave Magadan, 0 for 2 on the evening, took Roger's first pitch low, and second pitch high for a 2-0 count. He swung and missed on a good fastball, fouled off a slider to even the count at 2-2, and then fisted a single to right. Steve Labay got a late jump in right field, but it was a hard ball to read.

Rob Skates took the first pitch from Roger low, fouled a pitch back upstairs, and then flew out to Mike Trent in centerfield for the 2nd out of the inning.

Allen Stallings, the second hottest hitter for Alabama this week, was 1 for 2 tonight. Roger's first pitch was outside and got past Hearron. Magadan went to second on what was ruled to be another wild pitch. Roger hit the outside corner to make it 1-1, and then Stallings fouled off a pitch. Stallings hit a foul tip that

Hearron couldn't hold on to, but then Roger got him to swing on a nice curve to get Texas out of the inning – still a 2-2 game.

Top of the 7th

The #9 UT hitter, Bryan Burrows led off. He took a strike on the outside corner, and then a ball outside to even the count at 1-1. He took another breaking ball strike to fall behind in the count 1-2, but then lined a double to the wall in left! Skates must have thought he had a play, but the ball was on him so quickly that he couldn't even cut it off as he raced toward center. The ball skipped past him, allowing Burrows to take second.

Bill Bates came up, with Browne again looking at the top of the Texas batting order. Bill bunted the first pitch foul. Bates squared on the next pitch, but it was low, and he pulled the bat back for a ball. Velleggia threw to second, and Burrows slipped as he started back towards second and wasn't able to make it back to the bag to beat the throw. Alabama had the first out of the inning. Bates looked at another ball and took a pitch on the outside part of the plate to even the count at 2-2. He took a pitch outside to run the count full, fouled off a pitch, and then swung and missed on a big curve. 2 outs, and Browne had 7 strikeouts, tying Clemens for number of Ks at this point in the game.

Mike Brumley came up, 1 for 3 in the game. He took the first pitch high, fouled a pitch down the line in left, and then singled past Shipley at short. Texas was finally starting to get a few hits off of Browne, but Alabama already had gotten 2 outs in the inning. Brumley took a big lead off of first, but Gus gave him the sign to stay – not to try and steal second. And the gamble paid off.

Kirk Killingsworth took Browne's first pitch outside, and then hit a ball that the guys in the dugout thought was going out – but it hit high on the wall in left center, just over the leaping Allen Stallings. It went for a triple, and Brumley scored from first. Texas had its first lead of the game, 3-2!

The Bunt. All season long, José Tolentino had laid down a couple of practice bunts every day during batting practice, as did most players, before going back to swinging away and trying to groove his swing. And he had developed surprisingly good bat control. And all season long, he had been ragged by pitching coach Clint Thomas for hitting practice bunts. "Why are you bunting? You know you are never going to do that in a game!" Bill Bethea had told the players in one of his "skull sessions" about an opportunity to watch for in a game – a left-handed pitcher that fell off toward third base after a pitch, and at the same time having the right side of the infield playing back, leaving a possible hole for a good drag bunt toward second base. José saw Fermin Lake and Dave Magadan playing back on the edge of the grass and knew that Browne had been throwing pretty nasty stuff the entire game – so he saw the bunt as his best chance to get Killer home from third. After taking Browne's first pitch outside, Tolentino dropped a bunt toward second. The ball got past Browne, and by the time Fermin Lake could come in and field the bunt José was diving into first base, beating the throw, and Killingsworth had scored from third. Texas was up, 4-2! Dave Magadan, holding Tolentino on first, asked José if he had done that often. José told him, "First time all year." All Magadan could say was, "Damn!"

Jeff Hearron came to the plate 0 for 2 on the evening, but also having been hit by a pitch. He swung and missed at Browne's first offering, took a strike on the inside part of the plate for an

0-2 count, and then took an almost identical pitch for strike 3. Browne had 8 strikeouts, and Alabama was finally out of the inning – but Texas had taken a 2-run lead.

Bottom of the 7th

Frank Velleggia hit a 3 hopper to Bates on Roger's first pitch in the 7th for an easy first out.

Fermin Lake took a curve for a strike, and then a ball high for a 1-1 count. He swung and missed a good slider from Clemens, and then foul tipped a ball that Jeff Hearron hung onto for the second out of the inning. Roger was pitching well, but Gus just sent Killingsworth down to the bullpen to warm up, just in case he might be needed.

Dee Smithey, he of the home run back in the 5th, took a pitch high, and then a strike looking. Roger hit the black on the inside part of the plate for a 1-2 count, and Smithey fouled the next pitch back to the screen. Roger then threw Dee a high slider that dropped in, and Clemens had his 9th K of the game. It was 4-2 UT after 7 complete – and Texas needed 6 more outs!

Top of the 8th

Steve Labay led off, and on the first pitch from Browne singled between third and short.

Johnny Sutton squared to bunt, but pulled back and took the pitch outside for a 1-0 count. Browne threw to first, trying to hold Labay. Sutton then took a called strike after squaring early. On Browne's 3rd pitch Sutton did get the bunt down, in front of the plate. Velleggia threw Johnny out at first, but nearly threw the ball over Fermin Lake's head as he covered the bag. The sacrifice put Labay on second with one out.

Mike Trent took a pitch inside, and then a strike on the inside corner to even the count. Two more balls, low and then high, ran the count to 3-1. With Trent taking, Browne hit the outside edge to get the count full. Trent then flew out to Smithey in short right for the 2nd out of the inning.

With Bryan Burrows coming up, Alabama coach Shollenberger went to the mound and pulled Browne. The new Alabama pitcher was Troy Brauchle, 8-4 on the year, with 12 saves and a 2.72 ERA. The Alabama coach was obviously trying to keep the game close, and Browne did appear to be tiring a little. Brauchle was an "over-the-top" right hander, almost the complete opposite of Browne. And Brauchle did his job, getting Burrows to ground out to Lake on the first pitch to end the UT half of the 8th.

Bottom of the 8th

Craig Shipley led off for Alabama. Clemens blew a fastball past him on a very late swing for strike 1. Shipley took a pitch high and outside, and then fouled off a pitch in on his fists. He then hit a grounder to Tolentino at first. José had to block the ball, pick it up, and just beat Shipley to first for the out.

Alabama was back to the top of the order and Bret Elbin. Elbin, 0 for 2 on the day, took Roger's first pitch low, and then fouled a pitch into the UT bullpen. He took a pitch high, and then grounded to Tolentino for the second out of the inning. This was a much easier play for José, and it was pretty obvious he was happy to get an easy ground ball!

Designated hitter Ted McClendon hit a pop foul back to Hearron on Clemen's first pitch, and Texas was out of the 8th. 4-2 UT, and they just needed 3 more outs!

Top of the 9th

Bill Bates grounded up the middle on Brauchle's first pitch. Lake got to the ball over close to second base, but with Bates' speed he was able to beat the throw to first for an infield single.

Brumley dropped a bunt toward Lake, and beat it out, too! Texas had 2 on with no outs, and a chance to grab some insurance runs.

Kirk Killingsworth squared, but pulled back and took a strike. Velleggia threw to second, trying to get Bates, but Bill beat the throw back to second. Killingsworth then bunted, but it went right back to Brauchle on the mound, and he threw Bates out at third. Elbin fired the ball back across the diamond to first, and nearly got Killingsworth for a double play. Bates was the first out of the inning.

José Tolentino took a pitch outside, and then hit a one-bouncer back to Brauchle. He threw to Shipley at second, and the relay got Tolentino at first for a 1-6-3 double play to end the UT 9th.

Bottom of the 9th

Dave Magadan led off the 9th for Alabama. He fouled off Roger's first pitch, and then swung and missed for an 0-2 count. He then fouled off 4 straight pitches, making Roger work. And it paid off for Magadan. On the 7th pitch of the at bat he hit a ground rule double down the line in left field that bounced up into the stands.

Coach Gus went to the mound to check on Roger, and of course Jeff Hearron went out there, too. Gus asked Roger if he was OK, but didn't get the normal answer. Roger told Gus, "I'm hungry, coach!" Gus told him, "Well, get these guys out, and we can all go get something to eat." Gus did tell Roger to "Keep pumping them in there – keep challenging them." There was never any talk about pulling Roger.

After Gus returned to the dugout, Rob Skates hit Roger's first pitch right back up the middle. Clemens just got a piece of it with his glove, and the ball caromed to Bates at second. Bill was able to get Skates out at first, but Magadan made third base easily.

Allen Stallings then hit Clemens first pitch right up the middle for a clean single, scoring Magadan from third, and Alabama had gotten within 1 run at 4-3. How many times has Gus said the hardest 3 outs to get in a game are numbers 25, 26, and 27? That was proving to be true, once again! Alabama even sent another relief pitcher down to the bullpen, thinking they might get this game into extra innings.

Frank Velleggia followed Skates to the plate – the same Velleggia that had homered last night against Arizona State. He took Roger's first pitch low and outside, but then flew out to Mike Trent in deep center for the 2nd out of the inning.

Fermin Lake was Alabama's last hope. Roger fooled him on the first pitch, and Lake popped up to Mike Brumley in shallow left center to end the game. Both Johnny Sutton and Mike Trent might have been able to make the catch, but Brumley waved everybody off, and when the ball settled into his glove The

University of Texas Longhorns were the 1983 College World Series champions.

As they were running back to the infield to start the post-game celebration, Brumley asked Johnny Sutton why Sutton hadn't called him off on the fly ball – it is usually easier for an outfielder coming in to make a play than it is for an infielder backing up toward the outfield – but Sutton told him, "Can you imagine what would have happened if I had dropped that ball? I wasn't going to come near it!"

Roger Clemens had pitched a complete game, a 7-hit win. Texas had come from behind to win, as they had done in 4 of their 5 wins this week, including 2 games that went to extra innings. But none of that mattered. They were national champions! The attempted dogpile on the mound was pretty bad – probably because it wasn't something the UT team was used to doing. Everybody was screaming, hugging each other, and just trying to take in the moment. People reacted in different ways – Brumley couldn't quit jumping, but Alan Brown went and sat in the dugout and cried. The emotions of the moment were just too much, and Brown realized that he would probably never play in another competitive ball game. Alan had not had the best year – he had been a Junior College All-American last year, but this year only hit one home run. He did contribute in his one at-bat during the Series, hitting a pinch-hit sacrifice fly that tied the game against Oklahoma State, helping the Longhorns to get that game into extra innings. And he was one of the loudest cheerleaders on the bench, cheering on his teammates all week. During the interviews after the game Alan told Michael Kelly, the Omaha World-Herald's Sports Editor, "I just realized what a great game this is. I took it for granted. You can't take anything in life for granted."

Roger Clemens raced from teammate to teammate, shouting, "We're the national champs!" He was also yelling, "He was testing me upstairs that inning. He was testing me!" After the game, Roger told the press, "I got a little bit too excited. I even hyperventilated after the 8th. I started counting down the outs. I had to go back in the locker room and calm myself down. But I wasn't coming out."

José Tolentino, Deron Loy, and Bill Bates hurled their batting gloves to waiting fans in the stands.

After the game, when ESPN interviewed Gus, his first words were to his wife, Janie, who was ill back in Austin. "Janie, I love you, and I'll be home tomorrow, babe!"

Scott Wilson, one of the leaders of the Wild Bunch, got a great picture of Calvin Schiraldi's dad, Joe, doing "Hook Em Horns" in the stands after the game. Joe was a die-hard Aggie, and had told everyone that he would only show that Hook Em hand sign if UT won the national championship – and he did as he had promised!

Texas won this week even though they only hit one home run all week – the grand slam by Brumley against Michigan. UT played the last 4 games extremely close, outscoring their opponents by just 6 runs in those 4 games. Texas committed 12 errors during the week, the worst record of any of the 8 teams in the tournament. Kirk Bohls quoted Cliff Gustafson as saying, "That's just indicative of the kind of team this was. When you win on a cleanup hitter drag bunt, on a Mike Brumley grand slam, on a Johnny Sutton RBI single, it's really hard to evaluate how this team pulled it off."

Gustafson went on to say, "I began to sense something special in the making in the Regional tournament. I've never seen a team put its nose to the grindstone with an objective in mind like this one. It was as though they were not going to be denied. I can't explain what fate is, but if you believe in fate, you can take a lot of credit from what this team is."

Jeff Hearron said, "People were down on us early because we lost to clubs we hadn't lost to in millions of years." José Tolentino added, "We broke all the traditions – including almost winning at Omaha. We own the place. Well, maybe we made some payments. Maybe we couldn't hit the ball, but we could damn sure score some runs." He was probably referring to this last game against Alabama – out of the 4 runs UT scored, 3 came home on a bases-loaded walk, a fielder's choice ground out, and a drag bunt by Tolentino. Not exactly murderer's row type hitting, but it got the job done!

Calvin Schiraldi was named the Most Valuable Player for the Series. Catcher Jeff Hearron, shortstop Mike Brumley, and second baseman Bill Bates all made the all-tournament team.

Keith Moreland had been quoted after winning the CWS in 1975 that the championship in Omaha meant more to him than anything else – because he and his teammates would have that moment to remember, no matter what he did in the big leagues after college. This '83 team will feel that same way, forever.

The post-game party back at the HoliDome was epic. Players, fans, relatives, everybody had a great time. People got pushed into the pool, including the coaches. Some people were still pretty hung over on Sunday morning when the team had to go catch the plane to go back to Austin.

Sunday, June 12th

The Texas team plane was delayed about an hour in Houston, so they didn't get back to Austin until around noon on Sunday. There were several hundred fans on hand at the airport when they landed, and then when the bus got everyone down to Disch-Falk they found another couple of thousand people wanting to celebrate with them. The fans gave the team a standing ovation that seemed like it lasted about 10 minutes when the players walked in.

Gus told the crowd, "What a thrill it is to see this kind of support, and you are one reason we've been able to accomplish what we have." Cliff also acknowledged and thanked Bibb Falk, who had come out for the ceremony. Gus said they couldn't have done it without his assistant coaches, and he introduced Bill Bethea, Clint Thomas, and Howard Herrera. Gustafson then introduced each member of the team by number – and this time he got everyone's name right.

Kirk Killingsworth said, "I've been to Omaha, Nebraska three years and come up empty twice. They say the third time is the charm, and it really is, because we went undefeated."

Jeff Hearron (a transfer a couple of years ago from Cerritos Junior College in California) said, "I wish I had four years here at Texas instead of two because you fans are the greatest."

Roger Clemens closed out the speakers. He said, "I hope I didn't scare you too much the last inning. I really appreciate your support because it didn't seem like we had any fans for us up there. I don't know if they liked us or not. We had a lot of adversity, like people coming out of the stands, and we really didn't get any calls the whole time, but we still won it all."

The crowd sang The Eyes of Texas, and the 30-minute celebration was over, except for the signing of autographs for the fans. And during the entire ceremony John Turman, Gus' nephew and a student manager, held the national championship trophy like it was full of diamonds. The guys on the team hugged each other one more time in the locker room, and the season was over.

The Future

A lot of the guys off this team will be signing pro contracts in the next few days and weeks. Steve Labay has announced that he is quitting baseball, but Gus said he wouldn't be surprised if Labay changes his mind and comes back next year. Texas will have Bill Bates back, David Denny when he recovers from his injuries, Doug Hodo coming back as a leading hitter, and some young but talented pitchers – Wade Phillips, Eric Boudreaux, and Bruce Ruffin. David Denny will play summer ball in Alaska under Rice coach David Hall. Phillips, Ruffin, and Jaimie Doughty will play summer ball at Liberal, Kansas, while Deron Loy and Eric Boudreaux will play against their usual teammates in Liberal on a team in Hutchinson, Kansas. Texas doesn't rebuild – they reload. UT is bringing in another talented group of freshmen and junior college transfers. The expectations are that the Horns will be back in Omaha pretty quickly and going for another national championship.

Calvin Schiraldi said that lots of people "hate to lose" – but only a few develop the stronger emotion, a "burning desire to win." This team developed that desire, and did the work necessary to come out on top. That is why this team will always have 1983 to remember. A disparate bunch of returning stars who shouldn't have lost in Omaha in '82, some promising freshmen, and a scattering of junior college transfers, all of whom bonded into a team that was determined to win it all – and they accomplished just that. As the headline in the Austin American Statesman put it, this team was "Something Special." And that is why they deserved to have their story told.

Singing "The Eyes" before a game

Calvin Schiraldi on the mound

Mike Trent

Kirk Killingsworth
on the mound

Coach Cliff Gustafson getting his UT
Centennial Plaque from University
Vice President Shirley Byrd Perry

Kirk Killingsworth, Jeff Hearron, and
Mike Brumley congratulate Jose'
Tolentino after another home run

Jose' Tolentino corralling a low throw at first base

Mike Brumley taking a throw at second base,
with Bill Bates ready as a backup

David Denny scoring another run

Coach Gus thinking about another pitching change

Coach Gustafson with his dugout heater

Mike Simon

Coach Gus doing a mound visit with Jeff Hearron and Calvin Schiraldi

Wade Phillips

Johnny Sutton scoring against
Mississippi State

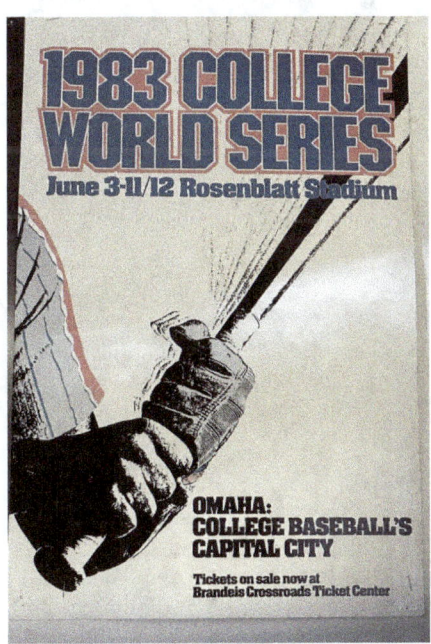

Doug Hodo at the plate against Oklahoma State

Picnic Day

At the picnic

Wild Bunch guys in Omaha

Scott Wilson, Vance Newland, Al Shepard, Doug Damewood, Greg Moore

Jeff Hearron congratulating Mike Capel after the Michigan game

Roger Clemens and teammates celebrating after the last out against Alabama

Dogpile!

Celebrating after the championship game

Coach Gustafson celebrating after winning the national championship

Singing the Eyes of Texas after the championship game

1983 BASEBALL

ACKNOWLEDGEMENTS

I want to first thank the players and coaches on the team for taking the time to share their memories of 1983 with me. Bill Bates, Bill Bethea, Mike Brumley, Mike Capel, Roger Clemens, David Denny, Jamie Doughty, Robert Gauntt, Jeff Hearron, Doug Hodo, Kirk Killingsworth, Steve Labay, Deron Loy, Bud Ray, Bruce Ruffin, Calvin Schiraldi, Johnny Sutton, Clint Thomas, José Tolentino, Mike Trent, and John Turman all contributed to what you have read.

Unfortunately, Cliff Gustafson passed away before I could get him to sit down and talk specifically about 1983 – but he will always have a special place in my heart as first my coach, and then later a friend. Sharing a peanut butter sandwich in his office and talking baseball was a highlight for me every time I had a chance to visit.

A lot of the game information comes from the great reporting from the sports writers at the Austin American Statesman and the Omaha World-Herold. Lou Maysel, Kirk Bohls, and Ken Murray on the Austin paper staff provided invaluable information. Michael Kelly, the Sports Editor for the World-Herald, and writer Steve Pivovar helped with articles from Omaha.

Most of the pictures are from the American-Statesman - USA TODAY NETWORK archives, now found at the Austin History Center. The History Center staff, especially Molly Hults, were very helpful in my search for pictures from 1983.

Several of the pictures, including the team picture, are from the UT Athletic Department's archives. Greg Moore, an old friend from my days in the Wild Bunch, also contributed pictures. Greg, thanks for keeping those photos for the last 40 years!

And a special thanks needs to go out to Scott Wilson. For those of you not familiar with Scott, he is the biggest University of Texas sports fan ever. He has attended almost 1500 straight UT baseball games, home and away, over the last 30-odd years. He has almost that long a streak attending UT football games. And he can often be found in the stands at any UT sporting event – volleyball, soccer, softball, rowing, basketball, tennis - whatever the sport, he is there! He was also instrumental in getting me in touch with a lot of the guys on the 1983 team, as he has stayed in contact with a lot of former players over the years. So, thank you, Scott. This book would not have been possible without you.

Any opinions expressed in the book are mine, and do not represent the opinions of the University of Texas or the UT Baseball Team.

If you liked the book, please leave a review on Amazon for me. If you wish to contact me or buy more copies of the book, I can be reached at jerryjohnson1@comcast.net.

www.ingramcontent.com/pod-product-compliance
Lightning Source LLC
Chambersburg PA
CBHW060903120626
46553CB00001B/188